GW00771702

The FORGOTTEN MAGE

The Magical Lectures of C.R.F. Seymour (FPD) concerning the
Ancient Mystery Religions and their relevance to magical
initiation today.

Nigel.

Christmas 92

The
FORGOTTEN
MAGE

The Magical Lectures of
of Colonel C.R.F. Seymour

Edited by
Dolores Ashcroft-Nowicki

With a Foreword by Alan Richardson, author of
Dancers to the Gods.

THE AQUARIAN PRESS LIMITED
Wellingborough, Northamptonshire

First published 1986

British Library Cataloguing in Publication Data

Seymour, C.R.F.
    The forgotten mage : the magical essays of C.R.F.
Seymour
    1. Occult sciences
    I. Title   II. Ashcroft-Nowicki, Dolores
    133   BF1411

    ISBN 0–85030–462–8

The Aquarian Press is part of Thorsons Publishing Group

Printed and bound in Great Britain

Contents

Dedication

To Christine with love and gratitude, and to the memory of 'Griff'. They danced in joy and worship before their gods and were not afraid to stand tall and straight before them.

Acknowledgements

I would like to render my thanks, firstly to the late Mr Chichester, formerly the Warden of the Society of the Inner Light, for his permission – given some years ago now – to reprint those articles that appeared in the House Magazine of the Inner Light in its early days. I remember him with great affection.

To Alan Richardson, a dear friend and colleague, and to Quest Magazine for allowing me to use his article on the Colonel as a Foreword.

To Christine Hartley for her encouragement, and to A.L. who loaned me some of her treasured Seymour papers – as she said 'Held for just this time to arrive'.

To Emily Peach and to my husband Michael, who have each in their way helped and encouraged me to put all the pieces together.

The Society of the Inner Light is still in existence, still a working school of the highest ideals. It has changed and grown over the years since these papers were written, as must all truly contacted schools. It was my privilege to be trained with and by them for many years. I wish them well in the future.

Foreword

By Alan Richardson

Colonel Seymour – The Moon Priest

No one ever liked him much at first meeting. He was too abrupt, too much the ex-colonel, and a man who had no tolerance for fools. In fact, his juniors simply called him 'the Colonel', the formality of the title helping to keep them at a safe distance. Those whom he allowed close almost idolized him, and they knew him as Kim, 'little friend of all the world'. That was a truer picture of him. He just had no time for cant or self-glorifiers. Whether they got close to him or not, no one who belonged to the Fraternity of the Inner Light in the 1930s had any doubt that he was one of the most powerful magicians of his day.

Dion Fortune and her husband, Dr Thomas Evans, called him Griffin, or Griff. They felt that the image of a winged lion's body with eagle head was a peculiarly apt symbol for the man's inner nature. When Dr Evans left his marriage and his Fraternity, it was the Colonel who took over the Power aspect; it was he who gave the group its scholarship and inherently pagan, Celtic direction at that time. In magical terms, he became the man behind Dion Fortune during the latter part of the 1930s. Now, he is very much the Fraternity's Forgotten Mage.

Charles Richard Foster Seymour was born in Ireland on 9 April 1880. He thought of himself as a Galway boy, but in fact his family seat, as one of the landed gentry, was at Killagally on the border of Galway and what is now County Offaly. Although his first commission was as an officer in the Hampshire Regiment, he soon transferred to the Indian Army. He fought in the Boer War, and took part in operations in the Orange Free State and the Transvaal, winning the Queen's South Africa Medal with four Clasps. During the Great War, he was wounded in German East Africa. After this, he took part in covert actions in Iraq, and was mentioned in dispatches. A multilingual man, but specializing in

Russian, he found himself as an interpreter on diplomatic duty in Russia in 1917. He travelled with his wife and daughter. The little girl took ill of a fever and died. His wife conceived again almost immediately; and Seymour was convinced it was the same soul come back. He went to Staff College at Quetta, in India. Among his pupils at that time were the likes of Auchinleck, Montgomery, Brooke and Slim – virtually a roll-call of Britain's greatest generals.

By 1930 he had retired and gravitated back to London. Upon the recommendations of certain friends he had in Freemasonry (he was a member of the Grand Lodge of Scotland) he found himself at the Fraternity of the Inner Light at 3 Queensborough Terrace, as run by Mrs Violet Mary Evans (née Firth) better known by her pseudonym of Dion Fortune.

Seymour's academic background and his long grounding in ritual, via his activities in the travelling masonic lodges that existed within the army, made the course of study in the Fraternity almost a formality. The cosmology of *The Cosmic Doctrine*, which was the core book, and which had wrecked the enthusiasm of many other students, proved no obstacle to his progress.

Before very long, he was editing the monthly magazine and writing many of the articles himself either under his own name, or signed with the initials of his Magical Name, F.P.D., which was Foy pour Devoir. It was a family motto, like most of the names within the Inner Light or its parent, the Golden Dawn. It meant 'Faith for Duty'.

His articles represented the very best of the outpouring from the Lodge. They specialized in what was termed the Western Mystery Tradition at a time when most people did not know that Britain had one. The basis of this tradition, in Fortune's interpretation, was that before Atlantis crumbled below the waves, small groups of illuminated adepts with their priestesses sailed away and carried with them the very essence of the ancient knowledge, and that this has survived today through myth, folklore and the magnetic resonance of prehistoric sites. Dion had written as much a few years earlier in her *Avalon of the Heart*, but she was essentially a popularizer. Seymour was able to give it all an academic basis. She had the knack of synthesis and charismatic delivery both in print and in person; he had the learning for her to draw upon.

Much of the magic practised within the Lodge used the

technique of creative imagination that had been pioneered by Ignatius Loyola. In one of his essays Seymour expressed it thus: that the magician should act *as if* the images were real, and *as if* the gods really were what they seemed to be. He was fully aware of the dangers in this, and was well versed in modern psychology, but he knew that man reaches a point when too much rationalization does no more than clip his wings. He favoured a possibly errant flight, to earthbound ponderings. 'A magician is *what* he believes himself to be; a magician is *where* he believes himself to be,' he wrote, adding that this was the path of true magic. It is a method that is particularly suited for the occult use of mythology – a mythology, moreover, that was the very essence of the British psyche in particular and the Western psyche in general. One of his long essays, 'The Old Religion', is virtually a manual of self-initiation into the Celtic Mysteries. The reader would take himself through controlled fantasy into the Celtic Otherworld, in the realms of the Sidhe, or Bright Ones. It is an essay that is studded with magical techniques, psychological comment, and some quite beautiful and evocative writing aimed at taking the student a few steps towards the heart of the Celt's inner landscape.

The essay had been written round the results of experiments in group meditation upon the use of ancient pagan symbols. 'These experiments had for their objective the linking-up of memories dormant in the subconscious minds of the members of those meditation groups with ancient cult memories that still live in the subconscious mind of the Great Mother of all-that-exists on this planet.' He goes on to add that most of the members of these groups have, in the past, served at the altars of pagan religions, and that if any one of the members had had a strong contact with a particular cult at a certain period then that individual could communicate these memories to others, and could link them with the cult memories that still lie within the Earth memories of Isis as the Lady of Nature. There is the confession, too, that in the early stages of such group meditation it was almost impossible to distinguish between fancy and the results obtained by the imagination trained magically. However, as the result of years of carefully recorded work, a system of cross-checking grew up, and a reasonable degree of probability was obtained. He insists that in the small cells with which he worked, the members had known each other in previous lives, and had served at the altars of these forgotten cults before. In his private magical records, it is revealed that Dion had certainly known him before, in Egypt, when he had been Nefer-su, a Priest of Ptah. And she had known him, too, at Avebury, when their sexes had been reversed, and she had been a menacing sacrificial Priest who had cut open the willing young female sacrifice that Seymour had been then, and let the blood flow down the sloping altar stone into a sacred cup.

No photograph has yet been traced with Seymour on it, but there is a word-picture of him in Dion Fortune's novel *The Winged Bull*: 'Brangwyn was a tall, slight, dark-skinned man; and his black hair, brushed straight back from the forehead, was greying over the ears and receding over the temples.' It is an accurate description, except that Seymour was not a tall man. One person who worked with him at the time described him as being of medium height, ostensibly an unassuming man, but with something inside him that was utterly, utterly powerful.

It was with the Colonel that Dion practised the Isis Rites which found their way into the novel *Moon Magic*, which in some ways was her most accomplished piece. The protagonist of that one, however, Dr Rupert Malcolm, was based upon her husband, Tom, who had by this time left her and moved to Buckinghamshire.

She gave Seymour a shadowy appearance in *The Sea Priestess*, too, as the lean and ascetic-faced Priest of the Moon who had the Atlantean Heritage that was *de rigeur* to the adepts of the Inner Light. It was this discarnate priest in the novel who directed the magical operations from the inner planes – although, to be strictly accurate, Seymour remembered himself as having been a warrior on Atlantis. The priest of the Sacred Clan who had come to Lyonesse bearing the initiatic title of Merlin was actually Dr Evans. Seymour had come along in the same boat as a guardian. Dion wove her last novels around composite pictures of the two men.

Her fraternity in those days was based upon the tripartite balance of power, love and wisdom. These qualities had their reflection on human and discarnate levels. From about 1927 onwards, when they had married, Dr Evans had meditated the Power; Thomas Loveday, appropriately enough, took the Love aspect; and Dion completed the structure at the angle of Wisdom, or Knowledge as it was at a lower level. Between the three of them, they sought to create a microcosm of the magical universe, a synergistic exchange of energies which would ultimately, they felt, affect the evolution of all humanity. When Dr Evans left, it was natural that Seymour took over.

Whatever Dion may have felt for him personally, it was never
entirely returned. There is a note in his magical diaries to the
effect that he had had about enough of the Isis Rites, which took
place at 3 Queensborough Terrace, Bayswater. As much as
anything, these might well have been Dion's attempts to
consolidate the sort of occult partnership with Seymour that she
had once had with her winged bull of a husband. In one sense, she
saw within the Colonel a copy of her own late teacher, the
mysterious Dr Moriarty, upon whose (non-existent) nursing
home the 'Dr Taverner' stories were based: they were both well-
travelled older men, with similar religious backgrounds and
masonic interests. By this time, however, 1937, her mage had
found another, far more congenial, priestess, a third adeptus by
the name of Christine Campbell Thomson. Known as CCT, this
40-year-old woman made a living as a novelist and prominent
literary agent. It was she who edited Dion's occult novels, as well
as the three detective novels she wrote in the late 1930s for light
relief from the gods. She was seen immediately as Dion's heir
apparent. When she first entered the Fraternity for one of the
public lectures that were given every Monday night, Dr Evans
was heard to make the curious aside, 'At last ... we've got a
priestess of Isis in the house.' In the early days of her training,
CCT had been given the role of onlooker, allowed to watch
clairvoyantly from the sidelines while the senior magicians
worked their rituals. By the time she became a fully contacted
adeptus in her own right, Seymour was aware that she was far
more suited to his occult schemes than her formidable and oddly
jealous mentor.

Dion, however, was a great woman. She would never stand in
the way of the Work.

That was the beginning of it. Their work took place at least
once a week for two years, and this was over and above their other
duties within the lodge which involved the publication of the
magazine, the senior group rituals, and teaching the juniors.

CCT then became the Colonel's Shakti: she provided the raw
power as only women can, and he directed it. Not naturally
having much in the way of sight himself, he needed the inner
rapport with his priestess to enable him to 'see' with the same
degree of facility. Emotionally, their relationship was never more
than a purely platonic one, his role that of an old man to his
granddaughter – even though the age gap was only one of
seventeen years. In their workings, they stimulated far memories
of previous lives which revealed links as far back as Atlantis and
earlier, in Egypt, in Avebury (she had held the cup into which

Seymour's blood had poured), along the Roman Wall, and in medieval Languedoc. Invariably, he had been her grandfather or father; always he had been a guardian.

In his heart of hearts, the old mage was a matriarch. He would have been at home – he had been at home – in the ancient Celtic tribes where the authority stemmed from the woman and was passed down matrilineary. Not surprisingly, he discovered another congenial co-worker by 1938, Paula Trevanion, whom he called his Wise Child. From then on, Deo, non Fortuna virtually disappears from his diaries, and the trio comprises himself, CCT and Paula: the Power, Wisdom and the Love respectively. If the Fraternity as a whole was a microcosm of the universe, then the small groups that Seymour favoured were microcosms of the Fraternity.

One can understand that Dion began to take exception to this. The parent organization, the Order of the Golden Dawn, had suffered because of the innumerable splinter groups that had formed. Yet it was never the Colonel's intention to create internal rivalries within the Lodge. It was simply that he preferred working in small cells. The fact that his favourite Tarot card was The Hermit helps explain this: a lonely and venerable figure on a mountaintop holding out his light to those willing to make the climb. Even so, in a variety of ways, Dion began to make it plain that his magical services were no longer required.

For his part, he had seen a change in her, too. He felt that she had suffered inwardly, somehow, for breaking her oaths in the writing of her masterpiece *The Mystical Qabalah*. She had lost something.

The onset of war decided matters. The Army called upon him once more in his advisory capacity, and he went off to Liverpool for a time. When he came back, 3 Queensborough Terrace had been bombed and Dion had taken rooms further along the street at 21B. He never saw her again.

He resumed his magical work under the aegis of Dr Carnegie Dickson and his wife Edith, who ran what was one of the last of the Golden Dawn Temples. And he resumed where he had left off with CCT and Paula, but this time using crystal magic of the sort pioneered by Dr John Dee – but without the anachronistic Enochian elements.

By 1943 he had worked out a magical curriculum for CCT for the next seven years, by going deeper into the Celtic and Arthurian mysteries with especial reference to the Welsh Traditions. He knew that he had seven years left to live and he wanted everything completed in that time. Adepts know such things. He had even found another priest for CCT because he was aware that he himself, as an ageing man, was no longer able to handle the levels of power that she was increasingly able to bring through.

Then, on Midsummer Day, 1943, without any warning, he died. It was a complete shock to everyone. His vision had failed him at the last.

In summary, Kim Seymour was a hard, lively, sad, protective and very humble man – with the sort of humility that only the very powerful can express. There was probably not a Christian atom in his body. And while he held the Power aspect within the Fraternity of the Inner Light, like Thomas Evans before him, he could make the place roar. If there was any real scholarship behind the Lodge at this period, then it came from Seymour, while Dion did a masterful job of synthesizing and popularizing it for public consumption. It is impossible and foolish to put magicians in league tables, as their followers are wont to do, because magic is manifested in different ways. But one can say that Seymour was every bit Dion's equal and, to a great extent, gave her direction during the 1930s. She was a great woman, but she needed her direction. She got it from the splendid adept her husband had been, and she was carried along the same route by Kim. Yet when he went, too, she lost something. If the group mind and soul is magnified each time one of its initiates is raised to a higher degree, then by the same token it must lose when its adepts leave and sever connections. By 1940 Dion Fortune had lost not only her most experienced magicians, but probably lost her pagan contacts too. That was what Seymour felt had gone missing in her.

CCT (Christine Hartley) and another co-worker held a ceremony of their own for the Colonel, building a Fire of Vision from the sort of woods described in *The Sea Priestess* and throwing onto it his adept's lamen, his masonic sash, and other ceremonial items. The magical side of him, the best part, floated into a cloudless Norfolk sky as so many particles of smoke. The forgotten mage went finally into the Otherworld he knew so well.

Alan Richardson is the author of *Introduction to the Qabalah, Gate of the Moon* and the forthcoming *Dancers to the Gods*. This Foreword first appeared as an article in its own right in *Quest* magazine, March 1984. It is reprinted here with the permission of the author and of *Quest*.

Editor's Preface and Introduction

Colonel C.R.F Seymour was a man of many talents and considerable occult skills. The friend and confidant of Dion Fortune, he worked with her and with his magical partner Christine Hartley for many productive years. The description 'an officer and a gentleman', could have been written specially for him. To his career in the Army, and to his magical work, he brought the highest of ethics, and both are areas where such integrity is imperative.

As one of those in the inner ranks of D.F.'s magical lodge he was a high priest in every sense of the word. The magical diaries of both 'Griff', as he was affectionately known, and Christine show the heights these two incredible people reached in their magical work. These diaries have been edited by Alan Richardson under the title *Dancers to the Gods*, also published by Aquarian Press and in many ways a companion volume to this one.

A magician and a high priest 'F.P.D.' most certainly was, but he was also one of the finest teachers of the occult arts to emerge in this century. But not for him the Outer Court. He saw his work as a teacher amongst those who had already taken the first steps towards the Adytum of the Mysteries. From time to time some of his written work appeared in the house magazine of the Inner Light, and occasionally both Gareth Knight and I have reprinted some of his articles in the house magazines of our own schools. Gareth Knight reproduced a section of his work in *The New Dimensions Red Book*, which is in the process of being reprinted by Helios Publishers as I write. But this was nothing to the amazing amount of work that he left behind and which has never been made widely available, yet what he had to say is very relevant to our needs and our times as we come to the end of the century.

It is time to turn the pages and allow the neophytes of a later era – and indeed those who teach them – to read, to share the ideas, wisdom and knowledge of this gentle man, who nevertheless did not suffer fools gladly, especially in his magical work.

He was, quite simply, a pagan – and a happy and fulfilled one at that, who also rendered to Christianity in its pure and original form the deference and acknowledgement due to that which stood behind it. He saw no real difference between paganism and Christianity in their ultimate endeavour to raise mankind to that divine place for which it was meant. His occasional asperity was reserved for those who have allowed Christianity to get sidetracked over the centuries.

Because all of these articles were written in the early thirties the terminology and the use of certain analogies are sadly out of date. I have slightly altered this wherever it has been possible without harming the text. F.P.D. was very given to quoting long extracts of poetry at the beginning of many of his writings. I have, with a certain sense of guilt, but with due deference, edited out the repetitions and some of the poetry. I hope he will forgive me.

'Griff' Seymour was a friend and contemporary of my own late teacher W. E. Butler, and it was from him that I first learned of 'F.P.D.' and was introduced to his writings. Years later, I was privileged to meet Christine Hartley and have spent many happy hours in her company listening to her recall her work with fellow members in the early days of the Inner Light. It is with her encouragement and blessing that Alan Richardson and I have taken on the task of reintroducing *The Forgotten Mage* to modern occultists.

Colonel Seymour left a daughter, Rowena, who married one Robert Crozier. Both Alan and I have made great efforts to trace them or their descendants in order to discuss the publication of these papers with them. So far, all our efforts have failed. Should they or anyone connected with them read this book, please get in touch with us through the publishers. We have also tried vainly to obtain a photograph of the Colonel, and if any reader has one, or knows someone who has, the publishers and I would be very grateful for a copy that might possibly be used in any future editions of this book.

Jersey, 1986

1.

The Meaning of Initiation

Kipling, talking of Englishmen of the nineteenth century, has pointed out that there is a 'divine discontent' that urges one on to seek beyond the skyline where strange roads go down.

As a rule it is only the restless soul, who, driven by this strange but divine feeling of discontent, seeks for the Ancient Mysteries of the Western Tradition. Thus, looked at from this point of view, Initiation into the Western Tradition may be said to be the goal of such a one.

It is also very true that the roads which lead to Initiation are among the strangest of the many strange roads leading beyond that skyline. During the nineteenth century, man sought to satisfy this restlessness by exploring the unknown territories of this physical globe. In this century, however, he is beginning to seek and explore the vast unknown territories that lie within the soul of mankind, and within the soul of 'that' which appears to our senses as physical nature.

Here we are talking in symbols, for this particular skyline is not that which bounds our view of the earth. It lies outside time and space, deep within the inmost self of those who seek truly.

The seeker after Initiation and its 'results' will find the roads he travels are many, varied and strange, yet all have one thing in common. If they are to lead anywhere they must first go deep into the consciousness of the one who seeks. Speaking generally, one may classify these roads under two headings: the solitary roads that lead, if you follow them far enough, to self-initiation; and the roads of ritual experience. Both lead to the same goal in spite of a preliminary divergence.

Those that travel the first road must leave (in their solitary meditations) the state of being we call the conscious consciousness far behind. To reach self-initiation they must go far beyond the restricted mental skyline that bounds the focused mind of man.

These roads must travel through the Ring Pass Not of everyday experience, and it is here that the weak fall by the wayside. Only the strong and very determined soul can force its way through.* Travellers may, in very rare cases, cleave their way through to that 'Thrice Greatest Darkness' lying at the heart of the Limitless Light of the fully developed mystic.† Here is that rare state of being that can only be described by means of a paradox. For while it is the fullest and most developed state of consciousness, it is also the utter negation of all consciousness as we humans understand the word. It is the true state of Nirvana.

But this is a type of initiation which is rare and so intensely personal as to be utterly beyond description. It may be dimly felt by those who have just touched the fringes of such an experience, but neither they nor the person who has fully experienced Nirvana can really describe what it is like.

The roads of the second type are broader, easier and more companionable. They have been worn quite plain and clear to the sight by the feet of countless thousands who have gone before. The ordinary man who is prepared to work and obey can travel with speed and safety along them, once he has picked up the trail of the Western Tradition and resolved to stick to it.

In modern Europe there are many roads along which the would-be Mystae of the Western Tradition can seek for the 'Grail' of ritualistic initiation. But, you may ask, what is meant by this?

Speaking generally – for no two people ever get the same result from the same ritual – we can say this much. The preliminary initiation ritual aims at linking the inner self with the unseen but conscious nature forces that have their existence behind the material world of the five senses. So, speaking in terms of the Alexandrian Graeco-Egyptian Mysteries, rather than those of Eleusis, we may call the early forms of initiation 'the Lesser Mysteries', which aim at lifting the 'Veil of Isis' and giving the initiate a better comprehension of his universe. In modern terms, he is being given his 'contacts'.

* Few people who come to the Door of the Mysteries fully realize the amount of hard work and discipline involved.

† Seymour speaks here of a very high level teaching, and is *not* referring to the usual connotation of the word 'darkness'.

From this necessarily condensed explanation it should be evident that an initiation into the Mysteries by means of ritual is a long-drawn-out process of self-development, that does not take place in a world of time and space. In this respect it differs from, say, a Masonic initiation which is an event in time and space and received from human hands.

In a genuine initiation few can say where or when or at what moment 'realization' came to them. It is not always understood that a Mystery initiation is a symbolic presentation to the conscious mind, while the *actual* initiation is a subconscious experience of the 'potencies' at work in the Temple – potencies that cannot be measured by psychic researchers or scientists in terms of physics.

Initio means 'I begin', and even the most successful initiation merely means a mental and spiritual process in the soul of the candidate. To this process there is no finality. It also occurs, however, in the much larger process of human evolution. Humanity as a whole is flowing slowly and steadily, but in most cases blindly, with the great tides of evolution. The ordinary man is unconscious of this progress. He knows not where these tides will bear him; nor does he much care, so long as he is fairly comfortable.

So we may describe initiation, as practised in this Fraternity,* as follows: Initiation is a ritualistic and symbolic ceremony which begins a spiritual and mental process that aims at enabling the candidate to become a conscious and competent co-worker with those beings who, from higher states of consciousness than this physical state, guide and guard humanity.

August 1934

---

* Since this was written, the Fraternity of which Seymour speaks (the Inner Light) has gone through many phases of growth, but the aim here stated remains true.

2.

Magic in the Ancient Mystery Religions

One might subtitle this essay 'The ABC of Magical Theory'. Besides a wealth of magical knowledge and know-how, the Colonel goes deeply into the god-forms of the ancient world and their functions as archetypal magicians. The place of myth in the world of magic is discussed with his usual thoroughness, and the reader is left in no doubt as to where the author stands in his personal beliefs. The power of the group souls of the ancient religions is seldom discussed or written about in any great detail, let alone with the clarity found here, yet it is upon its group soul that any religion ultimately rests. It is the core, so to speak, of all those believers that go to make up its body. Without the group soul as a secure base, any faith will crumble sooner or later – especially if it is damaged or tainted in any way. It was reading this essay that finally convinced me that these writings needed to be placed before a wider audience.

Part 1: Magic, Myth, Mystery
There are few words in the English language that can raise such strange reactions in the human mind as the word 'magic'. It is used equally to denote excellence, or the reverse. Poets speak of the magic of a woman's eyes, or of love, and they are right. But some cannot distinguish between a magus and a charlatan, and associate magic with conjuring, white rabbits, and top hats – and they too are right.

The word 'magic' has a way of revealing the inmost thoughts of the soul. Tell me a man's reaction to the word, and I will tell you, approximately, the state of his soul's evolution.

There is living today* a famous English preacher, a Bishop of

* December 1934.

the Church of England. Magic is for him the vilest and basest of superstitions because he cannot measure the magical workings of the Christian Sacrament of Communion in terms of chemical change. The same rite for Evelyn Underhill is an example of ritualistic magic. But magic's standard of measurement is not to be laid down in terms of chemistry; you cannot test its purity as you would a patent medicine.

Evelyn Underhill and Bishop Barnes stand at opposite poles of the magnet of religious experience. Both are right in what they say. But you will be committing religious adultery if you mix in your mind the plan of Bishop Barnes' religious consciousness with Miss Evelyn Underhill's.

The *Century Dictionary* gives the following definition of magic: 'Magic is the pretended art of controlling the actions of spiritual or superhuman beings.' This is a 'Barnesian' type of definition, and in its own way and on its own plane it is right. But it is not the *only* way. There are other ways and planes of thought about this matter.

'Magic', says the Byzantine writer Psellus, 'explores the essence and power of everything.'* This, put into terms of today's thought, means that magic is a technique of mental training that enables the mind to reach out beyond the visible surface of things, and by doing so, to get in touch with the mental side of Nature. To use a magical expression, magic is lifting the Veil of Isis.

It is a technique for training the body and soul of a man or woman and preparing them for initiation into a mystery cult. In the Mysteries one does not learn to control the actions of spiritual beings. Rather, by means of ritual and meditation the initiate learns to control his own soul, so that he is able to lift it temporarily out of physical consciousness. By doing so, the initiate becomes fully aware of the statement that 'The Kingdom of God is Within You'.

Thus the magic of the ancients enables a man to control his own soul, for good or evil, for magic has the power to make the magician either God-centered, and thus a power for good, or self-centered, and a more than common power for human evil.

Let us go into more detail and see what it is that the initiate of a Mystery school tries to do, whether he is an initiate of an Egyptian Mystery school in the year 2000 BC or of one operating in the twentieth century.

* Browne's *Magic and the Mysteries*, p. 51

What is magic as it is taught today? Dion Fortune has given us this definition: 'Magic is the art of causing changes to take place in consciousness in accordance with will.' (*London Forum*, September 1934, p. 174.) It is upon the subconscious mind that ceremonial magic works and upon nothing else. You have only to attend a Roman Catholic High Mass to realize this truth. The ceremony is unfamiliar, and in an unknown tongue,* and as a Protestant one's conscious mind is often hostile. But if you are an initiate, you will have learned the technique for sensing the atmosphere of a place, and you will quickly realize that a definite and highly magical ceremony is taking place. What is more, this ceremony is being consciously worked by a priesthood which has, and which *knows* it has, magical powers.

The most common subconscious powers of the mind as used in magic are telepathy, conscious suggestion, auto-suggestion and sensitivity to atmosphere. Everyone has these powers to a certain extent. In some they come naturally, and usually unsought, and sometimes they are developed to a high degree with no conscious knowledge of the actual technique. But in the initiate and the trained priest these powers are developed by means of a very definite technique, always kept secret, and which works very slowly.

The Church of Rome spends approximately seven years in training her young men to become priests. In the Mysteries it is generally reckoned that, with very few exceptions, it takes a minimum of seven years to make an initiate fit and ready to stand upon his own mental foundations.

In both the Church and those Mystery schools run on the lines of the Western Esoteric Tradition, these subconscious mental powers are set free, controlled, trained, and finally used as a means of ceremonial magic. Certain ceremonies are designed to work upon the imagination and to heighten the emotion, and it is by these ceremonies, frequently repeated, that the powers of the subconscious mind are trained and used. †

Magic, therefore, is a psychological technique. Modern psychology teaches that the mind is made up of various levels of consciousness, with barriers between them, and that deep down at the root of consciousness is the level of elemental energy.

---

* The author writes long before the saying of Mass in English became customary.

† He speaks here of the technique known as Pathworking.

Ceremonial magic aims at opening up and controlling this elemental energy, and pouring it in a carefully regulated manner into channels that have been properly prepared to receive it. Magic takes place in the realms of the mind. It uses mind stuff to build its engines, and mental energy to drive them. I repeat, magic is of the mental world, not the physical.

Part 2: Religion

Now let us turn to the word 'religion' and try to decide just what we mean by this term. As far as we are concerned, religion has nothing to do with any creeds, dogmas, rites or churches; and there is no need to believe in a personal deity, or indeed in any God at all. You may believe in all these things if you wish to do so, or, like my Buddhist teacher, believe in none. And yet your worship will come within the limits of this term 'religion' as used in these pages. We will use the term simply as a recognition of, and a communion with, the soul of *that* in which this visible Universe lives, moves and has its being. Here the term 'soul' means the emotional, mental, and spiritual states of consciousness, both in man and nature – nature being considered as an intelligent force.

You will see that here the word 'religion' involves two things:

1. Knowledge in contradistinction to belief.
2. Action that is direct communion with the Unseen, be it called God, a god, or a natural force manifesting as Law and Order.

The term 'Mystery religion' need not detain us long. In the past, mystery meant hidden, but not incomprehensible as it often does today. The Mystery religions were esoteric, selective and strictly limited brotherhoods. They had rigid laws and secret observances. In this way they were different from the State religions, which were free and public.

Having considered the meaning of the subjects given in the title, let us set out the object of these studies. Modern Christianity as understood by the extreme Protestant section of the Church of England and certain of the non-conformist sects, has been called (not altogether unjustly) a system of practical ethics slightly tinged by emotion and strongly obsessed by a fear of hellfire. It is claimed as a simple doctrine for simple people, and the simpler the people, the better the doctrine suits them. It has no esoteric teachings; all is given out. It is rational, above-board and practical, and its teachers declare that Christianity has no use for such things as magic, myth or mystery.

But when we turn to the past, we find that the three essential features of ancient religion were magic, myth and mystery. The first and last have been explained, but the term 'myth' is worthy of study. The word as it will be used does not mean a supposed historical story which may or may not be true. For us it means a sequence of symbols used as an aid to learning, memorizing and understanding a religious process, the true meaning of which is kept secret fom the uninitiated. Man always tries to define and synthesize his religious experiences. He rationalizes them and they become myth, with characters as symbols of the myth.

For the outer world, a tale in historical form is built up. For the initiate, however, the myth is the key to a psychological and mental process which is carried out within the soul of the initiate. It is not historical fact. For the cult initiate, things are not what they seem to the uninitiated. It was the ignorance and superstition of the Middle Ages that turned myth into supposed history.

Today, some Christians continue to confuse myth with history. Others deny that it has meaning, and look upon myths as fairytales for children. Both are wrong. Myth is a method for recording psychological experiences.

Let us turn now to the background of religious thinking of the Ancient Mysteries, and examine that phase which came under the influence of Neo-Pythagoreanism and Neo-Platonism, especially the latter.

It should be pointed out that Neo-Platonism when formulated was not a new system of thought. Plotinus (AD 205–70), who is looked on as its founder, had only gathered into a clear and comprehensive system the knowledge of many centuries of practical occult research. (Dodd, *Neoplatonism*, p. 10.) In this system Plotinus endeavoured to do two things: first, to give a clear and rational account of the reality implied in experience; and second, when understanding was reached, to place the student in direct contact with this reality, which – as was said earlier – may be called the Soul of Nature.

For Plotinus and the great Initiates of that time the history of the world was the history of the involution of a spiritual force into matter. This idea had come down from the writings of Plato, and it is certain that it was already an ancient idea 400 years before Christ.

To explain this teaching, Plato used the term 'On' to denote the Absolute or Unmanifest. The next stage in the world process was

'Ho ontos On', which means 'Real Being', that which really is, or has being, as contrasted with 'Genesis' or objective existence. With Plato, this Real Being is defined as 'essence', and described as formless, colourless, intangible and visible only to the mind or higher reason. (Iamblichus, *Egyptian Mysteries*, p. 29)

From the Absolute there emanated the gods of the Ancient Mysteries. Iamblichus (op. cit., p. 31) taught that there are the many gods that are the emanations of this Absolute God, and as such they were not substances, that is: real beings complete in themselves. You get this idea expressed in the 95th Psalm:

For the Lord is a Great God,
And a Great King above all Gods.

All over the ancient world at that time you get this same idea. The Hindus have Brahman, who is the God who is beyond Essence, and who is Absolute, while Brahma is the creator and is identical with essence or 'Real Being'.

The Parsis worshipped Zeroana, the Unlimited, and Ahura Mazda the divine creator. In like manner, the Egyptians at one period acknowledged Amoun the Hidden One as the Absolute, and Ptah was the Demiurgos or Architect of the Universe.

There is a point here which is unfamiliar to modern religious thought, and which should be explained for it is of vital importance if we are to understand the part that magic played in the Ancient Mysteries. These Gods were spiritual essences, and were formless in any sense that we can understand. They encompassed and permeated all things in the manner in which the Mediterranean encompasses and permeates the sponges that grow in its depths. Once a man became an initiate of the Mysteries belonging to a certain God, that man's soul lived and moved and had its being in the 'Real Being' of his particular God, in a special and peculiar manner.

The idea may be stated thus: the Ancient Mysteries taught that the god of a cult encompassed with his own divine life and energy the bodies and souls of the initiated members of that particular cult. St Paul was quoting the poet Aratus, and was using a Mystery teaching when he said to the Athenians: 'In him we live, move, and have our being ... for we are the offspring of God.' (Acts 17:28.)

Every initiate of a Mystery cult, by virtue of his initiation, became in a special manner the saving god of that cult. He was sealed and signed and often branded with the sign of the god. You will see this idea being kept up in the baptism of various sects in the Christian Church, where the baptism makes the infant, who is as yet unconscious of any religion, a member of Christ, a child of God, and the inheritor of the Kingdom of Heaven.

The Christian child is supposed to get all these benefits by virtue of a rite; he does not have to work for them. But in the Ancient Mysteries, the neophyte had to undergo long and careful training to obtain such benefits. He had to reach a certain standard of physical, emotional, mental and spiritual training before he could undergo the magical ceremony of initiation into a mystery cult.

Having reached that standard, he became a child of that saving god, and a participator in its protective essence. The god of a cult gave his followers protection in this world, and safe passage through the dark realms of the Underworld at death.

Let us sum up the chief points so far. The first point was that the ancients had a different idea of religion from the purely ethical conception common in Protestant circles today. For the ancient, the three essential features of religion were myth, magic and mystery. The second point is that the ancients used these words in a very different way from our modern usage.

Myths for the initiated were a telepathic presentment of certain pictures in the form of a drama, which imparted an intuitional awareness of the Cosmic Truth thus dramatized. They were a set of conventional symbols with a definite but secret meaning.

Magic as the ancients saw it was a secret system of physical, emotional, mental and spiritual training which aimed at giving the neophyte control over certain inner states of consciousness. He went through ceremonies of initiation which brought about certain kinds of psychic experience, experience which was expected to produce effects in the subconscious mind.

Plutarch (*De Anima*, p. 84) says: 'They who suffer death are as those initiated into the Great Mysteries, wherefore in deed as well as in name death is akin to initiation.' 'Telesthenai' is a Greek word meaning 'to be initated into the Mysteries', and in those Mysteries the dead were called 'Christoi'. Jesus, the Christ, uttered as his last cry at the point of death 'Tetelestai', a Mystery term meaning 'The Initiation is complete.'

Part 3: The Lore of Persephone

In Parts One and Two of these articles we considered the three aspects of the Ancient Mysteries: myth, magic and mystery, and finished up with the idea that 'They who suffer death are as those initiated into the Great Mysteries.'

In Apuleius is given a fairly full account of the initiation of Lucius into the Isis cult at Cenchreae. Lucius went through a long and arduous training for this event. He studied the ceremonial and contemplative devotion of the Egyptian liturgical tradition. Having undergone all this preparation, he was led into the innermost sanctuary to be given the culminating psychological experience. In *The Golden Ass*, he has this to say of that moment: 'I penetrated to the boundaries of death. I trod the threshold of Persephone, and after being borne through all the elements I returned to earth.' That is a definite statement by a man who lived, 2,000 years ago, a Mystery initiate.

All through the ages there have been those who have trained themselves to grasp the World Soul and enter into it. They have sought, successfully, to take the Kingdom of Heaven by force, the force of the directed will. The whole scheme of the Mystery teaching was based upon an idea which has been put thus: 'Behind this world of appearance lies another and vaster world with a thronging population of its own, with many populations, each absorbed in uttering its own being according to its own laws. There is a chain of "Being" whose top and bottom know nothing of each other at all.' And only rarely have we any intercourse with any but our own. We may, for convenience, call it the antechamber of this world. For the ancients, it was the world of Persephone. The old initiates believed there was a power and energy in this unseen side of nature which the trained adept was able to draw upon by means of special techniques. They based their scheme of training upon the beliefs that:

1. Man is the centre of concealed and potent forces; and
2. the unseen forces of nature are of the same kind as those that exist in the soul of man.

Thus man can draw from nature all the energy and power he needs. The greater his need, the more the adept can draw from this unfailing power source. 'Gnothi Se Auton'* was the greatest maxim that both neophyte and adept had to comprehend and practise. The cultivation of a student's powers began with

* 'Know Thyself'.

initiation and ended only with death. The first lesson in this lengthy process of self-knowledge that had to be mastered was the idea that 'nervous force is at the back of man's mental energy' while he is still in the body. It is this idea that lies at the root of the many strange and complicated rules of the Ancient Mysteries with regard to continence and chastity.

Demeter and Persephone were the two great goddesses of the Greater Mysteries at Eleusis. The realm of the dead was the kingdom of Persephone, the Queen of the Underworld, whose portress was triune Hecate. The statues of the latter were placed at the fork of roads looking each way. As a moon-goddess she was the patron of childbirth, of the sea and fishermen. She was also the goddess of night, darkness, ghosts and magic. Hermes, in his role of psychopomp, was the guide who presented souls to the rulers of Hades, Persephone and Pluto, her uncle/husband and King. Here are three great links which bind the Greater Mysteries to the 'Lore of Persephone'; i.e. Hermes the Guide or psychopomp, Hecate and Persephone herself.

'The dead are as those Initiated': in other words, the rite of initiation into the Greater Mysteries of Eleusis gave the initiate the Keys of Heaven and Hell – to use a popular phraseology. What it really means is that the initiate was made free of Hades, and Hades for them meant neither Heaven nor Hell. It meant that other and vaster world which lies beyond the veil of physical manifestation. The entry to this world was symbolized by the Veil of Isis, or the Helmet of Pluto, which is found as the Cap of Darkness in Norse mythology.

This system of thought was common to much of the ancient world. You get almost the same teaching in the Mysteries of Egypt where Anubis and/or Thoth takes the place of Hermes. A special note to make here is that these 'conductors of the dead' are also in many cases the instigators of the teachings of the Mysteries. Their role of 'Walker of Two Worlds' made them the guardian of neophyte and initiate alike, and both strove to become proficient in the ability to travel in worlds other than the physical.

Let us look at this 'Lore of Persephone' from the point of view of the Ancient Mysteries. To Iamblichus, it was the study of that astral knowledge pertaining to the creation of images from the generative energy. To the ancients, the term 'astral' meant the unseen world in general, and they believed that in this unseen world there were many classes of beings, as well as many different planes of consciousness. (Iamblichus, *Egyptian Mysteries,* p. 81.)

First, let us deal with the inhabitants of the world of Persephone. Scutellius gives us nine, a number that fits exactly with the Tree of Life, for he did not include in his system the Absolute or the Unmanifest:

1. the invisible gods;
2. the sky-gods;
3. archangels;
4. the angels;
5. the demons (remember that these were *not* devils);
6. leaders;
7. princes;
8. heroes and demigods; and
9. souls.

St Paul in the Epistle to the Ephesians gave the following classification:

1. princes;
2. authorities;
3. kosmokrators; and
4. the spiritual essences in the super-celestial spheres.

Damascius says that the Chaldean Mysteries held to the following list of Beings of the Unseen World:

1. gods that are pure mind;
2. gods subsisting before all subordinate dominion;
3. rulers;
4. archangels;
5. divine beings confined to no special place or service; and
6. beings with a special place and/or service.

The geography, if I may use that word, of the Unseen World was carefully mapped out in both the Egyptian and the Greek Mysteries, and the initiate was expected to have a sound knowledge of this celestial geography and to have been made free of these inner worlds before he started any exploration of the realms of 'death'.

Now let us examine the method by which the Ancient Mysteries taught their initiates to do their exploring. Mainly, it was a method of mind-control. There were numerous systems in vogue; but with a little effort, most can be brought within the scope of the following system which is based on the Qabalah.

First there was the condition of Unmanifestation called 'The God of Gods'. This condition was the All and the One, the Alone; and it was, and is, utterly beyond our comprehension. It could be given a name, but no attributes. It was the 'On' of the Neo-Platonists.

The next phase was 'Ho ontos On', or state of Real Being. It held all the various grades of being that lie between the completely unmanifest and the physical world which our senses reveal to us. This latter was called 'Becoming', or 'Genesis'. In the Ho ontos On there were four states of consciousness:

1. the spiritual;
2. the mental;
3. the emotional; and
4. the aetheric.

This last was a supra-physical condition. It was an inner world containing five elements; the fifth being usually called 'aether'. The physical world was held to be made up of earth, water, fire and air; and these four elements were held fast and bound to the form seen in this physical world by the fifth element of aether. The ancients taught that this fifth element acts upon the other four as isinglass acts upon jellies. It keeps them in their correct form.

You can put this information on the Tree of Life as follows:

10.   Malkuth is the world of the four elements.
 9.   Yesod is the world of the fifth element, the matrix in which Malkuth is embedded.
8/7.   Hod and Netzach form the emotional world – the form and force sides respectively.
6/5/4. Tipareth, Geburah and Chesed are the mental worlds.
3/2/1. Binah, Chokmah and Kether are the spiritual world.

Man is a child of the Absolute, the Unmanifest, and he belongs in the Cosmos which is his home. His Cosmic and as yet unmanifest self is called the Monad, the true Ego, and the Yechidah. It belongs to the On, or not being, condition of existence. When man comes into the realm of Ho ontos On, into the sphere of Real Being, he grows very gradually three dual-natured bodies: the spiritual, the mental and the emotional – that is, six inner plane bodies, and an aetheric body, which crystallize into the four elements of the physical body as we now know it.

So the soul of man has four states of consciousness which correspond to the four states of consciousness in the soul of the Great Earth Mother. (Soul here means all states of consciousness between the physical and the unmanifest cosmic monad.) Put another way, man has within him seven planes of Real Being corresponding to the seven planes of Real Being of the Earth Mother. 'As above, so below.'

Each of the seven subtle bodies of the soul of man belongs to and has a close link with the seven planes in the soul of the Great Mother. The relationship of each soul body to its plane is the same as the relationship of the physical body to the physical body of nature.

The nature and the real being of the soul of man is rooted in the nature and real being of the soul of nature, plane by plane. The Mysteries taught that if man could learn conscious control of his own soul, by his own subtler-than-matter bodies, then he could function consciously on the corresponding planes of the earth soul in exactly the same way as today he functions on the earth plane of nature. The ancient schools taught that an initiate could only hope to travel in safety on the other levels of being with the aid and protection of the god to whose cult he belonged. And he was given the protection of that deity after he had been initiated into the ritual of a particular plane of consciousness.

Part 4: The Inhabitants of the Realm of Persephone

Let us turn to the teachings of Iamblichus as given in his work *The Egyptian Mysteries,* concerning the inhabitants of the next world.

Iamblichus tells us that in the religious teachings given in the Egyptian Mysteries between 4,000 and 300 BC, and in the Graeco-Egyptian Mysteries between 300 BC and AD 300 – about the time that Iamblichus lived – it was a matter of faith that from the One Great God (Neter) there came the many, gods and men.

His teachings can be summarized thus. Behind all Being there is the causeless Cause of All. That Cause in itself is not Being; it is Amun, whose titles were the One, the Maker of All that have Being, the Hidden One. Proceeding from this One is the realm of Real Being. And in this realm are the gods and lesser divinities, who – with 'souls' – are the inhabitants of the Kingdom of Persephone. From this One, through the divinities in the realm of

Real Being, come the human and animal kingdoms that exist in the realm of 'Becoming', i.e. the physical world.

So between the Cause of All in the Unmanifest, and mankind in this realm of 'Becoming', there are many kinds of divine being, some superior, some inferior, to man. These beings exist and evolve in this intermediate state of consciousness which Iamblichus calls the realm of 'Real Being'.

This realm of Real Being is also described as the Soul of Nature, the Supreme Genetrix, by Ab-Ammon, the Egyptian priestly initiate who was the teacher of Porphyry and Iamblichus. The ruler of the realm of Real Being was 'Mind', the leader and king of the things that actually *are*.

The Divine Races of this realm, which could be reached by means of the sacerdotal technique of the Mysteries (*The Egyptian Mysteries*. p. 55), were divided by Ab-Ammon into two classes: the Superior Races, and the Inferior Races. The Superior Races were the gods and half-gods. The gods were spiritual essences. They were not bound to form as man is; but they governed the forms for which they were responsible from outside. They were – speaking with regard to man (op. cit., p. 41) – superior and perfect, while man is inferior and imperfect. These spiritual essences (relative to man) can do all things at once, uniformly and now; in contradistinction to man, who is unable to do anything completely or immediately, either speedily or individually.

These gods were completely formless, whereas man is circumscribed by his physical body. Ab-Ammon lays down the principle that 'Mind, the leader and king of all things that actually are, the Demiurge of the Universe, is always present with the Gods in the same manner, completely and abundantly, being established in itself unalloyed according to one sole energy.' (Ibid.) He contrasts this Universal Mind with the mind of man, which is derived from it.

What this important passage means is this: mind is the magical creator of all things that exist. It is creative energy. There is the Great, All Perfect Creative Mind of the Universe. This is the Demiurgos. Man, in a limited, feeble fashion can draw upon this creative mind of nature because he forms part of it. The gods, however, are actually aspects of that creative mind of nature, and are not limited, as is man. They, the gods, have direct access to it.

Below these superior gods, there come the half-gods, who were the teachers and directors of souls. Today, we would call them the 'Creations of the Created', for they were the results of the creating minds of those great spiritual essences, the gods. These half-gods are to be distinguished from the Archons or rulers over matter (op. cit., p. 79), whose characteristic seems to have been the force and disorder of creative energy when functioning in matter (op. cit., p. 83).

Of the same rank as the half-gods but of a different nature were the archangels and angels. 'To the Gods there pertain order and tranquillity, and with the figures of the archangels there exists a representation of order and quietude. With the angels there is the disposition of order and peacefulness, but they are not free from motion.'

Proclus says (op. cit., p. 83n) that in many Mystery rituals 'the Gods project many shapes of themselves, many changing figures; there will be a formless luminance radiating from them, now represented by a human shape, and now different'. Now these things were seen only by the Epoptae, the initiates of high grade who were being or had been fully initiated.

It must be understood that in the Mystery initiations the ritual did not aim at materializing an immaterial spirit. It aimed at raising the consciousness of the initiate above that of the physical level, and enabling him to function on a level that was in tune with that of the Gods, or selected Entities.

If a certain note is repeatedly struck on a piano then it will tend to set in vibration the strings of other pianos nearby which are tuned to the same pitch. In a Mystery ritual a certain spiritual note was struck, a note tuned to the vibrations of the spiritual essence which was the god of that cult. Those partaking in the ritual, if they had been trained to pick up this note and tune their consciousness to it, could pick up and receive the spiritual vibrations of the deity of that cult.

Those who entered the Mysteries were, and still are, given a long and very careful training in the art of 'tuning in'. To speak in terms of the wireless, you were taught which wavelength to use, which stations you might expect to pick up, and even the kind of programme you should be able to hear ... or see, for they had a spiritual television of a sort. You had only to watch yourself for error.

The advantage of this Mystery method is that it can be checked quite easily. Suppose you were a member of the Mystery school whose god was Thrice Greatest Hermes. You would expect to get the god Hermes in his symbolic form, perhaps as the Ibis-headed Thoth, or the winged Mercury with the caduceus, etc. You would pick up the appropriate symbols and attendants, and so on. But if you picked up a dog-faced demon with blood and thunder, or saw one of the Chithonian deities bearing down on you with a menacing air, you knew full well that someone had blundered. And it had to be you. You would have to explain to your justly annoyed superiors how it was you had called up the myrmidons of Pluto instead of the bright figures of the Elysian Fields.

Let us now sum up the points that have been considered. The Mystery gods were not immaterial ghosts in human guise, nor were they material idols. They were spiritual essences. They were part of the One God as a wave is part of the ocean. The forms in which they were contacted were the result of man's image-making faculty, for the gods are formless energies. They expressed an aspect of the 'Real Being' of the Unmanifest. They are *real* in their own way and on their *own* plane. Archangels, angels, half-gods and archons are realities of the same kind.

The initiate was trained to tune in by means of a ritual to the spiritual vibrations of the deity of the cult to which he belonged. When in this condition a more subtle set of senses opened up and the initiate could see and hear with the eyes and ears of the spirit. He did not see materializations with his physical eyes and ears; he was on a higher level of consciousness. Paul said: 'I know a man of Christ ... who was caught up into the third heaven. In body or out of it, that I do not know, God knows. I simply know that ... this man was caught up to Paradise and heard sacred secrets which no human lips can repeat.' (1 Cor. 12:1–4.)

Here you have in the words of St Paul an accurate description of the results of a Mystery initiation. This experience is exactly the same as that which the pagan Mysteries sought to give their initiates when taking their grade initiations in the saving cult of their particular deity, be it Hermes, Serapis or Isis.

Part 5: The Bridal Song
The Bridal Song of the Ancient Mysteries should start one's soul upon a journey that is not often taken today. Those who have studied the 'Sacred Marriage of the Qabalah' as taught in Israel about the time of the crucifixion will know this ancient road well. (Mead, *Echoes from the Gnosis,* Vol. XI, p. 32.) In the 'Wedding Song of Wisdom', taken from the Greek version, we find sung of the 'Maiden', the Bride-to-Be, the Secret Wisdom:

Her fingers are secretly setting
The Gates of the City ajar.

In the terminology of the time, this 'Maiden' is the Light's
daughter, the higher self, the one that sits in the bridal chamber of
the heart, an ancient term for the subconscious mind. She is the
one whose invisible fingers will open the gate of that inner city,
lying beyond the stairway of effort.

'The Religion of the Mind' was a term used to describe the
religion of the disciples of Thrice Greatest Hermes; men who
lived in an inner world of great beauty of thought and purity of
feeling. Here was a world created by the human mind, human
devotion and human intelligence of those who had been taught in
the ancient fraternities how to use the secret wisdom of Hermes.

Religion for them meant a combination of myth, magic and
ritual. But these words did not have the meaning they have for us
today. Myth was not fairytales, but the collective symbolism of a
psychological process. Magic was a process for training the mind
and making the will work upon consciousness, and ritual was a
method of using the five senses to aid the soul to lift itself above
the four elements of the physical world on to the spiritual
stairway whose lowest step is that of the 'Aether of the Wise'. One
step on that stairway leads first into the purple darkness of the
path of Saturn; then on, to the silver radiance of those moonlit
regions that stand before the orange-hued Temple of the Religion
of the Mind which Qabalists call 'Hod'.

Just as you have a higher and a lower self in your spiritual
make-up, so the priesthood of ancient Egypt – considered as a
class – had a higher and a lower self. The functioning priesthood
of the day formed the lower self, while Thoth was the
personification of the Group Oversoul. He was the higher self of
the Egyptian priesthood.

Within the Group Oversoul were stored all the experiences, the
knowledge, the memories of past and gone priests, priesthoods,
sacred colleges, and Mystery cults of ancient Egypt. The essence
of four, five or maybe more, thousands of years of religious
thought, meditation and magical working had gone to build up
the essence of that mighty Oversoul.

Out of the Oversoul of the Egyptian priesthood came much of
the Hebrew bible. The basic stories of the Old Testament have
come to us via Joseph, Moses and Solomon. Joseph married the
daughter of Potipherah, the Priest of On (Heliopolis), whose

ruins are near modern Cairo. On is probably one of the most
sacred, and certainly the most famous, university towns of ancient
Egypt. Moses was said to have been educated there – his Egyptian
name was Osarseph, a derivative of Osiris. Manetho says that
Moses served as a priest of Osiris. Not only did the Twelve
Patriarchs settle in Egypt, but all through the history of the
Hebrews there is a strong tradition of close relationship with
Egypt and Egyptian thought.

Out of the Egyptian Therapeutic system, as described by Philo,
grew up the monastic system of the Christian churches of Rome
and Constantinople, of Alexandria and Antioch. And it is as well
to remember that at Alexandria was born the group soul of the
Christian priesthood.

Hermes was the personification of the priestly oversoul of the
wisdom religion that grew up under the influence of the worship
of Serapis. This Hellenized religion was the child of the older
priestly religion of Egypt and had its centre of power in
Alexandria, and it held sway over the minds of men for some 700
years. Its powerful group soul expressed itself through the
teachings of Hermes Trismegistus. Out of this priestly group soul
of the Graeco-Egyptian religion, the group soul of Christianity as
a priestly religion developed. It gave us many of the ideas found
in the New Testament and in the traditions of the Roman
Church. It made the world of Jesus of Nazareth possible. 'Out of
Egypt have I called my Son' is a saying that is true in more ways
than one. The wisdom of Moses came out of the numerous
priestly colleges of Thebes, the city of No-Amon, destroyed by
the Assyrians; and of On at Heliopolis. The New Testament
wisdom came, in its turn, out of the priestly colleges of
Alexandria. Thoth and Hermes both stand behind Christianity's
sacred book, the bible.

No one is talking here of popular Christianity, either ancient or
modern. There is and was a wide gulf between the Christianity of
the priesthood of the Inner Christian cults and the Christianity of
the laity.

The group soul of the priesthood of any vital religion is a
specialized group soul within the greater group soul of the
followers of that religion. The group soul of the priesthood is
always more strongly knit, far stronger and more potent as a
magical instrument than is the less clearly defined, more
malleable, group soul of any religion as a whole.

In a Church such as that of Rome, you have today an example

of a group soul within a group soul. The priesthood are a class apart from the laity. They have their own special interests, their own religious knowledge, their own methods of teaching, learning and acting. They have their own ethical code, and in all these things this inner priestly code may be something which is quite different from that of the laity.

This point has been laboured to make the next point clear. Just as Jesus Christ is the personification of the male aspect of the group soul of the Church of Rome, and the Virgin Mary is the personification of the female aspect of the same group soul, so Hermes and the Sacred Wisdom form the male and female aspects of the Hermes Trismegistus Religion of the Mind.

Hermes is the male type, the great Teacher who saves. Isis is the Lady of all Wisdom and the Teacher of all Magic. (*Thrice Greatest Hermes*, Vol. I, p. 481.)

The New Testament tells us that the Virgin treasured the sayings of Jesus in her heart. And the Roman Church teaches openly that she taught the disciples in the upper room before the coming of the magical fire of Pentecost.

So too in the literature of the Trismegistic cults. Even the Lady of All Wisdom and the Teacher of All Magic gets her wisdom and her power from face-to-face instruction by the most ancient Hermes, with whom she gets into contact through spiritual vision.

For the celibate clergy of the Church of Rome, and especially for the monks in their cells, it is the Virgin Mary, the female force, that is attracted to them in their need for help and guidance. Nature will out, even in psychology. 'Mary Worship' is the natural result of the celibacy of the Roman Priesthood.

One can listen to the Catholic priests in their pulpits describing how Mary the 'Maiden Mother', comes to the tortured soul, inflamed by fasting and the sins of the imagination. She it is who gives to the fasting monk in his solitary hours the visions he longs for. Mary is the monk's 'Bride-to-Be'. It is she whose fingers are 'secretly setting the Gates of the City ajar'. It is she who sits in the Bridal Chamber of the celibate priest's heart.

Now let us return to the religion of the mind, and consider the methods of the 'Maiden' setting the gates ajar. As already pointed out, the Maiden is the secret wisdom of the higher self, and the common factor in the pre-Christian gnosis, the Pythagorean and Neo-Platonic gnosis, as well as the Christianized offshoot of the gnosis of Alexandria. All attempt to set ajar the gates of the inner world of the human soul, and to admit the influence of the higher self.

The methods used were a combination of myth, magic and ritual. You get the myth-making tendencies in the speculations with regard to the Fall and the sufferings of Sophia. You get the same thing in the Trismegistic lectures; in the story of the World Soul, of the Nous, and the creative aspect of the Logos.

Hermes is simply the Graeco-Egyptian name for Thoth. He is the creative word – not only of the Cosmic Absolute, but also, on a lower arc, of Amoun, the Absolute of the Universe. As such he assists both Ptah, the male creative aspect of the universe, and Isis, the feminine creative power of the universe.

Isis passes out of the realm of myth and into the realm of magic and ritual. The Lesser Mysteries of Alexandria were the Mysteries of Isis in her aspect of the Lady of Magic, the Teacher of Wisdom. In the three degrees of the Lesser Mysteries of Isis through which the neophyte had to pass before he could claim the right of admission to the Greater Mysteries of Osiris, the neophyte had to specialize in the magical use of the divine names and attributes, and he had to be summoned to the Temple by the Goddess herself.

This summons was given in the form of a theophany, the Goddess appearing to the neophyte when he was exalted by fasting and self-discipline in the Temple Sleep. The candidate was tested for fitness by a trained priest who would read his mind and thus determine whether or not he had reached the required standard. It was a sort of psychoanalysis. Fifty years ago, the idea of an examination of this type would have been considered foolish. Today, thanks to the researches of Freud, Jung and others, we know that trained psychiatrists – which the ancient Egyptian priests certainly were – can probe the soul and weigh it in the balance against the feather of truth in a manner that might well seem to our forebears to be miraculous.

Magic and ritual were, and still are, methods of soul training; and myth, magic and ritual were the fingers that set the gate of the inner city ajar. A ritual of Isis, which was performed regularly throughout the Graeco-Roman world to about AD 400, aimed at raising the impressions received by the senses of sight and hearing and inflaming them with emotion until the soul was swept out and beyond the limitations of the physical body into a state of consciousness that enabled the neophyte to feel the influx of the power of the All-Mother and to see her in the traditional form of Isis, Queen of Heaven.

Modern religious psychology provides us with numerous examples of this not-uncommon phenomenon. The Church of Rome recognizes this phenomenon and gives many instances in the lives of her saints. If we see its genuineness in this case, we cannot in fairness withhold the admission of its genuineness in the case of the Ancient Mysteries. That is not to say there has been no fraud, no simony, in those Mysteries. There was – and there has been such in the Christian Church. But no matter how many cases of fraud there may have been, the fact of its existence does not affect the authenticity of that Mystery phenomenon which the Ancients called 'setting the Gates of the City ajar'.

Part 6: Les Ténèbres de l'Ignorance

Before considering that period of history which has been well-named 'the Night of Ignorance', let us study the basic reasons that make the Mysteries – ancient or modern – so obnoxious to the organized priesthoods of Christianity.

In the first place, the ancient Mystery cults were secret societies. In the past, the attitude of the orthodox Church to the Mysteries was exactly the same as is the attitude of the Roman Church today towards the Freemasons. Then they had the power to slay and torture; today – thank God! – they do not.

The Mysteries taught that everyman can be his own priest. That makes organized priesthoods an unnecessary class. Naturally, the ancient priesthoods – both pagan and Christian – disliked having their privileges taken away from them, to say nothing of their tithes. You cannot blame a man for turning nasty when you interfere with his pocket.

Again, the adepti claimed to have the keys of heaven and hell in their possession. So did the Christians – but they claimed the power of admitting you to heaven or sending you to hell as the Church wished.

The true adepti claimed only to have each his personal key which unlocked for him alone the doors of the heaven worlds. He did not use his key to keep his neighbours out. Neither did he sell special 'through tickets' for purgatory. The Church of Rome said then as she says now: I alone hold the true teaching; belong to me or go to another place.

The initiate of the Ancient Mysteries said: Seek and ye shall find, knock and it shall be opened unto you. Anyone could seek and find. There was only one method by which one could be successful – hard work. It is still so in the Mysteries of today.

The Church of Rome said then, as now: Believe and support, then God's grace which is in the Church's Bank of Spiritual Grace, will see you safely into heaven.

The real key to the matter is this. The Mysteries taught, and still teach, that each individual is his own saviour. The churches teach that man is a miserable sinner, and only the Church can keep him out of hell. Only the Church can save a suffering humanity that is born and lives its whole life in sin.

Now let us turn to that 'Night of Ignorance' which the Church ushered in when she destroyed the ancient pagan civilizations. The story of the treatment of the Mystery tradition by the Church is, on the whole, sorry reading. In the third and fourth centuries AD the conquering Christian religion destroyed the gnosis, which had its chief centre in Alexandria. In the fifth and sixth centuries – having become a political instrument for imperial policy – it destroyed the pagan universities and schools in Greece and elsewhere, schools which had in some cases been teaching for over a thousand years.

Used as a political instrument, the Church proved fatal to a civilization tottering from age and corruption. Its teaching poisoned humanity instead of healing nations that were very sick. It is not unfair to say that the ethics and sociology of Christianity destroyed the fighting spirit of the Roman Empire just as effectively as the Roman free trade system in foodstuffs destroyed the livelihood of the Roman peasant – once the backbone of the Roman Army. While the food dole destroyed the independence and sapped the morale of the artisans of the Roman cities, Rome fell in the end because the Roman armies were largely officered by and recruited from barbarians, who placed Greeks and Syrians, as well as Romans, upon the throne of the Caesars.

By the seventh century, orthodox Christianity as a religious power was rotten to the core. The Western Roman Empire in Britain, Spain, France and North Africa had perished. In the Eastern Mediterranean, Mahommedanism had shattered the Eastern Roman Empire. Most of Asia Minor, Mesopotamia, Syria and Egypt became Mahommedan; and the Byzantine Empire as a Christian State sank to the lowest depths of vice and misery. Even in Italy, by the eighth century, the old Roman Empire had ceased to exist, and there the Christian Church ruled only by virtue of the protection of the Franco-German Holy Roman Empire from their headquarters north of the Alps.

By the ninth century the Saracens had conquered Spain, while

England, most of France, as well as Switzerland and Germany, had long before lapsed into barbarism. Learning had perished, and so had freedom. There was a single exception. North of the Pyrenees from the Bay of Biscay to the River Rhode, was a prosperous belt of country about 200 miles in width. This portion of south-western France owed its prosperity to the fact that the Visigoths, who conquered the country in the fourth and fifth centuries took special care to absorb without destroying the splendid civilization they found there. The rulers of Toulouse were the sovereigns of the only Christian state which remained happy and prosperous in the wreck of the western Empire of Rome. The rulers and upper classes of this little state were Arians, not Catholics. But in the course of time Arianism and Catholicism merged, and the country became – nominally at least – Catholic, and acknowledged the supremacy of the Pope.

The Mystery religions of the Graeco-Egyptian city of Alexandria had, in about the fourth century AD, taken refuge outside the Christian Roman Empire in Babylonia and Persia. Speaking very generally, it may be said that the Mystery religions of the Western Tradition reappeared in the fourth and fifth centuries as Manicheism. Like the conquests of Alexander nearly a thousand years before, the Mahommedans in the seventh century had broken up and scattered the Mystery centres in these countries. Some of the adepti passed into Bulgaria, Dalmatia and Hungary. In time these teachers worked up the valley of the Danube, the Rhine and the Po, then along the Italian and French trade routes to Toulouse, Orleans and Paris.

They were referred to by many names, of which 'Cathari' and 'Patarini' are probably the best-known. Their teaching was synthetic and built up from a Christianized form of Buddhism and Manicheism. It taught reincarnation, the avoidance of taking animal life, and the priesthood of the laity. It made mock of Churches, of priests, and of salvation by priestly officiousness. It recognized no priest as an intermediary between God and man. It taught that release from suffering and reincarnation could only be obtained through loss of desire for wealth and comfort, and it insisted on simplicity of life and service to one's fellow men as the way to happiness and release from rebirth and worry.

The religious and social conditions of the Christian Church at this time, between the ninth and thirteenth centuries, were deplorable. Bishops and priests vied with the nobility in vice and scandalous living. Both classes combined to grind the last farthing out of the merchant, the artisan and the peasant. It was hard to say which was worse – the feudal baron with his men-at-arms, or the Christian prelate with his monks, friars and nuns.

The Catharist heresy spread like wildfire in the eleventh and twelfth centuries. Priests, abbots, monks, nuns and whole congregations deserted the orthodox Church. The revenues of the papacy were seriously affected – and so the order was given to stamp out the Catharist heresy.

In 1125 St Bernard was sent to Toulouse, where a crowd hooted at him. In 1175 a council was held in the same city to stamp out the heresy; but as the courts of Toulouse and the feudal nobility had become open to secret heretics, the papal legate left in despair. The little town of Albi gave its name to a new heresy in that part of France. And so, in 1195 when Innocent III mounted the throne of St Peter, the word went out to all Christendom to start the Albigensian Crusade.

As Innocent III promised the German and French barons the lands and wealth of southern France as a reward for success in this crusade, plenty of 'good' Christian men swarmed to his banner. The military leader and representative of the Pope was Simon de Montfort – a man now infamous in history as one of the most brutal and bestial military leaders the world has ever known. Behind him, casting a halo of spirituality over this grim engine of destruction, stands St Dominic, founder of the Dominican Order, a man who in cold, calculating cruelty was in no way inferior to his military leader.

The troops of de Montfort swept over the rich provinces of France. Their first exploit was the capture of the small town of Beziers, in which 60,000 men, women and children – mostly fleeing peasants and even orthodox Catholics – had taken refuge. By order of the Abbot of Citaux, the papal legate, all were slain. The town was set on fire, and the entire population perished in the flames.

There followed ten years of ferocious warfare in which 500 towns and castles were destroyed. Open warfare and slaughter by soldiers were replaced – when peace (!) was made – by the activities of the Inquisition. In the end, the remains of the Albigensian heretics, reduced to a few hundred, took refuge in the vast natural cave of Ornolhac. The Catholic Governor of Toulouse walled up and guarded the only entrances – and that was the end of the Albigensian heresy in south-western France. Considering the methods employed by the Christians of that time, it was a merciful act. A once prosperous and highly civilized country had been brought back to the fold of the orthodox Christian Church. It came back as a desert with half of its population slaughtered in cold blood.

Before that time, the south of France was the only Christian country in Europe where the Jews had absolute religious and civil freedom. With the triumph of the orthodox party the Jews lost that freedom, and the once highly efficient educational organization of the State completely vanished.

As had happened some 800 years before, the Christian Church as a temporal power had seen its pockets threatened by the Mysteries and its professional clergy shamed by the purer life and teachings of the adepti. Once again, the sword and the flame destroyed the schools and the temples of the Mysteries, and restored its revenues to the papal college. But another attempt was soon made to bring the Mysteries back to Western Europe – this time by the Knights Templar.

The story of the Knights Templar is a curious one. In about AD 1120, Hugo de Payens and eight French Knights founded this Order in the Christian Kingdom of Jerusalem. Hugo de Payens and his comrade Geoffrey de Saint-Adhemar were not only fighting men, but were also mystically inclined. Saint-Adhemar, who came from Toulouse, was an Albigensian. Their protector was Baldwin II, King of Jerusalem, who for a year had been the prisoner of Emir Balak the Saracen.

The East at that time had a number of secret societies which were philosophical in their teachings and military in their actions. Then, the Mahommedan world was famous for its mind culture and learning. It was the age of Omar Khayyam and other great men.

In Palestine, Hugo de Payens found Theocletes, who was said to be the last Patriarch of the Gnostic sect of Johannites, and from him the Templars obtained their right to initiate. These three men, Hugo de Payens, Geoffrey de Saint-Adhemar and Theocletes are said by Maurice Magre (*The Return of the Magi*, p. 145) to have founded the Order of the Temple. It lasted for 184 years; for St Bernard approved the rule of the new Order in 1128, and Jaques de Molay was burnt, by order of Phillipe le Bel, in March 1313 after trials and torture that had lasted for seven years.

The Templars were a secret society with various grades of initiation. There was an Inner Order, which remained unknown and which governed the society under the nominal orders of the

Grand Master. There appears to be little doubt that they were in close touch, and often on friendly terms, with the Saracens. They grew rich and powerful. They had an immense army of highly trained men. They were exempt from military service, and could only be tried by the Pope. They had about 9,000 castles scattered in every country at the time of their destruction – all well-placed strategically.

It would seem that Phillipe le Bel suddenly realized that a great military power had grown up in France and outside his authority. On 13 October 1306 he arrested the Templars, confiscated their immense wealth and destroyed the Order in France. Thus finished, *so far as is known*, the last great attempt to win back for the Ancient Mysteries the material power and prestige they had enjoyed when Mithras was the cult deity of the Roman fighting man.

Once again the Religion of Love had triumphed. With the rack and the faggot the Christian teachers of the gospel of mercy and justice had crushed the Ancient Mysteries and stamped out their deadly teaching of the freedom of man's soul from sacerdotal bondage. Yet those Mysteries were not dead, only driven underground; and within the last hundred years they have once more come into the open. What is the power that lies behind them? What enables them to live on even when the outer form has been destroyed?

The power is the power of the divine pressing into manifestation. The ancient schools knew how to build channels for this divine power to use – and the power did the rest. The schools and their initiates are but the instruments of a mighty, conscious and intelligent will that is ultra-human.

The initiates of such schools know that reincarnation is a fact – though the doctrine they teach is not the popular one that today goes by that name. The temples of the Order in the physical world may be broken down, and their initiates killed; but the Temple of the Mysteries on the Inner Planes cannot be destroyed. Nothing can prevent the initiates from reincarnating or from recovering what they have learned of the ancient wisdom in past lives.

From time to time, a leader comes back and commences the work of rebuilding the outer manifestation of the Inner Temple. When that work begins, the initiates of that Temple who are in incarnation return to their Order and take up their work once more. Life after life, they who are of the ancient schools hear the call loud and clear. They feel the pull, and return to the Order to which they rightly belong.

December 1934 to March 1935

3.

The Esoteric Aspect
of Religion

There is a tendency today for people to seek 'instant occult knowledge', believing a rough (in some cases exceedingly rough) memorization of other people's work and ideas to be enough. There is little enthusiasm for digging out information from little-known sources, and from them developing one's own ideas. This was not the Colonel's way. He sought, sifted and summarized, happily and with undisguised enthusiasm, and on the basis of this he formed his own ideas and theories. The undoubted scholarship of the members of the Inner Light of that time was phenomenal. The Colonel was outstanding – but there were others who ran him close and who (like the unknown author of the letter criticizing his words concerning the American Indian Ghost Dance) could and would take him to task.

The encyclopaedic knowledge shown in this article is mind-boggling; and it is worth reading slowly and carefully for the information it imparts, quite apart from the occult advice it offers.

Although one can in no way compare the motives and high principles of the Inner Light with those of the Hell Fire Club of Regency days, both had members who could and did read Greek, Hebrew and Latin with almost as much fluency as their own mother tongue. Those days, alas, are gone. Scholarship of such high degree is rare in the occult these days.

Part 1: The Grey Dawn of Religion
The facts upon which these articles have been based are taken almost entirely from 'orthodox' sources, but the inferences drawn from these facts will seldom be orthodox. Also, the subject under consideration will be 'Religion' in contradistinction to individual religions, heretical or otherwise.

Professor W. Morgan, in *The Grey Dawn of Religion* (p. 1), tells us that, as a scientific historical study, the 'science of religion' is little more than half a century old, and that we know very little as to how, or why, or out of what, religion evolved in prehistoric times. And what lies behind that little that we do know, can be no more than a matter of uncertain speculation. He also warns us to be very careful how the facts about primitive religion which we may know are interpreted; and he tells us quite clearly that while the facts – for example, of totemism – are fairly clear, the numerous explanations given of them are in the highest degree hypothetical (p. 5). He adds that, with the information which is at present at our disposal, it is fairly clear that religion has developed from lower to higher forms.

This dictum as regards exoteric religion, or rather religions, may be accepted as being very generally true. The modern Roman Catholic Mass as a sacrament, is a far more civilized ceremony than either the ancient Taurobolium of Mithras or the sacrifice of his son and heir by Mesha, King of Moab, a sacrifice which was made when the King saw his capital in danger of being stormed by the troops of the King of Israel. But it is not all certain, when we turn from the outer forms of religion to consider its inner spiritual power, that the modern priest is in as close touch with the 'unseen world' as the priests of, say, 4,000 years ago, or even of the first century of the Christian era. Intellectually, the average priest of today may be superior to the average priest of long ago, but whether he is spiritually as well is open to question.

Professor Morgan seems to think that the religious ancestors of the priest and prelate of today were the magic-working priesthoods of the ancient religions, that is, the mediumistic sorcerers of the remote past. He is also of the opinion that often they were witch doctors of a type similar to the shaman of the Ural-Altai tribes of today. In this respect, he is in agreement with the famous Professor Otto of Marburg, who thinks that religion must have started from the sense of the eerie and uncanny. And there is little doubt that both Otto and Morgan are right, and that ceremonial religion, as we know it, has grown out of magic. The Roman Catholic Mass, for example, is a potent magical ceremony.

Now having gone so far, the learned Professor Morgan ceases to probe any deeper into the remote beginning of religion. 'Nothing' he says, 'is more futile than to go with Durkheim to primitive phenomena for an understanding of what religion essentially is' (p. 29). Nowhere, however, does he explain what 'religion' in its inner essence is. And very charmingly he covers this omission and ends his book with the verse:

A fire-mist and a planet, a crystal and a cell,
A jelly fish and a saurian and the caves where the cave men dwell
Then a sense of law and beauty and a face turned from the sod;
Some call it evolution, and others call it God.

Let us now turn to Dr Geden, also a well-known authority on the comparative method of studying religion. He tells us that the object of this new science is 'to gather and assimilate truth from all sides, to winnow the chaff from the wheat, and to follow the truth thus found wherever it may lead'. Also its object is to rid religion of any connection with magic, for, by the way, magic is Dr Geden's bugbear.

Now, as Professor Morgan has failed in his book to give any idea of what religion, as opposed to religions, is, it is necessary to see if a definition can be found of what this very common word means in the science of comparative religion. Again, unfortunately, Dr Geden, great authority though he is, can give little help. He points out that to give a definition of religion is difficult (p. 17), and he adds: 'The simplest terms therefore in which to define Religion and to distinguish it from Magic, with which in reality it has little to do, are probably those of *worship.*' There he, perhaps wisely, leaves the matter. But as this definition is not very helpful, Dr Geden must be left for yet another modern authority.

Dr Carpenter, principal of Manchester College, Oxford, is much more thorough in his comparative study of 'religion'. In his little book, *Comparative Religion* (p. 42), he tells us that Varro, Cicero and Lucretius – in about 50 BC – discussed the derivation of the word *religio*. Cicero connected it with the verb *legere*, to string together, to arrange, to read. Lucretius, however, found its origin in *ligare*, to bind, to tie fast.

Marcus Terentius Varro is interesting, for he treated 'religion' under three heads and declared that 'in the form presented by the poets' tales of the gods, it was mythical. Founded by the philosophers upon Nature (physis) it was physical. As administered by the priests and practised in cities, it was civil.' (Varro's *Antiquities*, section entitled 'Divine Things'.)

Here is 'the old notion that Religion was a legal convention imposed by authority for purposes of popular control; and Varro does not disdain to declare it expedient that States should be deceived in such matters'.

From the point of view of the individual man struggling through life, and often not very happy, this kind of treatment of religion, while informative and interesting, does not help much. For when a man begins to think seriously about 'religion' as opposed to religions, he comes up against the problem of what religion in itself really is. 'How can I find out for myself?' is today a very common question.

Even the various Christian Churches can help one but little. For example, a pamphlet entitled 'What are Monks for?' – which has received the imprimatur of the Church of Rome, defines (p. 6) religion as follows: 'The word "Religion" is one of the most venerable in the vocabulary of men. It may be taken to signify a collection of doctrines or dogmas, that God has revealed, which the Church teaches, and which we are bound to believe.' This is certainly not a definition of 'religion'; it is no explanation whatever of what 'religion' in itself really is; but it is an interesting statement of the views of the Church of Rome about religions. The Church teaches, and therefore you must believe! And, to use a colloquialism, that's that.

As regards the Protestant sections of Christ's Catholic or Universal Church, Jacobus, in *The New Standard Bible Dictionary*, defines 'religion' thus: 'Regard for what is believed to be Deity.'

As a somewhat half-hearted attempt to define religion while saying nothing that might be considered too definite, or be attacked as too unorthodox, or even too orthodox, this Protestant definition is the antithesis of the one given by the Church of Rome. The latter at least knows what it wants to say, and it has the courage, as well as the knowledge, to say exactly what it means.

The agnostics cannot help us much in our search for the essential meaning of 'religion'; for a great deal of modern sceptical – that is, rationalistic – literature is prepared to define 'religion' as a pathology; and after all, there may be something in that, for religious mania is just as well-known a disease as, say, alcoholic mania.

So having got very little help from the professional religious teachers, and having discovered that their opponents, the rationalists, look on religion as an aberration which indicates intellectual deficiency, it is interesting to see what an unprofessional writer on religion, a philosopher, has to say about the subject. Professor Whitehead is a Fellow of Trinity College, Cambridge, and Professor of Philosophy at Harvard University. Although he is not a professional theologian, his books which touch on 'religion' are influential, and are probably more widely read by the educated laity than are those of any modern clerical writer. He has no axe to grind. He is not a paid servant of the Church, and it would seem that he does not care a 'tinker's damn' for either orthodoxy or rationalism. In his book *Religion in the Making*, and just before he gives his definition of religion, he makes the following statement:

> ... we have the gravest doubt as to what religion means so far as doctrine is concerned. There is no agreement as to the definition of religion in its most general sense, including true and false religion; nor is there any agreement as to the valid religious beliefs, nor even as to what we mean by the truth of religion.

And a little further on (p. 7) he points out that 'in considering religion, we should not be obsessed by the idea of its necessary goodness. This is a dangerous delusion.' No wonder Professor Whitehead is regarded with such a wary eye by the professional priest. He defines (p. 6) religion as follows: 'Religion is the art and theory of the internal life of man, so far as it depends on the man himself and what is permanent in the nature of things. This doctrine is primarily a social fact.' Again, Professor Whitehead says: 'Religion is what an individual does with his own solitariness.' This is rather unorthodox. Some 2,000 years ago, Christ said that the sabbath was made for man and not man for the sabbath – a phrase that was blasphemy to the priests and the Pharisees of the time. Whitehead, in the lines quoted above, has really said that the various religions are made for man, and not man for the religions. From the institutional point of view, this is an extremely dangerous type of teaching. Many a priest would treat it as rank blasphemy. It is a threat to a vested interest.

Professor Whitehead, in explanation (p. 7) of his definition continues:

> Thus religion is solitariness; and if you are never solitary, you are never religious. Collective enthusiasms, revivals, institutions,

churches, rituals, bibles, codes of behaviour, are the trappings of religion, its passing forms. They may be useful or harmful; they may be authoritatively ordained, or merely temporary expedients. But the end of religion is beyond all this.

It is not until belief and rationalisation are well established that solitariness is discernible as constituting the heart of religious importance. The great religious conceptions which haunt the imagination of civilised mankind are scenes of solitariness; Prometheus chained to his rock, Mohammed brooding in the desert, the meditations of Buddha, the solitary Man on the Cross. It belongs to the depth of the religious spirit to have felt forsaken, even by God.

Today, thanks to the exploration in North Africa and in Western Asia, we know that the idea that religion is solitariness was very common in paganism, as well as in the early forms of Christianity. And, taking the word 'ritual', in its common, 'lay' meaning of 'any ceremonial form or custom of procedure', it can be seen that there is such a thing as the 'ritual of solitariness'. Thanks to the discoveries of papyri, and to the decipherment of inscriptions in temples and in tombs, it is known that 2,000 years ago men went out into the deserts of North Africa, into the wilderness of Syria, to the mountains and forests of Asia Minor, hoping to find, after patient searching and prolonged training, the essence of 'religion' in this 'ritual of solitariness'. The great Mystery centres were in the 'hidden places'.

There are Christian Orders today whose members seek, in the ritual of long-continued meditation, to get at the heart of religion; and these practices are also common to almost all the religions of the East. Solitariness in some form or other is considered to be a vital aspect of the religious life by practically all sects and religions, except those of extreme Protestantism; that is, by sects who have forgotten how to meditate.

That any individual who sets apart a few minutes every day for silent meditation in the 'inner chamber', can carry out the 'ritual of solitariness', is a statement which cannot honestly be denied, and should not be objected to. Yet when *Religion in the Making* was first published, the suggestion that 'religion is solitariness' seemed to strike quite a new note in the ordinary popular thinking of Protestantism. And the reason is not far to seek. Training in the science of meditation has almost vanished from the practical religion of the Protestant laity. And Professor Whitehead's definition has come as a welcome reminder to the twentieth century that there are two sides to any religion: the form and the force side, the spirit and the letter.

The organization of Boy Scouts, Girl Guides, Parish teas, etc., are but passing forms of a semi-religious hobby. They are not 'religion', though they are often mistaken for it. They are extremely useful and interesting social side-shows, and they are no more part of real 'religion' than was the selling of doves, or the changing of money in the Temple.

Only too often it may with truth be said that when the Protestant minister finds that he has failed as a prophet, he begins to rely on filling his church by means of parish teas and whist drives. This is not to say that there should be no parish activites, but these things should never take first place, as they often do in the life of the parish priests of the Protestant sects. Always on the go – no time to prepare; is a complaint that is often heard on the lips of the clergy. The man who says this condemns himself. He may be an organizer, but he is no true priest. He may be an ordained priest, but he is not a functioning one.

There is only one way to keep the force tide of religion running strongly in a parish priest or in a layman, and that is to insist on the daily performance of the ritual of solitariness, *for* a fixed time, *at* a fixed time, and, above all, *in* a fixed place. One must, if possible, have the fixed place, for meditation is the link between the outer world of matter and the inner world of spirit. One cannot, unless one is an exceptional person, link up with the unseen anyhow and anywhere.

Anyone who has been in touch with the rising generation and with modern religious thought and its methods of expression will know that the 'key' to most of the 'free' religious thinking of today can be summed up in the phrase, 'From authority to experience'.

Can personal religious experience be obtained today in the way it was in the ancient Mystery religions? The answer to this question is that anyone of average intelligence and common sense who is prepared to pay the price demanded can arrive at a direct experience of religious truth. Such persons can unveil for themselves the mystery of death; and they can 'know' – not merely believe, but 'know' – the truth of the conception of a 'reality' behind this world of experience and utterly different from it.

In the exoteric religions of individual churches the laity will find the form side of religion fully developed and open for all to use, and to use with great benefit to themselves. But the force which will turn this outer form into a living inner reality must be created by each individual for himself. No man can light the spark, or tend the flame that burns in the soul of another. You may, as a teacher, pass the match and the box, or shelter for another a feebly flickering flame, but you can neither kindle the sacred fire in the heart of another, nor keep it burning when once it is lit.

'Religion', as Whitehead puts it, 'is Solitariness.' And the way to 'experience' lies through the 'ritual of silence' – a ritual which every individual must carry out for himself. 'If you are never solitary, then you are never religious.' (*Religion in the Making*, p. 7.) And when reading the religious history of those forgotten centuries, it must never be forgotten that the key to any clear understanding of that which the pagan religions on their esoteric side strove to do and to teach lies in a sympathetic study of their use of meditation, i.e. of the 'ritual of silence', to attain to 'reality'.

Again, it must be understood that it is only when a certain facility in meditation has been acquired that the great adventure of 'religion' really begins. For the pagans, as well as for those early Christians whom we call the 'Gnostics', the gnosis was a practical religious experience rather than an intellectual process. They taught that the gnosis can only be got through the 'ritual of silence', an esoteric teaching which stretches back to the grey dawn of religion.

Part 2: The Living Past

Let us go back in thought to the living past that lies hidden in the Graeco-Roman religions, and see what it can teach us today. To begin with, it may be said that, so far as the outer world of English Protestantism is concerned, one of the great discoveries of the last fifty years has been that 'intuition' (i.e. 'knowing by instinctive apprehension', or 'knowledge reached without reasoning by an inexplicable and unconscious process of thought') is a mode of awareness which forms the basis of the great religions. Intuition used to be considered a 'desire', such as desire for good, or for God, etc. It was thought to be an extension of consciousness which came to a favoured few by chance, or by a sort of good luck. Also, that the person thus favoured had to wait passively for this intuition to descend, and that it could not be commanded.

Within the last few years, thanks to modern psychological research, and a more careful study of the ancient Mystery religions, it is now known that such an extension of consciousness can be a matter of voluntary experience. It can be taught to all and sundry by means of a technique, just as music can be taught to all and sundry. The results, will, of course, vary in individuals, just as they vary in teaching individuals music. But there is a process of attaining to 'intuitional' religious knowledge, and it can be taught.

Now in studying those ancient pagan religions, from the esoteric point of view, the fact that the process of getting 'contact' with the unseen – the numan – could then be taught as a technique to suitable students, must not be forgotten. The Mystery religions cannot be understood unless it be remembered that the ancients had this regular and definite system for obtaining personal religious experience, which was taught to, and which could be efficiently learned by, most men.

Contacting the 'numen' was for them not merely a momentary flash of inspiration; it was a definite process, and it led to a very real result. It is a waste of time to study the Mystery religions if it is not kept constantly in mind that the background of pagan religious thinking was based upon this idea of the 'numen' as a hierarchy of spiritual powers which stretched between the human and the divine.

In an interesting book on the history of European thought, entitled *The Living Past*, by F. S. Marvin, there is (p. 3) the following sentence: 'Metaphysics apart, we know in fact that "thinking backward" has accomplished and inspired a new and passionate effort for "living forward".' Following up this idea – which, by the way, is pregnant with possibilities from the point of view of the comparative study of 'religion' – Professor Marvin points out that capacity for the organization of knowledge is the main difference between mankind in a state of civilization, and man as a savage. Professor Marvin, then taking these ideas for his thesis, develops his study of European history. Here it is proposed to apply this idea of 'thinking backward' in order to 'live forward' to this study of the esoteric aspect of religion. Further, it is proposed to add yet another idea, this time from the orthodox Christian aspect, a somewhat more revolutionary one. Nevertheless, it is an idea which is vital to any unbiased study of 'religion' as opposed to sectarian comparison of religious organizations. This additional idea is that 'all religious systems deserve to be valued by the practical test of their functional significance for human society'.

The Christian priests, as a class, would certainly not agree with this statement; for, put in other words, this phrase means that all religious systems, be they so-called divinely established churches, or merely humanly established societies, without any exception, must be regarded as socially conditioned products. Their value must lie in the extent to which they meet the actual needs of individuals and groups at any given period.

Many of the more broad-minded Church writers, such as Angus – the author of *The Mystery Religions and Christianity* – freely admit that the Mystery religions of 2,000 years ago did meet the actual religious needs of their age, and so they flourished, for they were fulfilling a very definite want.

From this point of view, which could be that of any disinterested student of comparative 'religion', it necessarily follows that in religions there can be no absolute standard of truth – whether delivered once and for all to Apostles, or to anyone else. For since religions are now generally recognized to be, on the whole, evolving towards higher levels with each passing age, it follows that religions are always changing, and usually, though not necessarily always, developing. Thus there can only be a relative standard of truth, one which varies with the standard of the age, and with the mentality of the nation or nations which use any particular religion, or set of religions.

No religion, as taught by man, or by any collection of men, such as a church, is absolutely true. All have erred in the past, and there is every reason to think that all will continue to err in the future. And the history of the past shows quite clearly that all religions, so far as is known, have contained some truth and some error. So by 'thinking backward' we can learn the useful lesson that much which appeared to our ancestors (both near and remote) to be divine truth, was in reality but human error. Also, by 'living forward' we can comprehend how much that appears to us today to be vital Christian truth may well appear to our grandchildren, in the light of their fuller knowledge, to be childish and biased.

To study thus the history of religious thinking should have the excellent result of making us humble, as regards our capacity for absorbing religious truth. It ought to make us today more sweetly reasonable as judges of the past; especially when we remember that it is difficult to arrive at any even approximately accurate knowledge of what the ancient Mystery religions taught. For Christian iconoclasm has destroyed the shrine, and Christian ignorance has burnt, as far as was possible, all the literatures and the liturgies of the Mysteries. The Christians of the fourth and fifth centuries were even more wantonly destructive than the savage and ignorant Mohammedan soldiery of the seventh and eighth centuries. The researcher into the Ancient Mysteries has to overcome yet another difficulty which is additional to that of the destruction of their literatures. The early Christian Apologists (Angus, *Mystery Religions*, p. 41) misrepresented the Mystery cults in such a way that one is sometimes compelled to question how they ever exercised such a potent spell over ancient religious minds.

For the researcher of today there is no fact which stands out more clearly and strongly in the history of the Mystery religions than this: 'They were something which was a great deal more potent than a system of ethics divinely sanctioned.' Can this be said of that religion which today passes for modern, cultured and rational Christianity?

Few of those who have attained middle age realize, unless they have kept up an interest in ancient history by reading good modern historical works, how misleading was much of what they were taught at school or at college on the subject of the Graeco-Roman world of some 2,000 years ago.

The spade of the archaeologist, the zeal of the seekers for ancient manuscripts and papyri, have now brought to light information which has revolutionized our ideas on the civilizations of the Mediterranean Basin in the millennium which lies between 500 BC and AD 500.

Thirty-five years ago, much of our information with regard to these great pagan civilizations was drawn from the writings of the Church Fathers. Their views on these matters were considered to be authoritative; being called saints, they must speak only the truth; and the fact that they might be biased was not given much consideration. Their unfavourable view of the pagan civilizations was further supported by the extant writings of the great Roman satirists, who, as we know, dealt only with the cruelties of the idle rich, then, as now, a small and foolish class. Today we know that an early Church Father was usually as prejudiced against the Roman state as a modern Russian Bolshevik is against an English Conservative government. We also know that the average educated Roman of that age looked on the Christians as a set of fanatics who were not only pacifists, but also unpatriotic; whilst the uneducated Roman world in general looked on the Christians as an atheistical sect who in their hate of mankind were seeking to overthrow the religions as well as the social order of their time and to wreck the Roman state.

As each side hated and completely misunderstood the other, so each sought to vilify the other. Now that we are in a position to check much that the early Christian Fathers have quoted in their writings about the Mysteries, it has been discovered that, though they may have been very good Christians, and even excellent bishops and brave martyrs, most of the Fathers had a very undeveloped sense of historical accuracy, and they had no idea of fair play for an opponent. Modern historical research has shown us that the pagan world was not as bad as it was supposed to have been, and the pagan religions were not the evil cults that the Christian Fathers, in their zealous propaganda for their own 'ism', tried to make out.

There were great social and religious movements for alleviating the suffering of humanity, movements which had achieved a considerable measure of success long before Christianity began to be a power. There were religions of redemption with an effective method of salvation and a very high standard of morals and ethics long before Christ was born. It can fairly be said that there is no important dogma, rite or ritual in the exoteric Christian Church which was not in existence, in a similar form and with a similar function, long before Jesus was born. Francis Legge, in *Forerunners and Rivals of Christianity* (I.XLIX), and Angus, in *The Mystery Religions and Christianity* (p. 4), both endorse the view that, speaking of the six centuries from Alexander the Great to Constantine the Great, it can fairly be said that 'there has probably been no time in the history of mankind when all classes were more given up to thoughts of religion, or when they strained more fervently after high ethical ideals'.

It is true that there was much superstition, folly and ignorance, but do these not exist in the Christian countries today? Are there no quacks to be found in London today? The state and many of the national religions of Rome, Greece and Egypt were over-prosperous materially, and in a state of decline spiritually but is not the same thing often said of the Christian churches of today?

The great state-supported temples were the safest banking institutions of the ancient world; commercially, as we now know, they were functioning with power and had a very high prestige for commercial honesty. And as regards this point, it is not always remembered today that it was a characteristic Roman belief that the chief interest of religion was to serve the interests of the state. And to a great extent the official Roman religions acted as the bankers and the recorders of the Roman state. They were a part of the state machinery, and an efficient part. Many of the priests were regular members of the civil service, and had little or nothing to do with the care of individual souls; for the state religions were devices for keeping the group mind of the nation in a healthy condition and contented with their government.

Now the gradual development of the state religions into business concerns led to the growth of private religious cults, whose ministrations soon filled the vacuum thus left in the religious life of the individual. But of course the individual had to be sufficiently developed to feel that there was a vacuum which needed filling; and the Mystery religions only appealed to those who felt this need. And so, speaking generally, these private religious cults, which later on grew into the great Mystery traditions, catered only for the fairly well-educated. Unfortunately for the students of today, they have kept their teachings and methods of working very secret. But this we do know: they gave a definite teaching, by means of a symbol system, and they insisted on prolonged meditation on that teaching. Also, to develop intuition and to encourage its use the priesthood of the Mysteries used certain special symbols, which varied according to the cult, and they insisted on regular and prolonged meditation on these symbols, as a method of spiritual training.

Theurgy, or working with the aid of, or in the power of, the divine, i.e. the 'numen', was the chief result of this method of training. And so a new type of priesthood, with functions which were very different from those of the former state priesthoods, grew up gradually in the countries around the Mediterranean Basin.

As has already been said, the priests of the old state cults were, as a rule, men of the world, absorbed to a great extent in their civil duties, or in the routine commercial business of the great temples. The performance of religious rites was only a subsidiary function attached to their civil status, and they made no pretence of being in charge of the religious training of individual souls, at least so far as we can tell. On the other hand, the Mystery school type of priest was first and foremost a religious teacher, and it is now suspected that he was a sound practical psychologist as well.

In the Mystery religions the priesthood was trained in the care of souls — sick or otherwise — just as carefully as are the Roman Catholic clergy of today, and some of the Anglican clergy. The priestly initiates of the Mysteries knew how to co-ordinate certain of the religious powers of the soul, powers which are still but little known to the clergy of today. These priests knew how to enter upon certain valid and potent states of consciousness by means of a combination of ritual and meditation. As priests of a particular cultus they had for their own use a definite meditation technique, and they were able to build up for others a definite life of religious experience by means of study, meditation and sacramental rituals.

We know now that the Mysteries taught a very definite and very effective religion of salvation, where the word salvation meant spiritual and mental health here and now while in the flesh. Salvation did not mean for them a problematic escape from burning lakes and hungry spiritual worms in the life after death. These Mystery religions strove to make man a free and joyous citizen, not only of this world but of the next, the world of the life after death. And their guarantee was that of personal experience, not that of a supposed divine authority which was incapable of being verified by firsthand experience.

Within the secret brotherhood of a Mystery religion, the great adventure of religion became for the initiate a matter of personal experience – an experience which could be enjoyed by means of the cult's meditation technique and through their religious rituals. 'Religion' for the best of these pagan Mystery schools was something which went far beyond the teaching of a system of ethics. Their religion was a practical life process, which involved continuous mental, spiritual and emotional development.

Meditation developed the faculty of intuition, and intuition in its turn developed the faculty of spiritual realization, and the latter led to 'regeneration', or being born from above. Thus will the comparative study of religion show that 'thinking backward' into the 'living past' can inspire new and passionate effort for 'living forward'.

There is much in the history and in the teachings of paganism which is inspiring and helpful to men today, for these Mystery religions were essentially religions of vitality, joy and freedom of thought. It may be said, too, that if the organization of knowledge is the measure of a civilization, then the civilization of the Graeco-Roman world was a high one, at any rate from the religious point of view.

Finally, the fate of the Greek and Roman state religions is a plain warning to modern Christians that the value of any religion depends on its functional significance for the society of its age. Some 200 years ago Wesley called the Church of England of his day 'A dead Church worshipping a dead Christ'. Roman history shows only too clearly what a drag upon the evolution of humanity a dead church can be; and the history of the Reformation, some 500 years later, confirms this.

There are many today who say quite openly that the great Christian churches are drifting into the same position as the state religions of the Roman Empire at the beginning of the Christian era. If so, one wonders what till take their place.

Part 3: The Background of the Pagan Mysteries

One can have no grasp whatever of the inner or esoteric aspect of the pagan Mystery teaching unless one constantly reminds oneself of the following point of view. For the pagan initiate, that which strikes upon our senses from the outer world, 'the *form*', is not the whole of the phenomenon. Behind, or within, or without, or somewhere in another dimension, there is a reality of which the form in question is but a manifestation. Concealed behind all form there is a 'deeper being', to use a phrase from Keyserling. Unseen behind that which strikes upon the senses, there is, as it were, a living soul, which is imprisoned – as man is in his body – in the form which we see or touch.

Further, the Mystery schools veiled their teachings behind a mystical imagery to which we have very often not got the right key. Without that key, the symbolism of the Mystery religions often seems to be incomprehensible to us. Nevertheless, their teachings, so far as we can understand them, as we are now beginning to find out, are based upon practical knowledge and sound psychology.

Mystical experience – which we might call vaguely direct contact with the numen – was the central meaning of the Mystery initiation. Unless this point is clearly understood, it is useless to study the Mystery religions.

Let us now look at the general conditions of social life while the Mystery religions flourished. The period from 400 BC to just before the birth of Christ was one of social destruction, and it saw the breaking up of many states and most empires. Alexander the Great, in about 330 BC, destroyed the Persian Empire. His generals and their successors carved out kingdoms for themselves, and then fought incessantly with each other. Finally the Romans came and conquered the whole of the Mediterranean Basin. During 350 years of military destruction, all the little independent states had vanished; many cities were destroyed altogether; others were sacked time after time by the various conquering armies. Whole classes of once prosperous citizens had disappeared or were reduced to slavery.

It is calculated by reliable historians that during the first century AD three out of every four persons inhabiting the great towns of the Roman Empire were slaves, or had been in slavery. In many countries the once great and politically powerful middle classes had vanished. There were left only the very wealthy, and the very poor. The lawyers, doctors and school teachers, as a class, were usually slaves. The agricultural classes of Italy and some of the European provinces, had been ruined by foreign-grown wheat brought from Egypt, and issued as a dole to the urban unemployed of Italy and Greece. It has been truly said that in the Mediterranean Basin these three centuries had been centuries of prolonged suffering and destruction which cannot be compared with any other period in the history of the Western World. The Emperor took, in 13 BC, the title of Pontifex Maximus, and the peace which Augustus and Tiberius gave to a war-weary world led to the Emperor Augustus being ranked as a god – the God of Peace.

Now this long period of suffering, both mental and physical, had wrought great changes in the attitude of the European nations as a whole towards religion. In the first place, it had altered men's ideas about the local religions and gods of the small states. Before this period (say 600 to 700 BC) each little state had its own god and its own form of religion. That god, who functioned through a priesthood maintained by the state, looked after the general interests and safety of the state. Religion was then a matter for the group rather than for the individual. For example, in the whole of the Old Testament – as written in the Hebrew – there is no reference to individual immortality. It was the immortality of the Jewish nation that was considered to be important. Religion was a system of ritual for the 'salvation' – that is, for the safety – of the State. It hardly concerned itself with the fate of the individual, and it made little attempt to provide him with a reasonable hope of salvation in the next world or happiness in this one. Gradually the destruction of the petty local states led to a considerable loss of confidence in the local gods and in the local group systems of religious observance.

As modern historians such as Angus point out, man began to demand from religion, not a strong god who was able to save his city from pillage and rapine, but a benevolent god who would be kind enough to 'save' an individual, be he poor or rich, sick or well. And to meet this demand the great Mystery religions grew up slowly in an age of insecurity, of suffering, and of misery due to incessant warfare. The national religions, although they were in a state of spiritual weakness and decay, continued to function, often with great magnificence. The popular feasts were held, and popular rejoicing took place on the various festal days in much the same way as we keep Christmas Day – which, incidentally, was the birthday of Mithra, that of Jesus being unknown. (Our Lady Day, 25 March, was formerly the Annunciation of Mithra.) But the educated classes, as the writings of Marcus Terentius Varro and other authors show, had as a rule abandoned official religion for philosophy. While the educated priesthood of the official pagan religions seem to have been just as sceptical with regard to their religion as were the Sadducean priests of the time of Jesus. For example, we know that Scaevola Pontifex Maximus in the first century BC enumerated three kinds of gods: those of the poets, who are futile; those of the philosophers, who do not suit the state owing partly to their being superfluous and partly to their being injurious to the people; and those of the statesmen. (Angus, *Mystery Religion*, p. 33.)

In the time of Augustus, many of the state religious foundations had lapsed because the educated, the well-born, and the middle classes would no longer enter the temple schools; and the state priesthood was being filled from the ranks of the uneducated plebeians.

We must then distinguish between the three types of religion which existed at this period. There was the religion of the uneducated, which was popular superstition. It was a mixture of spiritualism, astrology of a very low type, and the official religion of the state in its lowest and most debased form. Then there was the official state religion, a religion for the group mind which was almost entirely formal. And thirdly, the religion of the educated classes – when they had any – which was a special type of personal religious experience. This was probably only to be found at that time in one or other of the numerous Mystery cults or secret brotherhoods, which specialized in a definite type of religious experience, under the patronage of a definite cult deity.

Now these secret brotherhoods had, as a rule, come from the East. Multitudes of slaves captured in the Roman conquest of the world were brought to Rome and Italy. They formed a world of their own within the Roman world. They formed their own private cult association – and they initiated their conquerors into their Mystery religions.

So once again we see that a careful study of the social conditions of any period is necessary before we can begin to understand the religious conditions of that age. And 'thinking backward' brings out into strong relief this maxim of the comparative method of studying religion – 'Religions are socially conditioned products and their value must lie in the extent to which they meet the actual needs of the individuals and groups of any given period.'

The old state religions had once met a very definite want, and while they met that want they flourished. Later, human religious needs changed. The state religions were unable to change with the times. And as they could not meet the demands made upon them, they fell into disrepute.

Now, speaking very generally, and for the sake of convenience, we may classify the Mystery cults as follows. First there were those that came from Asia Minor, the chief of which were the Magna Mater, and the great religion of Mithra, the soldier's religion. Broadly speaking, these cults appealed to the emotions. Next there were the numerous types of the Graeco-Egyptian Mystery religions, out of which emerged orthodox Christianity, which as we know it now is but a shadow of what it once was spiritually. Again speaking very generally, we can say that the appeal of the Graeco-Egyptian religion was to both the emotions and the intellect, but chiefly to the latter.

Now let us study the actual religious needs of that time and then consider how the Mystery religions as a whole satisfied those needs.

First, as has been pointed out, the state religions catered almost entirely for the group. They failed because they could not satisfy the restless questing individualism of the New Age that set in with the conquest of Alexandria. The chief religious characteristic of the Graeco-Roman age is the rebellion of the individual against the corporate body. The Sophists had created this spirit of individualism in Greece by teaching 'Man is the measure of all things', while Socrates, who died in prison for the rights of conscience in religion, and for the privilege of private judgement, probably quite unwittingly undermined all religious authority by teaching the eternal value of the individual. For Socrates and his pupils the ultimate basis of moral action was not in the laws, or in the religion of the state, or in tradition, but in man's own reason and conscience. This doctrine revolutionized the religious conceptions of the Ancient World; and Socrates was thus the Greek forerunner of Jesus.

The Mysteries catered to the fullest possible extent for this new spirit of individualism, for their basic idea was the unfolding of the personality, and they strove to make, by means of a specified spiritual training, life freer and fuller for all. In the religious fraternities of the Mystery cults, rich and poor, noble and slave, artisan and merchant prince – all met on a footing of absolute equality. Women were on a footing of equality with men. The Mysteries held out to all their members, be they high or low, man or woman, virtuous wife or mistress, the possibility of contacting the divine powers.

Secondly, there was another reason for the sudden development of the Mystery cults. At the time when this movement towards individualism was in its first flood, Alexander the Great broke up the long established and exclusive priestly colleges of the Euphrates valley. This drove hosts of priests out to earn their living by teaching their esoteric knowledge. Thus his conquests had religious consequences as far-reaching as the capture of Constantinople by the Turks in AD 1453, when the Greek scholars were driven westward to bring the Renaissance to Europe. It is curious how often in history we see the breaking up of a religion in one country leading to a religious advance in another land – usually a far distant one.

There is one point we must never forget, and that is that the ancient Greek was a fine missionary. He was intellectually curious and fond of innovations, and he was fortunate in living under a system in which all thought was free and unhampered by clerical conservatism. He was also intensely conscious of the unity of the divine. And for the educated Greek the various gods were an abstract conception of the One God. Take the speech of 'Isis of a Thousand Names' as given by the initiate Apuleius in his *Metamorphoses*, or *The Golden Ass*.

Parent of nature, mistress of all the elements, the First-born of the Ages ... whom the Phrygians adore as the Pessinuntian Mother of the Gods, the Athenians as Minerva, the Cyprians as Venus, the

Cretans as Dictynian Diana, the Sicilians as Prosperina, the Eleusinians as Demeter, others as Juno, or Bellona, others as Hecate or Rhamnusia; while the Egyptians and others honour me with my proper name of Queen Isis.

To the initiates of the Graeco-Egyptian Mysteries it was a matter of experience to know that behind all objects manifesting in matter, there exists, although it is unseen, an ideal object – that is, an ideal pattern which is seeking to become manifest upon the physical plane.

The third factor in the development of the Mystery religions was the passion which existed in the ancient world for the formation of trade unions. When life was so insecure, the individual, helpless against oppression, combined with fellow workers and formed a collegium or sodality. These collegia met, like the modern freemasons, with due 'rites'. Very often they were linked to a temple which was dedicated to an orthodox deity. Religion, and a sort of club life, as well as trade unionism, worked peacefully side by side. In some cases the religious aspect became more and more pronounced; in others the secular aspects prevailed. The former developed slowly into religious brotherhoods, worshipping a particular deity; and eventually many of them grew into Mystery schools. You can trace much the same idea in the development of the monastic orders in the Church.

But the most important of all the factors which contributed to the growth of the Mystery religions was the popularity of the practice of meditation which grew up out of the failure of the state religions to retain their hold over the more educated members of the community.

With the coming of individualism came 'conscience', which is a stoic term. Reliance on an outside religious authority gave place to subjectivity. The local type of decalogue was seen to be out of place. And the disciples of Socrates, together with the Pythagoreans and the Stoics, substituted for this authority the habit of self-examination.

Seneca writes, for example:

Every day I plead my case before myself. When the light is extinguished, and my wife, who knows my habit, keeps silence, I examine the past day, go over and weigh all my deeds and words. I hide nothing. I omit nothing; why should I hesitate to face my shortcomings when I can say 'Take care not to repeat them, and so I forgive you today'.

Thus we see that the pagan Mystery religions, by their emphasis on the importance of man as an individual soul, by their doctrine of the numen, and by their training in self-analysis and meditation, gave new religious hope to a world that was spent and war-worn, as Angus points out: 'The Mysteries brought a fresh spiritual impulse to a social system that had long lost that optimism which was such a conspicuous feature of the classic days of Greek freedom and greatness.'

Part 4: The Ritual Theurgy of the Mystery Religions

As the ritual theurgy of the Mystery religions is a thorny subject it is advisable to start by defining the terms employed rather carefully.

Ritual as used here means: 'Any ceremonial form or custom of procedure' (*Century Dictionary*, Vol. XVIII, p. 5195). For example, a poet writes:

> False are our words, and fickle is our Mind;
> Nor in love's ritual can we find
> Vows made to last, or promises to bind.

Ritual is easy enough to define, but to give a clear definition of 'theurgy' is not so easy. Here 'theurgy' means the combination of ritual and meditation, in a specially prepared sanctuary, for the attainment of certain particular religious ends. This is not a good definition, for it involves a number of obscure expressions. But the difficulty is this: theologians who write on the subject are quite ready to define 'theurgy', but, usually, they are not ready to admit of its existence. Now to define, that is, to declare the essence of, to make clear an outline of, a thing which one believes not to exist, seems to involve a contradiction in terms. To define that which does not exist, seems rather like painting an Academy masterpiece with a paintbrush dipped in distilled water only.

Here, however, is an attempt taken from the *Century Dictionary*, Vol XXII, p. 6286: 'Theurgy is the pretended production of effects by supernatural agency.' But the Greek word *theourgos*, that which is the effective of theurgy, also means a priest; and so this definition is not very illuminating. Also, it seems to cast aspersions on the ancestry of the priesthood. Are they the spiritual descendants of fraudulent miracle mongers?

Now that orthodox writer Vaughan, in his *Hours with the*

Mystics (i.36), gives the following 'good' definition of theurgy. He says: 'I would use the term theurgic to characterise the mysticism which claims supernatural powers generally, works marvels, by the virtue of talisman or cross, demi-god, angel, or saint ... .' The *Hastings' Encylopaedia of Religion and Ethics* (Vol. XII, p. 319) has this to say on the subject:

> The Celestial Hierarchy of Dionysius and the benign daemons of Proclus, the powers invoked by Pagan or by Christian theurgy, by Platonist, by Cabbalist, or by saint, alike reward the successful aspirant with supernatural endowments; and so Apollonius of Tyana and Peter of Alcantara, Asclepigenia and St Theresa, must occupy as religious magicians the same province. The error is in either case the same – a divine efficacy is attributed to rites and formulas, sprinklings and fumigations, relics or incantations, of mortal manufacture.

There is good sound British common sense; there is sound Protestant opinion backed by sound Protestant scholarship. But as a definition, it completely misses its objective, just as a man who shies at a coconut misses it if it does not exist. *Hastings* (Vol. XI), in a fine article on Neo-Platonism, deals pityingly with the theurgic tendencies of Porphyry, Iamblichus and Proclus, the famous successors of Plotinus. The author likewise puts up a coconut which, according to him, does not exist even in his own imagination, and then proceeds with great skill and impartiality to knock it down.

But there is this drawback to the otherwise sound scholarship and the concrete knowledge of Vaughan, and others of that ilk. They believe theurgy to be a pretended art and, as such, to have no actual existence. If they deny its actual existence, then of course they can give, no matter how much they may write on the subject, no *positive* information about theurgy. Because, for them, theurgy does not exist and so, by their own showing, they know nothing about it.

Perhaps it is better to go to those writers who had a definite and positive experience of theurgy, and see what the theurgic art meant for them.

Much of the information with regard to the theurgy of the ancients comes from the writings of the Gnostics, both pagan and Christian, and from the Neo-Platonists Plotinus, Porphyry, Iamblichus and Proclus. Now the basis of theurgy is contained in the following extracts taken from the teachings of Plotinus. He taught (op. cit., Vol. IX, p. 316) 'that the Universe contains many beings more divine than man – daemons, and gods, who are daemons of a more superior order'. Also, 'that the great sin is selfishness or self will, which makes us forget our father'. Moderns would perhaps replace 'father' with 'higher self'. Again, according to Plotinus, and indeed almost all the teachers of the Mystery religions, 'Death only means that the actor changes his mask', for death, in the Mystery teaching, is something very different from the 'holy dying' of the Christian religion of this age.

The system of Plotinus was a dynamic pantheism – the doctrine 'that the living forces of the Deity permeate all nature' (op. cit., p. 309). This is often taught today in Eastern religions and philosophies, and it is a very ancient Mystery teaching, which the Stoics taught openly well over 2,000 years ago.

Matter, for Plotinus, was not the matter known to the human senses. 'It was impalpable, intangible, all but nothing.' (Op. cit., p. 310). In other words it is the substance of physical matter, which becomes 'divine matter' when enriched by the spirit poured into it. We might call it the etheric background of matter.

For the Neo-Platonists, 'sensible reality' is but a shadow of the true reality. The sensible world is a reflection of the eternal world in the mirror of matter. And 'divine matter' is real, on its own plane, just as much as sensible matter is real on this physical plane. (Op. cit., p. 311).

Further, Plotinus laid down that 'a feeble contemplation makes a feeble object of contemplation'. With regard to this very significant admission, it is known now that a special type of 'dynamic' or active meditation was the method used by this school, as well as by the other schools of the Mysteries, to obtain the 'beatific vision' – the highest crown which is reserved for only the very highest type of mystic.

But in addition to these very rare 'great ones', these ancient contemplative schools, by means of a special technique, turned out hundreds of highly trained initiates, who were able to teach and work with power because they were able to enrich 'divine matter' by pouring spirit into it.

So we are now a little closer to understanding what theurgy really is. First, it is a psychological process, and it goes on in the mind. Then, theurgy makes use of 'divine matter' or, as we should call it in terms of the twentieth-century theology of Professor Otto, the numen. This theurgy 'informs' for it vivifies this 'divine matter' by ensouling it with spirit. In modern terms, the theurgy of the Mystery schools was the dynamic use of meditation to obtain personal religious experience.

What we rather vaguely, and in popular language, call religious 'ritual' is, in its essence, nothing more than meditation expressed in action. One can understand what this means by watching a Mass worked by Roman Catholic priests. In this case meditation is dual-natured, active and passive, and it deals not only with definite symbol systems, but also with symbols and symbolic actions.

So a more detailed explanation of what is meant by theurgy might run as follows. Theurgy is the continued use of meditation and ritual, in a specially prepared sanctuary, for the purpose of obtaining certain direct religious experiences. Its central teachings – at any rate in the earlier stages – deal with the 'birth from above'. It is a natural process, partly mental and partly emotional, which has nothing whatever to do with the supernatural, though undoubtedly it is, for the majority of Westerners, supernormal.

For the ancient 'knower' – the Gnostic of the Mystery schools – theurgy meant a technique of meditation and ritual by means of which a man in the flesh strove to unite himself consciously with his higher self, by finding the Kingdom of God within.

In one of the descriptions of initiation handed on in the Trismegistic sermons [Mead, *Echoes from the Gnosis,* Vol. I, p. 19, The Gnosis of the Mind] in which the candidate is reborn, or born in mind, he [the candidate] is amazed that his 'father' and initiator here below should remain there before him just as he was in his familiar form, while the efficacious rite is perfected by his means. The 'father' of this 'son' is the link, the channel of the gnosis; the true initiation is performed by the Great Initiator, the Mind. In other words, the 'initiated' is also the 'initiator'. Once again, it is evident that theurgy, at least in its simpler stages, is a process for making the higher and lower self combine, consciously, and for a definite purpose.

So Vaughan, though worthy and orthodox as a teacher, has in this particular instance misunderstood the issue completely. And his remarks about the efficacy of sprinklings and fumigations, which are of mortal manufacture, are beside the point.

There is nothing supernatural in theurgy. For the whole process is, and was, purely psychological. It is only those who are ignorant and without practical experience who talk about this 'pretended art' not realizing that the Christian Last Supper, Holy Communion, Mass, Eucharist – call it what you like – from first to last, is a theurgical operation. And so far as Protestantism is concerned, it is only too often badly worked and ineffective.

Now recalling the statement that theurgy is the combined use of meditation and ritual, in a specially prepared sanctuary, for the purpose of obtaining religious experience, consider the workings of the Roman Catholic Mass. Here is a modern example of ancient theurgical ritual, one that is still a very potent rite if you understand it, or if you are a welcome member of the group soul of the Church of Rome. For the purposes of this article the 'Order and Canon of the Mass', as explained by Dom Fernand Cabrol OSB is used. He tells us (p. 2) that attendance at the whole Mass was originally reserved for the initiated and baptized alone, there being two parts to a Mass. The first part is styled 'The Mass of the Catechumens', and the uninitiated were dismissed before the Offertory. The second part was 'The Mass of the Faithful' and the 'rites of this second part all relate directly to the Sacrifice of the Eucharistic Banquet' (p. 4).

The prayers called the Preface and the Canon, of the second part of the Mass were for a long time kept strictly secret (p. 6). The priest had to recite them from memory, for they were not allowed to be written down, and they were not translated into the vernacular until about 1850. The consecration of the Elements is called by the Church of Rome 'the Mystery of the transubstantiation of the Elements of Bread and Wine [into the body and blood of Christ]' (p. 7). An idea is here expressed that is familiar to any student of the sacred meals partaken of in the Ancient Mysteries.

Now the word Eucharist comes from a Greek word meaning a giving of thanks; and it is, even in Protestantism, essentially a sacrament, while the Roman Church defines the Eucharist as 'both the Sacrament and sacrifice of Christ truly present under the appearances of bread and wine' (Addis and Arnold, Catholic Dictionary, p. 323). In other words, the Christian Mass is a theurgy, worked by the initiated celebrant and his assistants. That modern authority on mysticism, Evelyn Underhill, somewhere describes the Mass as a ceremony of a magical nature, and she is perfectly right, because the Mass is a magical ceremony pure and simple, when worked by a properly initiated priest. It is *not one* when worked by an untrained ministrant for *then* it lacks *intention*.

As has been said, the initiates of the Ancient Mysteries held that there were subtle and potent invisible worlds which stand behind this visible and material one. Amplifying this doctrine, they also held that behind the material form which we call the man's body there are other and more subtle bodies – bodies which enable the man, when he can control them, to function in those other worlds which are invisible to us while in the flesh. These subtle bodies are constituted from the subtle matter of these inner worlds.

This teaching came apparently into the Greek Western Mystery Tradition from the two great Wisdom traditions of Babylonia and of Egypt. (Mead, *The Subtle Body*, p. 29.) The Pythagoreans and the Mystery teachers of that time were not unfamiliar with the use of the Augeoeides or Astroeides, or subtle vehicles of the 'soul in its purity' (p. 46). And these vehicles seem to be the same as the 'soma pneumatikon' – 'Spirit Body' – of St Paul (p. 48). These terms do not have the same meaning as the 'astral' body of the modern Spiritualists and Theosophists. The modern term 'astral body' really refers to that body which was termed by the ancients the 'image', i.e. eidolon, imago, simulacrum. While their 'shade', i.e. skia or umbra, is what we now would call the etheric body.

Plato, in the *Phaedrus* (op. cit., p. 49) uses the very evocative words, 'We are imprisoned in the body like an oyster in its shell.' And these ideas of the inner constitution of man and of his intimate relationships to the inner constitution of the world are essentially theurgical, and they have a very definite bearing upon the aims of the Mystery religions. The historian Plutarch (AD 50–120) says on this subject: 'When a man dies, he goes through the same experiences as those who have had their consciousness increased in the Mysteries.' (Mead, *The Vision of Aridaeus*, p. 13.)

It is a very curious coincidence, if it be a coincidence, that in Greek the verbs 'to die' and 'to be initiated' are almost identical. *Teleutan* is to die; it is a form of teleutao, to complete. *Telesthai* is to be initiated, and it comes from the active verb *teleo*, which also means to complete, to accomplish, to perfect. And it is so used in the New Testament, for example, in 1 Cor. 2:6 'But we speak wisdom among the perfect' – i.e. among the initiated.

Now Plutarch held high office in the Temple of Apollo at Delphi (op cit., p. 10). He was also connected with the Dionysiac Rites, and had a profound knowledge of the minor grades of the Osiric Mysteries. His teaching, as given above, is corroborated by that of the Neo-Platonists whose school came into existence after his death, and by the Orphic Traditions which were being taught centuries before his birth.

So far as our limited knowledge of these ancient Mysteries goes, this 'living death' of the 'perfected' or the high grade initiate, was common to all the Greater Mystery teachings, and this living death was the aim of their ritual. It was also the ultimate objective of the long years of training in the technique of solitary meditation which was given in most of the reputable Mystery schools.

Closely connected with meditation, as a theurgical system of getting in contact with the divine, is the system of incubation. Incubation, or, in popular language, 'the Temple Sleep', denotes in comparative religion the practice of sleeping (or at least passing the night) in a shrine or other sacred place with the object of receiving a divine revelation or divine aid. (*Hastings' Encyclopaedia of Religion and Ethics,* Vol. VII, p. 206.)

The basal theory is given us in the book of Job (33:15–16): 'In a dream, in a vision of the night, when deep sleep falleth upon men, in slumberings upon the bed; then he [God] openeth the ears of men and sealeth their instruction.' Jacob's ladder, Joseph's and Pharoah's dreams, Solomon's dream in Gibeon, in which he asked for wisdom, are all instances of a similar idea.

This practice was extremely common in Ireland when the Druids were in power. It is common today in Mohammedan countries, and prevails widely in countries ministered to by the Greek Orthodox Church, where it is now used for the cure of disease, and for divination.

Jayne, in *Healing Gods of Ancient Civilisations,* p. 50, gives a mass of interesting information on this subject which is up-to-date and, above all, accurate. He suggests, as the result of his study of the healing cult of the Graeco-Egyptian god Serapis, that the methods used were those 'that are now known as hypnosis and suggestive therapeutics'. He also tells us that 'the priest physicians' of ancient Egypt were persons of education and social standing, famed throughout the orient from earliest historic times ... men who stood forth as noble and beneficent figures of Egyptian civilisation'.

In Greece there were medical schools attached to many of the healing temples. 'Many cities had physicians under salary who were heads of public hospitals with a full equipment of consulting rooms, pharmacies, and operating rooms with instruments.' (Op. cit., p. 239.)

'Asklepios was the deified head of the Greek cult, and his shrines and healing temples were judiciously selected with a view to general salubrity, pure air and water, and general attractiveness.' (Op. cit., p. 252.) They were put outside the cities so Plutarch tells us (op. cit., p. 256) in order to get a more healthy site, and there were large and beautiful sanitoriums attached to the shrines of the more wealthy type.

Theurgy has, and had, a very real existence in its own state of being, which is psychological. It makes use of a combination of meditation and ritual to attain its ends, which should be religious. In the olden days, the Mystery priest was, by virtue of his office, a trained theurgist. In theurgy the immediate objective was the strengthening of the influence of the higher self over the lower self, and the giving to the initiate of more control over his subtler bodies, as well as purification and exaltation of his soul. The ultimate objective, to which only an initiate of the very highest type could hope to rise, was the 'beatific vision'.

So it will be seen that theurgy in these Ancient Mysteries was a psychological method. It was not a matter of formulas or incantations or fumigations, as certain modern writers seem to think. Its object was the purification of the man, and the exaltation of his consciousness.

Part 5: The Egyptian Tradition

If the methods of training used by the various Mystery schools are correlated, it soon becomes evident that, in spite of a wide diversity in details, most of the schools are working to a common pattern. So far as archaeological research can take us it would appear that the common working basis of the pagan Mysteries of the Mediterranean Basin (between 500 BC and AD 500) is to be found in Egypt. There are other explanations of this common factor which are given by the initiates when teaching in their schools, but these will not be considered because it is impossible to produce any historical or geographical or archaeological facts to corroborate these theories.

The Mysteries of Greece and Grecian Asia Minor as well as those of the Grecian Islands are according to Spence (*Mysteries of Egypt*, p. 17) the offspring of those of Egypt. Mr Spence has made this subject his special study for forty years and he may be right. Though it is open to question whether the Ayran (or Wiro) Mystery systems are based on the Egyptian system, there is no doubt that they have been strongly influenced by it.

Their similarity, however, can be explained in another way. Suppose the Mystery teachings with regard to the mind-side (including memory) of nature be true, and suppose that 'initiated persons' are able to commune with mind (used in the Plotinian sense) as the Mysteries declare, then the common pattern is not to be found in Egypt or elsewhere on this physical plane; it is to be found in mind. This is a simple explanation which moderns – without practical experience of the Mysteries – will find difficult to accept.

If the Orphic, the Pythagorean and the Neo-Platonic Mystery systems, as used in Alexandria, are examined and compared with the systems of Egypt it will be seen that they have, one and all, not only a common basis but also a common objective. It is their method of attainment that varies so much. Again, when the books written by modern authors on the subject of the Ancient Mysteries are studied, one is inclined to wonder how in the face of the evidence which they accumulate, their authors can consider (as so many do) the Ancient Mysteries to have been collective illusions. For example, Professor Macchioro in his book *From Orpheus to Paul* has collected an immense number of important facts about the Ancient Mysteries, also references to them from classical authors and from wall paintings, vases, etc. The net result seems to be that, in this professor's opinion, the entire Mystery system, as a method of gaining religious experience, was a delusion. It was the result of collective suggestion such as that which the Belgian hypnotist d'Hont used to demonstrate by way of experiment (op. cit., p. 100). Indeed (Chapter 3) this learned professor's object seems to have been to reduce the Ancient Mysteries to the status of a Ghost Dance religion, making them similar in their teaching and methods to those spiritualistic revivals which broke out among the American Indian Tribes during the nineteenth century (p. 53).

In spite of this bias the professor has done much good work in clearing away many sectarian prejudices, and in treating his subject with unusual sympathy. He has at least recognized that in the Orphic Mysteries mental phenomena played a very large part. He emphasizes the fact that the Greek Lesser Mysteries at Agrae and the Greater Mysteries at Eleusis were carried out without the aid of scenery (p. 63ff). As a result of modern exploration the construction of the Telesterion of Eleusis, the room where the neophytes were initiated, shows that there was no scenery, and that no dramatic performance, however simple, could have been enacted in this room where nothing but pillars could be seen. Formerly it was supposed that the visions seen at initiatory rites such as those described in *The Golden Ass* were stage effects produced by means of elaborate machinery, such as that used in our theatres today. Excavations show that these telesterions rested on solid rock and that such machinery could never have existed. And the excavation of the Kabirean Telesterion of Samothrace supports this conclusion.

From the results of archaeological research, as well as from a study of the accounts given by the ancient authors themselves, it is practically certain that the Mystery rituals were dramas, acted without scenery or movement, and without a visible and material stage. It seems also clear that magical symbols were used to invoke certain mental pictures in the imagination of the neophytes as well as of the initiates (p. 65). As the professor points out, myths became living facts through symbols. 'Symbols invoke the myth, and bring people into touch with it. Such symbols become the starting point of a whole series of visions and emotions.' Here the professor has possibly said a great deal more than he knows.

Thanks to Clement of Alexandria, the symbols which were exposed in the Orphic Mysteries are known (p. 67). These were a whip top, dice, a ball, apples, a rhomb, a mirror and a fleece. All these symbols referred to the story of Zagreus; it is said that they recalled the games by means of which the Titans distracted the mind of the young god while they killed him. But is this all? Chapter 10 of Harrison's *Prolegomena* suggests quite another explanation.

Proclus refers more than once to the fact that the symbols themselves exerted an influence upon the initiates which rendered them sensitive to the ceremonies and led them to divine communion. And this is an important point if any clear understanding of the Mystery methods is to be hoped for. It is not easy to explain ancient symbolism unless one is prepared to admit that it had a suggestive influence on those who knew its sacred meanings. Macchioro also comments (p. 68) on the sacred images, which he seems to think were statues or Xoana, and he describes them as savage idols replete with tremendous power, perfectly capable of killing or making a person mad or sick. This is, in some respects at any rate, an error. The sacred images which were replete with power were not of necessity physical images.

These facts and theories which he puts forward are extremely valuable to any student of the Greek and Egyptian Mysteries, for he closes many blind alleys. Sadly, for the probable reason that he has had no actual experience of the inner workings of a Mystery drama, Professor Macchioro has missed the real meaning of much of what he so ably describes. Nevertheless, his book is worthy of close study by all students of the Mysteries. He has missed some of the inner meanings because he has attempted to understand the Mysteries solely through the workings of his rational mind. The Mysteries were, and are, to a large extent based on the workings of the irrational mind. They are as irrational as is a man's love for a particular woman, and his desire for complete and ecstatic union with her.

They are irrational because the primary urge which drives the initiate into action is love; irrational love for an aspect of the divine and for a complete and ecstatic union with this aspect of the divine. The Ancient Mysteries must remain as a sealed book to the reader unless he can *realize* that the divine loves, and can be loved by, the human, and that ecstatic union with divine forces is possible here and now.

Professor James in *The Pluralistic Universe* (p. 13) when discussing the various types of philosophical thinking, points out that the distinguishing mark of 'a philosopher's truth is that it must be reasoned. Argument, not supposition, must have put it in his possession.' Contrast with this Aristotle's statement that is was not necessary for the initates 'to learn anything, but to have their emotions stirred'. (See Angus, *The Mystery Religions and Christianity*, p. 62.) This does not mean that there was no reasoned teaching given in the Mysteries; such teaching was given and is still given. It does mean, however, that during the actual ceremony of initiation the burden of the appeal was (and still is) laid upon the unconscious mind, and not upon the conscious or reasoning mind.

This point is of importance when studying standard authors such as Angus, who returns again and again in his books to the practical efficacy of the Mystery cults as living systems for producing religious experience. He writes for example:

> Another way of escape [from pessimism and the evils of dualism] was by the religion of ritualistic *Henosis* or union with God by rite and sacrament, represented chiefly by the Mystery religions and subsequently by the Magical mystical Christian sacraments. Such union was secured not so much ethically as ceremonially and

emotionally. The correct ritualistic process released the divine element to make its ascent to the higher world. The Mystery furnished the initiated soul with the password to bliss. By sacramental efficacy akin to contemporary magic the material man was in rebirth transmuted or remade into immaterial and therefore immortal substance. A guarantee of the immortality so passionately longed for was given here to each member of the Mystery fraternities. Initiates were 'demortalised', and being thus rendered divine, were endowed with deathlessness. (Angus, *The Religious Quests of the Graeco-Roman World*, p. 42.)

Such convictions and guarantees can never have been the result of matter of fact reason. No philosopher's truth can give one conviction in the realms of religious experience. The reasoning mind can check facts and fancies, but it cannot make religious truth real and living. That is the province of a part of man's soul which is not the reasoning mind.

A great writer on ancient Egypt – M. Moret – has put this point admirably in his book *Kings and Gods of Egypt* (p. 198):

The Votary of Isis, wrapt in ecstasy at the feet of the goddess, interpreted the revelation not in the word, but in the spirit, according to the need of his heart, in the glow of his faith. From that day mysticism lived. The Isiac became his own priest; the god no longer a far distant entity, a remote state providence, deigns to converse with him, becomes his tutelary friend, and as it were 'a thing of beauty and a joy for ever'. Each man possesses the God who is the father of all.

'The Isiac became his own priest.' This sentence elucidates the age-long hatred of the orthodox Christian priesthood for the initiates of the Mysteries. This priestly hatred explains why we know so very little about the Egyptian Mysteries, for the Christians destroyed everything belonging to the Mysteries upon which they could lay their hands. The Ancient Mysteries, like the seventeenth-century Quakers and certain other sects, threatened vested interests. The initiate scoffed at the idea of a paid and professional priesthood standing between God and man. They threatened a powerful and wealthy class and that class, in defence of its own pockets, destroyed its enemy thoroughly and systematically – a very natural thing, from their point of view, for any priesthood to do.

In these Ancient Mystery brotherhoods there was an accumulated knowledge of religious psychology which had been amassed through more than a thousand years of practical working. Thanks to the Christian habit of destroying, as heretical, anything that is not understood, or is considered dangerous, this knowledge was lost to the Western world for nearly 1,500 years. In the East, however, a higher type of civilization – and a less bigoted type of priesthood – has resulted in the preservation of much of this psychology in the form of yoga. This the West has now begun to study at a time when by patient scientific research, the medical and scholastic professions, freed from the haunting fear of the rack and the stake, or social and religious ostracism, are rediscovering in the domains of psychology and psychotherapy much that was once well-known to the ancients.

Today only the outer shell of the ancient cults remains. We have the stones of the broken temples, their mural decorations and those of the rifled rock tombs, and a few relevant papyri. There are a number of notices in the classical authors of Greece and Rome, and books written by such teachers as Iamblichus, Plotinus, Proclus and other philosophers, the scanty remnants of a once vast literature. We have also the furious denunciations of the early Church Fathers. Once these men were considered to be most reliable, but today modern historical research has shown, by checking their evidence with new sources of information, that they were generally biased witnesses, often ignorant, and in many cases deliberately untruthful. As Miss Harrison puts it *(Prolegomena to the Study of Greek Religion,* p. 538), 'Their wilful misunderstanding is an ugly chapter in the history of human passion and prejudice.'

In spite of concealment by those who favoured the Mysteries, much can be learned from the outer forms of the exoteric Egyptian religions once the Mystery technique has been acquired. A study of Moret, Breasted, Budge, Petrie and Weigal, although they deal chiefly with the popular and exoteric forms, is absolutely necessary before one can make much of the many hints which are given in Herodotus, Plutarch, Iamblichus, Apuleius, Porphyry, Arnobius (a Christian Apologist), Diodorus and Lactantius. The Hermes Trismegistic literature, which has been so ably edited by Mead, is really outside the scope of this manual.

There is also the so-called 'Book of the Dead', the real title of which is said by certain authorities to be 'The Book of the Master of the Hidden Places', or as Budge translates it in the rubric to Chapter 163 'The Book of the Mistress of the Hidden Temple'. This is especially valuable because a prolonged and careful study of the pictures and the symbols which are used in it has a curious and far-reaching effect on the subconscious mind of the student.

The modern authorities mentioned above, with the exception perhaps of M. Moret and, with certain reservations, Professor Budge, seem to think that the Mysteries of Egypt, like the exoteric religions of that country, grew up from crude beginnings. The anthropologists of today, like their predecessors of two thousand years ago, cling to the popular idea that all these religions were the offspring of the imaginings of savage negroid races from central Africa.

M. Moret certainly does not hold this theory, and Professor Budge has qualified it by saying that the religion of the educated classes should be excepted. But if, as has been pointed out, the idea can be accepted that the ultimate source of the Mystery teachings is not to be found in the physical brains of humanity, then the question of savage origin of the Mystery religions does not arise.

That this non-physical theory of the origin of the Mysteries was held by the ancient initiates is clear from the following quotation which is taken from Iamblichus' essay on the Egyptian Mysteries (p. 256):

> The Egyptians do not say that all things are physical. Indeed they separate the spiritual, the intellectual and the natural life from one another – not only in the universe but also in man ... and they acknowledge the existence of a vital power, pre-existent to the heavens and subsisting therein. They also establish a Pure Intellect above the world; and another which pervades all the spheres.
>
> Moreover, they do not survey these things by mere reason alone; but they announce that they are able, through the sacerdotal theurgy, to ascend to the more elevated and universal essences ... For there are according to them, many principles and many essences; and also supermundane powers, which they worship through the sacerdotal rite. (See also Spence, *The Mysteries of Egypt,* p. 61.)

In so far as the Egyptian and Graeco-Roman Mysteries are concerned, this 'sacerdotal theurgy' has the same meaning as the modern term 'the Western Mystery technique', and this is sometimes referred to as the 'Wisdom of the West' or the 'Yoga of the West'. In its essence it is a body of knowledge dealing with religious psychology. It is not a dogma, nor is it a teaching with regard to scientific or religious phenomena. It is really a technique for controlling the mind; and it is analogous to the yoga systems of India in its fundamental principles. Its empirical methods, however, are, speaking generally, different from those used in India, or by the Buddhists of Tibet, China and Japan.

This Wisdom of the West is a method of mental and spiritual training which has its roots in those Mysteries of Ancient Egypt which have come down to us through the Alexandrian schools. It has also been influenced considerably by the Chaldean and Greek Mystery traditions as regards it methods of training its students.

The mental training of the Yoga of the West in its early stages aims at teaching the student how to get in touch with his own higher self and then how to secure and to maintain (a much more difficult matter) a conscious link with that which Fechner called the World Soul. The Egyptian Mysteries also in their elementary stages (commonly called the Lesser Mysteries of Isis), taught their students how to get into conscious touch with the soul of the great Earth Mother, i.e. with the Green Isis.

It is necessary to explain here exactly what is meant by this term 'getting into conscious touch with the soul of the Earth Mother'. The explanations which are given here are by means of analogy; for it is impossible to explain in terms of brain consciousness the exact meaning of getting into conscious touch with a something that transcends brain consciousness.

One can explain to a certain extent by means of analogy, but one cannot describe. Those who have had this experience will realize what the analogy strives to convey. Those who have not had this experience will find it difficult to accept any explanation whatever.

Man has four states of consciousness: physical or brain-related; emotional or astral; mental; and spiritual. A saint lost in adoration of the Majesty of the Godhead is, so we should say, functioning in a spiritual state of consciousness. He is oblivious of his physical body, and he is no longer functioning consciously in his physical state of consciousness.

Again, consider the apocryphal mathematician who, absorbed in some abstruse problem, was found to be boiling his watch for his evening meal and noting the time by means of an egg held in his hand. The physical world had become for him unreal, for he had failed to notice the functional difference between his watch and the egg. The man was functioning on the planes of the mind. He was no longer in conscious touch with the realities of this physical world, which as a plane of consciousness had become for him subconscious. In technical terms he had risen above the plane of sense consciousness.

The genuine musician functions in the same way. His physical actions are subconscious and his consciousness is far away in that world of beauty and rhythm, and of sound as harmony, which is sometimes called the astral state of consciousness.

The understanding of the technique of the Mystery training which was given to the ancient initiates depends entirely upon our comprehending the idea (which has just been set forth in the recent quotation from Iamblichus) that, just as man is a living entity with these four states of consciousness, so this planet earth is a living conscious entity with states of consciousness which are analogous to those of man.

It is not here stated that the earth as an entity is conscious in exactly the same way that a man is conscious. The conditions may be analogous; but it is not said that they are identical. Man's consciousness is part of the consciousness that pertains to the earth's in exactly the same way that a bubble of foam on the surface of a wave pertains to the ocean upon which it floats.

The ancient Egyptian in the early stages of his initiation was taught that just as a man's body in obedience to man's will consciously draws its physical nourishment from the Earth Mother's physical body, so man's soul can draw nourishment from the Earth Mother's great oversoul. Man's emotional, mental and spiritual states of consciousness are part and parcel of the states of consciousness of the earth soul. Man's soul is individualized out of the soul of the Earth Mother, but it is not, in any way whatever, separated from it.

Man's soul, so the 'sacerdotal theurgy' taught, can get, and keep, and thrive upon, conscious contact with the soul of this planet – that is, with Isis. And in the Lesser Egyptian Mysteries, the neophyte was taught a special technique for lifting the veil of Isis, a thing which no 'mortal' could do – for the initiate was taught how to put on immortality before lifting the veil.

This term 'lifting the veil' in modern language means getting into conscious touch with the emotional, mental and spiritual states of consciousness which the ancient initiates personified as the goddess Isis – the Divine Mother of us all.

Part 6: The Cult of Isis and Osiris

The Laments of Isis and Nephthys
(Invocation of Isis – Berlin Papyrus 1425)

Come to thy Temple, come to thy Temple, O An!*
Come to thy Temple, for thy enemies are not!
Come to thy Temple!
Lo, I, thy sister, love thee – do not thou depart from me!
Behold Hunnu,† the beautiful one!
Come to thy Temple immediately – come to thy Temple
  immediately! Behold thou my heart which grieveth for thee;
Behold me seeking for thee – I am searching for thee to behold thee!
Lo, I am prevented from beholding thee –
I am prevented from beholding thee, O An!
It is blessed to behold thee – come to the one who loveth thee!
Come to the one who loveth thee, O thou who are beautiful Un-
  Nefer,‡ dead.
Come to thy sister – come to thy wife –
Come to thy wife, O thou who makest the heart to rest.
I, thy sister, born of thy mother, go about to every temple of thine
Yet thou comest not forth to me:
Gods, and men before the face of the gods, are weeping for thee at
  the same time, when they behold me!
Lo, I invoke thee with wailing that reacheth high as heaven –
Yet thou hearest not my voice. Lo, I, thy sister, I love thee more than
  all the Earth –
And thou lovest not another as thou dost thy sister!

(Taken from *The Burden of Isis; The Wisdom of the East* series,
p. 20.)

There is a difference between the gods of the Egyptian Mystery
religions and those of the popular and state religions which are
described by Professor Budge in his famous work, *The Gods of the
Ancient Egyptians*. The gods of the Mystery religions are drawn
almost entirely from what may be called the Osirian Cycle. The
other gods, it is true, appear in the Mystery rituals and systems of
training; but as far as is known, their role was a subsidiary one,
and a beginner does not require a detailed knowledge of their
attributes, forms and numerous symbols.

The Lesser Mysteries centre around the wanderings and

* The moon-god form of Osiris.

† A sun-god form of Osiris.

‡ A title of Osiris. *Osiris* is so named because he is the dispenser of
benefits, a form of the Absolute; one Egyptian dogma makes Osiris to
be *Hes-Iri*, which would seem to mean 'the seat of Isis'. (See
Iamblichus, *The Egyptian Mysteries*, Part VIII, Chapter 16.)

sorrows of Isis; the Greater Mysteries deal with the sufferings and resurrection of Osiris. Generally speaking, in so far as the neophyte is concerned, the former deal with the generation of worlds and souls, the latter with the regeneration of the human soul and the cosmos, the return to the divine.

The part played by Thoth, the teacher of the Lady Isis, is that of the Lord of Initiation and the God of Wisdom; it is one of the most important in the rituals. Then a little more in the background are the great cosmic deities such as Amoun – the Hidden One; the Ra cycle of the sun-gods; the moon-god cycles and the nature or elemental deities. (See Iamblichus, *The Egyptian Mysteries*, Part VIII, Chapter 16.)

The Egyptian Mysteries were essentially magical in their nature and their initiated priesthood seemed to have relied largely on ritual, as well as on meditation, for the magical training of their neophytes. The word 'magic' as used in this book may be defined as follows: 'Magic is the art of causing changes to take place in consciousness and in accordance with the will.' This is a definition which is well understood by most modern initiates. In other words, it is a technique for using the mind.

Von Hügel has written (*Essays and Addresses*, p. 251): 'Magic begins only when and where things physical are taken to have spiritual results apart altogether from minds transmitting and receiving.' The term magic has evidently changed its meaning. For the ancient initiates it meant mind-training, and the development – by means of such training – of man's transmitting and receiving faculties with regard to things spiritual and mental. In most modern Mystery schools magic still has this connotation. And it is curious to find an eminent Roman Catholic such as Von Hügel, who is famous as a philosopher and mystic, applying this ancient religious term to things material and removing it altogether from the sphere of the mind. One can understand a Protestant divine, or an anthropologist making such an error, but not a Roman Catholic. Perhaps the Church magic is from God, and all rival systems are from Diabolus!

In the Egyptian ceremonial magic, the *modus operandi* for obtaining magical power and concentrating it to a desired end, was usually that which is known as the assumption of a god-form, and the whole of these magical rituals and rites derived their effectiveness from the ability of the officiating priest (or priestess) to identify himself with the god (or goddess) being personified.

It is difficult to explain to anyone who has no experience of this peculiar magical rite, which is known as the assumption of a god-form, what effect this operation has on the operator and those working with him. Perhaps the best way of explaining this is by means of an analogy. An actor of genius is playing the part of, say, Hamlet or Othello. This, for the time being, is the person whose personality he assumes, and it is the historical or legendary personality of Hamlet or Othello that acts and reacts upon the audience and the other actors. The difference between such an actor and an amateur who merely knows his lines can be felt mentally and emotionally by all in the theatre.

Up to a point, this will explain to the non-initiated the validity of the effects of the assumption of god-forms in a Mystery ritual. But it must be remembered that for initiates the character or personification which was called Isis or Osiris represented not a human being but vast cosmic forces, which were mental, emotional and spiritual in their natures. There was behind these initiates a real power whose intensity was therefore greater than that behind the conception of any literary or even historical character, however famous. But remember this is only a rough analogy by way of explanation.

This class of magical ritual is sometimes called in comparative religion 'imitative magic', and it is extraordinarily common even today. The Roman Catholic Mass is an elaborate ritual for causing changes to take place in human consciousness in accordance with the will. It is efficacious, it is holy, and it is beautiful; it is extremely helpful for those who are in sympathy with it; and it is a fine example of modern imitative magic. Consider quietly and without religious prejudice the implications of the phrase 'Do this in remembrance of Me' – i.e. *in imitation of Me.*

The Communion rites of the Greek Church are an even more primitive form of imitative magic than that of the Roman Catholic Mass, for portions of the Greek ritual are worked by priests behind closed doors and out of sight of the congregation.

The Communion rite of the Church of Scotland which is celebrated in the Scottish National Church at Crown Court, London is another example of imitative magic, for you may have in this beautiful rite a duplication of the happenings at the Last Supper, the elders taking the place of the Apostles, and the ministrant that of the Lord Jesus. This ceremony, simple and ordinary as it may appear, with its actors clad in the garments of the twentieth century, is an exceedingly potent rite for causing changes to take place in consciousness. The Real Presence is there, and it can be felt in this particular case, just as effectively as in the much more elaborate ceremonies of the Greek or Roman Catholic Churches.

The Egyptian initiate's concept of a god was something very different from the idea which the idol-hating Protestant of the twentieth century usually holds. This difference is best explained by an analogy. In the Roman Catholic Church you will see devout worshippers praying before statues of the saints. If you study Roman Catholic literature you will discover that the informed Roman Catholic does not worship the saint; the latter is a medium through which divine power can be manifested for the benefit of the worshipper. You will also learn that the amount of power available is to a great extent regulated by the faith of the worshipper. In other words, the saint is really a psychological device for focusing the worshipper's mind upon a certain aspect of the divine power.

As an example of this, consider the following cutting taken from the *Daily Express* of 2 February 1935:

A PRIEST BLESSES THROAT SUFFERERS

Two hundred people suffering from throat complaints yesterday attended the Church of the Holy Apostles, Claverton Street, Pimlico S.W. for 'the blessing of St Blaise for throats'.

They were blessed by the Rev. Harry O'B. England, a Chaplain at Westminster Cathedral. He made the sign of the cross before the throat of each worshipper with two lighted candles twisted into the shape of a St Andrew's cross.

St Blaise was an early Christian Martyr who cured a boy with a bone in his throat. Roman Catholics now believe that he is the special protector of the throat.

The Egyptian god was also a psychological device for focusing the worshipper's mind upon a desired aspect of divine power. For the initiate, the god was a focusing point upon which he could concentrate when getting in touch with the sources of power which indwell the earth soul. By means of the god-form he focused upon these divine powers as the Roman Catholic with throat trouble concentrated on St Blaise. In the Egyptian religion there were many gods; in the Roman Catholic religion there are many saints. Gods and saints are but different names for the same thing. Both religions use the same methods, for the magic of the Roman Church came from the Schools of Magic in Alexandria.

The Roman Catholic saints are fellow workers with God. They serve the 'One God'. The pantheon of the Egyptian Mysteries was but a manifestation of the Egyptian 'Absolute' who is generally called Amoun or Amen, the Hidden One. Budge tells us that in his opinion the educated Egyptians were monotheistic 3,000 years before Christ. (See also Iamblichus, *Egyptian Mysteries*, Part VIII, Chapter 16.)

From the point of view of the Mysteries, there were three great religious centres in Ancient Egypt. The first was Heliopolis, near modern Cairo, the centre of the worship of the sun-gods. Here the specialized teaching was a technique for getting in touch with those Cosmic Forces whose general symbol is the sun, and whose overlord is the Logos of our system. This Mystery deity was some one or another of the many forms of Ra, or of Osiris when he became identified with Ra (see ibid, paragraph entitled 'Many Names of god formation of Matter', p. 253).

The second great centre was at Hermopolis Magna, some 200 miles to the south of Cairo. Here were the schools which were dedicated to Thoth, the God of Learning, and the Lord of Initiation. From this centre in later times grew up much of that literature which is known as that of Hermes Trismegistus (see ibid, note to p. 259.)

The third centre was at Thebes, some 400 miles south of Cairo. Here were the colleges pertaining to the Mysteries of the great Cosmic Builders and those of the moon-gods and earth-gods. Here was the centre of Amoun, the Unmanifest of the Egyptians (p. 254) and the divinities of Yesod and Malkuth, to use the terminology of the Qabalists.

If these three types of training are examined, it will be seen that generally speaking their special religious teachings deal respectively with the training of the superconsciousness, consciousness and subconsciousness.

As a rule, the moon forces represent the contacts of the Lesser Mysteries, the sun forces those of the Greater Mysteries, while the colleges at Hermopolis Magna trained those priestly initiates who stood behind the Greater and Lesser Mysteries as the members of an unnamed Order which governed and guided the former.

The classification given above will not cover the deities of the exoteric Egyptian religions. It will, however, be found sufficient by the beginner to act as a pointer and to indicate major divisions in the classification of the macrocosmic and microcosmic forces, which were used by the ancient initiates. It is not exhaustive and it is not meant to be. But the enquirer will find an immense quantity of somewhat confusing information in the following books: Iamblichus, *The Egyptian Mysteries;* Budge, *The Gods of the Egyptians;* Spence, *The Mysteries of Egypt;* Mead, *Thrice Greatest Hermes,* Vol. 1, Chapter 9. It is only fair to add that unless the student has a fair working knowledge of the Qabalistic technique for using the 'Tree of Life' he is wasting his time and his energy in trying to fathom the depths of the Egyptian pantheon. He will find this technique given in full in *The Mystical Qabalah,* by Dion Fortune, a book he is advised to study carefully. Here is the key Omar Khayyam failed to find.

In the ancient Osirian religions the central figures around which the rituals were constructed are Isis, Osiris, Thoth and Horus. Speaking generally, the Egyptians believed that Osiris came from heaven as a great teacher and that he died for his people. Also it was believed that by his death and resurrection Osiris became the ruler of the next world and the supreme judge of the living and the dead.

Even for the non-initiated Egyptians the central point of the Osirian religions was the sure and certain hope of resurrection immediately after death in a transformed body; and this hope was assured to the worshipper by the death and resurrection of Osiris, the ideal man.

In the esoteric concepts of the Osirian Mystery religions this sure and certain hope became something much more explicit – it was an experience to be undergone whilst still in the body. And this resurrection, as well as the symbolic death in the Mysteries, gave to the initiate the certainty of immortality.

The 'Veil of Isis' may be taken as a mystical technique term equivalent to the 'Censor' in psychology. It is a psychological factor which prevents man while still in the physical body from functioning consciously on the inner planes. A mortal could not lift the Veil of Isis, but the initiate who had died the Mystery death and who had risen as an immortal (and thus obtained control of the Censor!) was able to penetrate the Veil by virtue of the powers conferred upon him at his initiation.

So far, no real consecutive life of Osiris has been found. Professor Budge thought that the story was so familiar to the ancient Egyptians that all writers appear to have taken it for granted. They mention only such incidents as are necessary.

Budge tells us quite plainly that the 'classical writers and the

Christian commentators have no exact knowledge of the meaning of the history of Osiris, and none of them really understood the details of his cult'. Plutarch in his *Isis and Osiris* (Mead, *Thrice Greatest Hermes*, Vol. 1, Chapter 9) warns his readers that the real meaning of the cult teaching is other than the apparent meaning of the exoteric and popular story. Plutarch's treatise runs to about 100 pages, and to the modern mind, taking what he says literally, it is completely unintelligible. He was an initiate and a hierophant, and it is evident that in this treatise to Klea he is using expressions which he knows that she, as an initiated priestess, will understand, but which the non-initiated will not understand. Budge seems to think we are better off than classical authors such as Plutarch because we can decipher the Egyptian hieroglyphs, which these classical writers could not do. As regards the practical working of the Mysteries, this is an exceedingly doubtful assumption. For, if the object of this book has been made clear, it will be evident from what has already been said that the Mystery technique is not a dogma, and neither is it a teaching. It is a method of using the mind in order to obtain certain experiences in the domain of what might be called, rather generally, 'religious psychology'. And, if there is any truth in this conception, it is evident that an ancient initiate who had had these experiences was less dependent upon a knowledge of the Egyptian hieroglyphs than a modern archaeologist or anthropologist.

From a study of the hieroglyphs, modern anthropologists, like those whom Plutarch made fun of some 1,900 years ago, have derived the cults of Osiris and Isis from a primitive hero-worship which has added to it elements from numerous nature cults, some of them very ancient. In reality, the anthropologists derive these cults from a primitive form of spiritualism. Osiris was a dead hero who had become identified with the spirit of the growing crops and with the grain god; and thus eventually he represented the spirit of vegetation in general. Isis was his chief assistant, for she taught men how to use the fruits of the earth. Later, these two nature spirits, with the growth of the human imagination, became, according to the anthropological school (who certainly cannot be accused of imagination), the rulers of the Underworld and the saviours of humanity.

History today is opening up vast areas that hitherto have been called prehistoric, and archaeological research is pushing back by many thousands of years the beginnings of civilization. For the religious 'fundamentalist' the creation and civilization of humanity began about 4000 BC. The historical fundamentalist also used to be in the habit of deriving historical civilized life from primitive beginnings which took place at about 4000 or 5000 BC.

This habit of deriving all religions from the spiritualistic imaginings of peoples of that time, and that of considering man's fears to be the true source of man's pantheon, are slowly being abandoned. Scientific research and new discoveries in the psychology of religious thought are bringing to light the curious fact that the more we learn of these ancient religions and the better we understand them, the higher becomes our appreciation of their metaphysics.

The origins of Osiris and Isis have little practical interest for the student who is seeking to master the technical training which was given in the Osirian Mystery cults, and it is better – in the beginning – not to bother about such matters. For such a student is in the same position as a learner driver who wishes to pass the driving test. The latter is not interested in the history of the petrol engine, nor in Archimedes as a professor of primitive engineering, but in the practical work of learning how to drive and how to avoid reducing the man-power of the nation.

In the same way the type of student for whom this book is written is not interested in the history of Osiris and Isis as such, but in the acquirement of sufficient skill in the mental training which was used in the Egyptian Mysteries between say, 500 BC and AD 500 to enable him to get in touch with those numerous powers which gave life to the Ancient Mystery cults at that time.

For the ancient initiate of that period, Isis (as regards the Lesser Mysteries) was the Great Mother of all. She had two aspects to her nature. She was the Virgin sister and wife who dwells within the soul of the neophyte; and as Apuleius tells us, the neophyte had to await the direct and individual appearance of the goddess herself, before he could presume to demand the rite of initiation. She was also the Cosmic Mother of all, a role which pertained to the Greater Mysteries.

With regard to the first-mentioned aspect, that of virgin sister and wife, a little thought will enable us to put into modern language the ideas conveyed by this symbolism. One of the promises made by the goddess to worthy neophytes was that after initiation she would never forsake them, but in this life and in the life to come she would be the friend and helper, the guide and the protector. In other words the 'Isis within' is the higher self with which the neophyte has been put in touch by the technique of the cult training.

The Cosmic Mother of all, the Isis of many names, is that ocean of primordial mother spirit from which the gods and humans alike are born. The individual 'Virgin Isis', the Isis within the human soul, is part and parcel of this greater Cosmic Isis, in just the same way that a bubble gleaming on the foam of a sunlit wave is part and parcel of the great ocean.

In the Lesser Mysteries, the neophyte was taught, by means of meditation and ritual, the art of centring on the 'Isis within'. He learnt the technique of going into the Silence, and of waiting until the goddess herself appeared to him. The visions of the ancient neophyte who spent many months, sometimes years, in his little room in the college which was attached to the temple, are of exactly the same nature, and have exactly the same religious validity, as the visions that today come to the Christian monk in his cell in an English monastery.

The process of attaining to the vision of the 'Isis within' and to conversation with her, is – in method – the same today as it was 2,000 years ago; for man changes but little.

The 'Isis within' is but a symbol which stands for the same power that the modern Christian mystic calls the 'Christ within'. This physical training is a discipline which aims at rendering the body a more efficient tool of the spirit; and in most of the ancient fraternities, as well as in some modern brotherhoods – especially those of the Roman and the Eastern Churches – this discipline is given by daily toil for a definite number of hours in the open fields. The ancient initiate, by this means, day by day, rebuilt and renewed consciously the link that binds the 'Isis within' to the 'cosmic Isis'.

A bubble on the crest of a wave vanishes in a moment when the attenuated film of water that surrounds it loses its proper amount of moisture. So, too, with the relationship with the Isis Within and the Isis Without. Unless the tie be renewed and the life force be kept constant in its flow, the would-be initiate will fail to become initiated. He will be unable to pass the tests at the 'portal' and here pretence is of no avail. For the guardian at the gate is his own higher self.

Bearing in mind these remarks, the story of Isis and Osiris as given by Plutarch (first century; see Mead's *TGH*, Chapter 9) may be summarized as follows: Osiris was the divine son of Nut, the sky-goddess, and Geb, the earth-god. He became the god-king of Egypt and taught the savage Egyptians the arts of civilization and gave them a code of laws. He left Egypt to travel over the world and to instruct other nations. Until his return his wife and sister, Isis, ruled Egypt.

After his return, his brother, Set or Typhon, murdered Osiris, throwing his corpse, in a sealed chest, into the Nile. The chest floated out to sea and was washed ashore at Byblos. A large erica tree (a species of heather) sprang up, and it enclosed the coffin. The size of the tree was so extraordinary that the local king had it cut down and incorporated it into his palace. Isis, aided by children and by the jackal god Anubis, came to Byblos and made friends with the king, Melcarth, and his wife, Astarte or Ishtar or Ashteroth. Eventually, Isis brought the coffin back to Egypt and hid it in an out of the way spot in the Delta. Set, who was now King of Egypt, hunting by moonlight, found it, and cut the body into fourteen pieces which he scattered throughout the country.

Isis collected them all except the phallus, which was eaten by the fishes, and she built a shrine to Osiris over each piece. Taught by Thoth, and aided by certain goddesses, she performed a magical ceremony, that brought Osiris back from the dead, and enabled her to conceive the younger Horus, that is: Harpocrates. The latter came into the world prematurely and was lame. When he grew up, aided by the elder Horus – the sun-god – and by Thoth, he conquered Set, the evil one, whose symbol was a black pig.

This is a very brief rendering of the exoteric Isis and Osiris myth as given by the initiate Plutarch. It appears to be a history of certain human personages and certain divine beings. The uninitiated Egyptians probably mistook it for history, as do some uninitiated scholars of today. For the initiate, the above story is part of a myth which is designed as an *aide mémoire* to enable the human mind to attain to certain experiences which are of a religious nature.

In the Egyptian telestic or theurgical rites, the personages in this myth represented and personified certain qualities in the world soul; qualities which are reproduced in the human soul; and one of the objects of these rites was the linking up of the microcosmos with the macrocosmos. Iamblichus (*Egyptian Mysteries*, p. 26) tells us quite plainly that the object of the Mysteries was to enable the worshipper to participate in the god – i.e. a spritual essence.

In the Lesser Mysteries of Isis, the various rituals represented various parts of the sorrows and sufferings of Isis in her search for the lost Osiris. In their dramatized form, the neophyte, by means

of the use of the technical system of the cult of Isis, was enabled to
merge his human being into the wider and more vital part of that
divine force which was personified under the name of Isis or of
one of the other gods of the cult. This merging was one of the
main objectives of the Lesser Mysteries, and much of their system
of technical training was designed to this end.

Part 7: The Grecian Tradition

Iacchus at Eleusis

Chorus (unseen)

Iacchus, O Iacchus!
Iacchus, O Iacchus!

Thou that dwellest in the Shadow
Of great Glory here beside us,
Spirit, Spirit, we have hied us
To thy dancing in the meadow!
Come, Iacchus; let thy brow
Toss its fruited myrtle bough;
We are thine, O happy dancer; Oh our comrade, come and guide us!
Let the mystic measure beat:
Come in riot fiery feet
Free and holy all before thee,
While the Charities adore thee,
And the mystae wait the music of they feet!

(Aristophanes, *Frogs,* in J. E. Harrison,
Prolegomena to the Study of Greek Religion, p. 540)

Strange as it may seem to many, Mithraism from Persia, the
Pythagorean and Orphic reformation in Greece, Druidism in
Gaul and Britain – all have in their inner traditions a common
stock of great religious root ideas and root symbols. That the
Greeks of the fourteenth century BC are linked in some way with
the Celts and the Aryan invaders (Wiros) of Persia and India is
accepted as a fact by critical historical research. That the
Hyperboreans, who may have been Celts, sent offerings to the
wolf-god, Apollo Lykeios at Delos is a historical fact; as is also a
fact that the citizens of Croton, where Pythagoras settled on
leaving Greece, gave to Pythagoras the name of Apollo
Hyperboreus.

It was from Italy that Pythagoras started his reformation of the Greek Mystery religions, somewhere about 540 BC. He founded an inner school which influenced the Orphic tradition strongly. In this school the initiates were trained to work 'with power' at Croton in the south of Italy about 100 miles east of the Straits of Messina. This school of initiation spread all over the Mediterranean in a very short time. It had, in most of the great Greek cities, small shrines founded by the initiated disciples of Pythagoras. These latter were extremely unpopular and they were persecuted with great severity. For example the initiates who formed the headquarters at Croton were massacred, only two members escaped, and the movement was for a long time driven underground. But it had behind it some vital force which kept it alive and vigorous. For, like Orphism in its early days, Pythagoreanism was a sort of spiritual leaven which in time pervaded the whole of Greece. It was unpopular and despised by the official religions and by the populace. It was often, and justly, ridiculed by the comic poets, for like modern cults it had its eccentrics! But an educated man like Plato is extremely cautious in mentioning its doctrines, and he abstains as far as possible from mentioning its name when quoting these doctrines. It is known that many famous men belonged to this Order, but they kept the fact a secret, for reasons which, at present, are not quite clear.

Pythagoreanism as a cult was closely connected with the cult of Apollo at Delos. The latter became the sun-god of the Greeks, and he equates as a Mystery power or force with Mithras and Ra. Like Mithras, he was the patron of athletes – and of the ideal of manly youth and beauty. And it is now recognized that the Pythagorean cult was a strong, though secret, influence for regeneration in the exoteric and esoteric worship of Apollo.

It is worth noting that there are some strong resemblances between Pythagoreanism and Buddhism, such as abstinence from animal flesh, the doctrine of rebirth, and the purification of the senses. But very little is known about the former for after the massacres of the initiates somewhere about 500 BC it led a concealed existence in connection with the Mysteries of Dionysius and Orpheus, and it only came out into the open as the Orphic-Pythagorean esotericism about the time of Christ, and later on as Neo-Pythagoreanism.

What then was Pythagoreanism? Really it was the occultism of the ancient Greeks and it had its secret method for obtaining 'power' through a life led in close touch with the nature forces, i.e. the numen, or what may be called the mind side of nature. In this it closely resembles the Greater Mysteries of Mithras and the modern Tibetan and Indian yoga cults.

Here once again, we have come up against the root principle of all these Mystery religions – whether it be the religion of Mithras or Buddha, of Xenophanes, of Pythagoras or of Orpheus – that the personal 'religion' of an initiate is based on 'power' obtained from the numen by the ritual of meditation, i.e. by a dynamic mysticism.

With regard to this point there is much to be learned from Xenophanes (576–480 BC), the founder of the Eleatic school of philosophy. He taught that the universe which we see is unity, and that 'God is the One'. For Xenophanes and his school God is not only immanent in the universe, but also the Transcendent One. He is the principle of unity which pervades this universe as well as the principle which brought it into existence from himself And from the fragment which is quoted on page 156, it appears that Xenophanes had passed that childish stage which makes the Absolute, or the Unmanifest, or whatever name is given to the 'Source of All, and the Maintainer of All' a personal God who can be influenced by a professional priesthood.

For him, as for many of the mystics of Greece, nature 'sees and thinks and hearkens', and between that great Transcendent Immanent Principle which he calls the One and mortals there are hierarchies of the gods. Xenophanes – as Miss Harrison so clearly points out (*Prolegomena to the Study of Greek Religion*, p. 258) – 'knew that till man becomes wholly philosopher, his gods are doomed perennially to take and retake human shape ...' and he saw that making God personal confines the Finite-Infinite and the manifested-unmanifest within the limitations of the worshipper.

For most men, if one is going to touch the power of the numen one must personalize, and personalize as clearly and as definitely as possible. But one must recognize that this personalization is merely a psychological trick which enables the human mind to pick up its contacts with those divine sources of power which are implicit in nature. Here the term Nature is used as in the *Poemandres* of Hermes Trismegistus; it is the formative principle behind all matter; it is a manifestation on its own plane of being of what Otto calls the 'numen'.

Miss Harrison gives a very clear idea of how one should look upon the use of this 'trick' of personalization in the Greek religions (p. 163):

At the outset one preliminary caution is imperative. Our minds are imbued with current classical mythology, our imagination peopled with the vivid personalities, the clear-cut outlines of the Olympian Gods; it is only by a somewhat severe mental effort that we realize the fact essential to our study that *there were no gods at all*, that what we have to investigate are not so many actual facts and existences but only conceptions of the human mind, shifting and changing colour with every human mind that conceived them ... There is no greater bar to that realising of Mythology which is the first condition of its being understood, than our modern habit of clear analytic thought. The very terms we use are sharpened to an over-nice discrimination. The first necessity is, that by an effort of the sympathetic imagination, we should think back the 'many' we have so sharply and strenuously divided, into the haze of the primitive 'one'.

Nor must we regard this haze of the early morning as a deleterious mental fog, as a sign of disorder, weakness, oscillation. It is not confusion or even synthesis; rather it is as it were a protoplasmic fullness and forcefulness not yet articulated into the diverse forms of its ultimate births. It may even happen, as in the case of the Olympian divinities, that articulation and discrimination sound the note of approaching decadence. As Maeterlinck (*Sagesse et Destinée*, p. 76) beautifully puts it: 'la clarté parfaite n'est-elle pas d'ordinaire le signe de la lassitude des idées?'

It is said that in one of the higher initiations of the Greater Mysteries the candidate is led into an empty shrine; a voice whispers in his ear: 'No god exists.' He that hath ears to hear, and eyes to see may understand this for Miss Harrison has given to him the clue in the passage quoted above.

Once again, in the Greek esotericism, we have come face to face with the same mental background that is found to exist in the Mithraic or Chaldean Mysteries and in the Graeco-Roman Mysteries. There is a neutral unpersonalized sea of cosmic force in which this universe lives, moves and has its being. This sea of cosmic force is mental in its nature and it is supra-physical. Man is an individual bubble floating among the waves and currents of this sea; and because he is an individuality – and thinks himself to be separate and apart from this common ocean of primitive mind – he individualizes these forces, waves or currents, and calls them Apollo or Ra, or Hermes, or Thoth, when he wishes to identify them.

It is man's conceptions of the gods that take form and exist. The forces he calls gods are beyond our finite existence. A god is *impartibilis et impassibilis*, to use words from the Church of

England Prayer Book (Thirty-Nine Articles, I).

The gods are devices of the human mind which enable it to attain to mystical union with the numen. And this mystical union is its fullness is Nirvana, but it can be obtained, for the most part in flashes only, here and now.

> Spirit, Spirit, lift the shaken
> Splendour of thy tossing torches!
> All the meadow flashes, scorches:
> Up Iacchus, and awaken!
> Come thou star that bringest light
> To the darkness of the rite,
> Till thine old men dance as young men, dance with every thought
>   forsaken
> Of the dullness and the fear
> Left by many a circling year:
> Let thy red light guide the dances
> Where thy banded youth advances
> To be joyous by the blossoms of the Mere!

(Aristophanes, Frogs, in J. E. Harrison,
Prolegomena to the Study of Greek Religion, p. 540)

When one studies the Greek religion as set forth by great scholars such as Mr Gilbert Murray, Miss Harrison or Sir James Frazer, one often closes their books with a feeling which is akin to despair. They tell one so much and they give one so little. One is overwhelmed by a flood of facts and contradictory explanations of those facts. As one broods over these things one is inclined to suspect that even writers of insight, such as Dr Verrall, have confined their work almost entirely to historical facts, or to those curiosities and immaturities of the primitive forms of religions which delight the anthropologist.

These authors seem to recognize that for the ancients themselves the facts that they record (usually with pity) were psychological, and that they had a psychological reality for the persons who experienced them. This psychological reality, however, does not appear to exist for the writers who have been mentioned: they seem to represent an extreme of scepticism.

In Mr Thomas Taylor we have an author who has gone to the other extreme. For him the psychological side is all that matters, and one could wish that he had paid more attention to the acquisition of linguistic technical knowledge than he did, because 'his work has been the subject of repeated criticism and his translations are not accepted by classical scholars', and this fact has had a cramping effect on one's appreciation of 'that intuitive perception of the interior meaning of the subjects which he considered'. (*The Eleusinian and Bacchic Mysteries,* p. 27.)

The truth of the matter seems to be that the Ancient Mysteries are incapable of concrete and written explanation. One has to be able to find them for oneself, and to bring them through some deep hidden stratum of one's own being – or fail to understand them. One can find the facts, but their interpretation cannot be put on to the printed page.

A study of Miss Harrison's book makes it pretty clear that as regards the history of the Mysteries we need bother no more than to recognize the truth of the ancient saying: *Quot homines tot sententiae, quot sententiae tot Dei.* From the point of view of the Mysteries during the period we are studying (500 BC to AD 500) one can scrap the whole of the elaborate pantheon of classical Greece.

So far as the reader of this book is concerned there are only five gods – or rather, one should say, five distinct god-forms – that are important to the student, at any rate in his early days. First, there is the Earth Mother variously called Ge or Demeter or Cybele; then she is Proserpina or Pherephatta, the Queen of the Astral World, who is also called Kore, the Virgin, and the daughter of Ge. In reality Kore is the inner aspect of the Earth Mother, and she represents the power that is known to the Qabalist under the god-name of Shaddai-el-Chai, Ge being the Greek equivalent of Adonai.

Next there is the child of these two mothers. In the Eleusinian Mysteries and those of Agrae he is Iacchus, a spiritualized aspect of the popular deity Bacchus. This golden child of the Likhnon is the child of earth and heaven, Zeus and Persephone-Ge, the Mother and the Virgin. Zeus is the third form, and he is the equivalent of Kether; in the conjunction of Zeus and the Mother and the Virgin we have the Mystic Marriage that produces the Saviour; or, to use the Qabalistic terms, Kether and Malkuth in conjunction produce the Christ principle at Tipareth.

The most important of the remaining gods of the Mysteries are Hermes, the fourth god-form; and Venus Aphrodite, who rises from the green sea that is in Netzach. She is the fifth important god-form.

If the student will read Mr Taylor's *Eleusinian and Bacchic Mysteries* with care, and then proceed to study Chapters 7–12 of

Miss Harrison's *Prolegomena to the Study of Greek Religion*, he will acquire a wide and varied background to his thinking about the Mysteries. Also by confining his practical training in meditation to the five god-forms just mentioned, he will avoid losing himself in a maze of irrelevant matter, and will save much time and energy.

An analogy will perhaps explain clearly what is the object of this restriction. Suppose one wished to study the Mystery of the Real Presence at the Roman Catholic Ceremony of the Mass. It would be a waste of time to study the curious semi-Christian semi-pagan ceremonies which are found even today in the West of Ireland and in the less civilized Christian countries. To study the doctrine of the real presence, it is quite unnecessary to consider the custom of circumambulating holy wells or of affixing beetles and other small frogs and coloured rags to thorn bushes at these wells. The student of the Ancient Mysteries who wishes to gain touch with *that* which lies behind them is merely wasting his time in studying the Anthesteria (the ritual of ghosts and sprites), the harvest festivals, the women's festivals, the curious use which is made of snake symbolism and the demonology of the Greeks.

In the chapters which have been suggested for study, the reader can skip, if he wishes, the Omophagia (feast of raw flesh), and the hero feasts. These all refer to early primitive rites which were common to large bodies of the members of these primitive tribes. Even the magnificent choruses of Euripides and other authors, though they are worth careful study for the atmosphere they produce, should not give a student his idea of the background of a Mystery initiation in a fully developed Mystery cult. There were many Mysteries to many gods; each of the five above-mentioned gods had his own set of Mysteries, his own rituals; and each cultus had its own method of preparing the candidate. The Mysteries of Eleusis and Agrae were but the Mysteries that were peculiar to Athens; their chief deities were Ge and Kore, Zagreus, and the babe Iacchus (at Agrae, Dionysius), and Hermes. But at Delphi, Apollo and Dionysius were the chief gods of the local Mysteries, and their rituals, though similar in type, were not the same as those at Eleusis and Agrae.

In Dionysius, under his various aspects, we have the impulse of life in nature (op. cit., p. 426) and he signified, for the town-bred Athenians, a return to nature. This was the ritual in the Outer Court, so to speak. But within the temple, for the trained initiate who had passed beyond the rank of mystae, Dionysius was the god of spiritual ecstasy. He was not the god of wine and intoxication and of a country holiday – on the lines of a modern bank holiday. The wild rushings to and fro upon the mountains, which are parodied by Aristophanes and other poets, were condemned by Plato and the philosophers, and they had nothing in common with the rites of initiation that were given in the Inner Temple in the *telesterion* (place of initiation). In the telesterion at Eleusis, at Agrae, and at Samothrace, there was no possibility of enacting noisy dramatic rituals – there was no room for them, and no stage. Further, the noise and movement alone would have precluded the 'efficacious rite'.

In the secret recesses of a Mystery temple the method of initiation appears to have been something as follows – there was a long period of disciplinary preparation by teaching and fasting. The neophyte retired for a time from the world and took a chamber in the temple of the cult into which he sought initiation. We know that he was taught the various stages of the science of meditation, and when the appropriate stage was mastered, he was taught how to contemplate the sacred symbols and given their inner meaning. By daily attendance at the temple rituals, he learnt the method of bringing the numenous power of the cultus into manifestation.

Speaking generally, the actual ceremony of initiation was divided into three parts. There was the veiling and the unveiling and then that silent, almost motionless, drama which was the actual initiation itself. The latter took place within the trained mind of the neophyte, and its effects were reinforced by the workings of the minds of those who had preceded him through the portal.

The student will find modern examples of this type of initiation given in the works of Madame David-Neel and Dr Evans-Wentz. They will help him to understand those of the ancient Mystery schools. (See also Chapter 9.)

In the Egyptian and Chaldean traditions (Chapter 9), the sources from which the Mystery cults drew their rituals of initiation are comparatively clear and straightforward. The sources of the rites of the Greek Mysteries are to a great extent a matter of conjecture, and new facts, as they appear, would only seem to add to the existing confusion. The Orphic Tradition is sometimes put down as Greek, sometimes as Cretan, and sometimes as Thracian. Many excellent occultists consider Orpheus to be as mythical, as a man, as Homer. Many of the

Orphic hymns are now considered to be the work of Onomakritos (*Prolegomena*, p. 472). Probably Orpheus came from Crete, was naturalized at Athens, where he recognized and reformed the exoteric Thracian rites of Bacchus.

Where the Dionysiac rites at Agrae came from is also a matter of conjecture. But the Mystery rites of Dionysius must not be confused with the popular and exoteric rituals of Bacchus. The Dionysius of the Mysteries, as Miss Harrison points out (p. 436) is the male correlative of Kore, the Virgin.

The rites of Bacchus were probably brought from Thrace. They were crude, for Bacchus is the god of vinous intoxication. The Dionysius of the Mysteries is probably derived from the Cretan pre-Greek myths of Zagreus; the Zagreus myth being the Mystery of the Babe of God, and a 'motherless' mystery. Demeter and Kore are Nature goddesses, who may have come from the north with the invading Greeks. They certainly absorbed the duties and responsibilities of the mother goddesses of the pre-Greek population. This will explain the likeness between Demeter and Cybele, for both are Greek nature goddesses, the one of the Greeks of Greece, the other of their cousins who conquered Phrygia.

The Dionysius of the Mystery religions is Dithyrambos, a title which expresses the Mystery of his birth, which was the cardinal secret teaching of the Lesser Mysteries. The word comes (according to the ancient Greeks) from *di* and *thura* – the double door, and they took it to mean 'he who entered life by the double door', i.e. the womb of his mother and the thigh of his father. In Christianity it is sometimes called *mystically* the 'birth from above'.

As Dithyrambos is the babe mystically born, so the more advanced initiate became a mystically born babe in that rite of initiation that came just after the Sacred Marriage (op. cit., p. 436).

The rituals of Agrae as well as those of Eleusis are unknown. That they concerned the rite of the sacred marriage and the birth of the Holy Child we know from both pagan and Christian sources, and that both these rites were mystical is also known. Further, that the initiate in a mystical manner became a 'Bacchus' is also certain (op. cit., p. 500). In the Egyptian Mysteries, the initiate became an Osiris by the virtue of a rite which is known as the assumption of the god-form. In the Chaldean, we have a considerable part of the actual rite for the assuming of the god-form of Mithras (see Chapter 9). But in the Greek Mysteries how 'the culminating ritual acts, by which union with the divine, the goal of all mystic ceremonial, was at first held to be actually effected, later symbolized' (op. cit., p. 563), we do not know.

The Greek Tradition, from the point of view of history and religious study, is extremely unsatisfactory. We do not know how they got their results except that in a general way they used an intensive system of meditation and combined it with sacred rituals; sometimes this ritual seems to have been of the nature of a Mystery play; in other cases it appears to have been a ritual which was carried out in silence, and probably in darkness. It was an example of what is today called group meditation.

Once one has grasped the fact that initiation is the beginning of a long and secret process of mental and spiritual training which goes on within the hidden places of the man's own soul, and that it is assisted by ritual, but is not the end result of a ritual, one ceases to worry overmuch about the gaps in our knowledge of Greek Mystery rituals.

It is perfectly possible for the earnest seeker, who is prepared to spend the time and trouble required of him, to touch for himself those inner powers that are personified by the names of Demeter, Kore, Iacchus, Hermes and Venus Aphrodite. The sacred marriage and the birth of the Holy Child must take place in the man's own soul if he is to be truly initiated. The Master, Jesus, when talking to Nicodemus, told him this, and wondered at the latter's failure to understand. But then, as an ancient Orphic text puts the matter (op. cit., p. 473): 'Many are the Wand-bearers, few are the Bacchoi.'

Part 8: The Chaldean and Roman Traditions

> Mithras, God of the Midnight, here where the Great Bull dies,
> Look on thy children in darkness. O take our sacrifice!
> Many roads thou hast fashioned – all of them lead to the Light,
> Mithras, also a soldier, teach us to die aright!
>
> Rudyard Kipling, *The Hymn of the Thirtieth Legion: c. AD 350*

One of the sanest, and to moderns the most attractive of the pagan Mystery religions is that of Mithras. It is far more ancient than Christianity to which it is similar in type, in much of its teaching,

and in many of its rituals. Being older it is even more
encumbered, in certain respects, with primitive survivals and
crude modes of thought than is Christianity.

Today it should be of interest to us, and to Germany, for it is an
Aryan, and not a Semitic, or Hamitic type of religion. It is a clean,
manly religion, well-suited to the healthy-minded. It has no use
for drivelling by 'sick souls', or for the pathologies of 'world
flight'. After a long and rather slow period of development it
became the religion of the fighting man of the Roman armies, and
the basis of its ethic is that life is a struggle, and he fights best who
fights hard and fights with clean hands.

It failed to conquer Christianity largely because it had no place
for women, and nothing to offer them emotionally, mentally or
spiritually. The wife and female relatives of an initiate had to join
one or other of the many cults of the Great Mother.

Mithras is probably one of the oldest of the Aryan divinities, for
his name is found in the religion of both the Eastern – or Indian
branch – and the Western or Persian branch of the Aryan race. In
the earliest times, the name seems to have had the meaning of
'The Friend of Man'. In the Vedic religion as 'the light of day' he
is linked with Varuna – to whom belong the thousand eyes of
night.

Among the Iranian peoples, Mithras or Mitras worship attained
to far greater an importance than it did in India. The Varuna of
the Vedic religion equates with Ahura Mazda the Absolute or the
supreme God of the Persians. Mithras then would seem to be that
which St John and Philo call the Logos or the Creative Word. In
the library of Assur-bani-pal there is a tablet which identifies
Mithras with the Babylonian god Shamash. And in the Persian
Empire, before its overthrow by Alexander the Great, Mithras
took a prominent place beside Ahura Mazda, as` a sort of
beneficent creative aspect of the Absolute.

In the Zoroastrian Reforms – probably about 700 BC – the
Yasht says (op. cit., p. 753): 'Thus spake Ahura Mazda to the
holy Zarathustra: "When I created Mithras, Lord of wide
pastures, then O Spitama, I created him as worthy of sacrifice, as
worthy of prayer as myself Ahura Mazda." '

Everywhere through the Yashts or sacred writings of the
Zoroastrians we find Mithras in the role of a good shepherd, the
one who cares for the poor. He is the strong, the sleepless, the
vigilant watcher. 'He it is who sees that the compact [Mithrem] is
not faithlessly broken.' Mithras also protects the poor in the

world, and in the next world he it is who guides his followers through the 'Valley of the Shadow'. Essentially, Mithras is the god of battles but always fighting on the side of right and not might, 'a quality which led hundreds of years later to his becoming the favourite deity of the Roman soldier, and the heavenly representative of military justice, virile manliness, and patriotism'.

The conquest of Babylon by the Persians effected a considerable change in the status of Mithras (E.R.E., Vol. VIII, p. 753). As so often happens the religion of the conquered race influenced strongly the religion of its conquerors. Ahura Mazda withdrew to the management of the Cosmos. Angra Mainyu, that is Ahriman, the Prince of Darkness, became Lord of the Underworld, while Mithras became the 'Mesitees', the Mediator, and Lord of the Universe of Light – this world. So it seems that the Christian and the Jewish idea of 'God and the Devil' came from Babylon.

When the Persian Empire was broken up (330 BC) by Alexander the Great, Mithras became the chief deity of a cult, in place of being one of many national gods. He occupied, it would seem, exactly the same position then that Jesus Christ occupies in the Orthodox Christian theology of today. He was the divine saviour who mediates between a rather uncertain-tempered God and a somewhat perverse mankind. As a man, you were saved by and through Mithras and not by your own efforts. Into this new Mithras cult was poured much of the occult learning which had been kept secret in the great priestly colleges of the Euphrates, for when the priests were rendered homeless by Alexander, many of them were forced to earn their daily bread. They founded Mystery schools and taught their own occult lore throughout South-West Asia.

> Thus the political downfall of the Persian state released a tremendous spiritual impulse which had been locked up in these ancient Chaldean temples. This spiritual impulse took, in Mithraism, a form which rendered it suitable for world conquest, and so Mithras started his 700 years of world conquest and of unbroken victory.

First Mithraism passed into Asia Minor, where it became a state religion and was assimilated to the indigenous deities. Mithras was identified with men, the moon-god of Pontus, and elsewhere with Attia. An alliance was also formed with Cybele – the Great Mother of Anatolia – probably because Mithras was a god for men only.

This latter alliance is hard to explain, for Mithraism was an extremely pure and chaste religion, with as high a standard of ethics as Christianity at its best, and the worship of the Great Mother was certainly not ethical.

In the mystical teaching of the Mithraic religion there was a peculiar conception known as the 'glory' (E.R.E., Vol. VIII, p. 754). This was conceived as a kind of spirit body, a mystical effulgence or aureole, derived from the heavenly light. And this apparently is where the idea of the nimbus of the Christian saint came from. In the Mithraic story of the Fall, or the ancient myth of Yima, sin, i.e. the descent into matter, entails the loss of remembrance of the spiritual body. This 'glory' or *hvareno* was the talisman of the Royal House of Iran. And it was known among the Hellenized Asiatics as *Tykee Basileus* or 'the King's Luck'.

This 'glory' or aureole, which appears as an oblong halo surrounding the figure, explains much. It has a very definite bearing on the symbolism of Mithras; not as the sun itself, but as the light which is before and after the sun at sunrise and sunset. Also, it explains the ancient idea of Mithras manifesting himself as a sort of faint glow which lights the surface of the earth during the hours of darkness.

Here it is evident that we are not dealing with a religion whose sins come from chewing apples and other anthropomorphic ideas and symbolism, nor with a sordid, frenzied type of religious ecstasy such as was found in Ancient Greece and in Asia Minor. Instead, we have a type of mysticism which is really, in many ways, almost beyond the comprehension of the ordinary concrete-minded modern who is not in close touch with the 'numen' as a real and almost tangible phenomenon.

From the mystical point of view Mithras is the light and life that stands behind visible nature; that visible nature that is the outer garment of God, and the veil of the Absolute of our Creation. He is the bringer of life and light to a fallen mankind.

The initiate of Mithras believed that, just as there is this living mystical light which gleams from behind all visible nature, and which forms the Earth Mother's Glory or spiritual body, so there is in every man a living aureole, a spiritual, Mithraic body of light and life and divine purity. As has already been said, this 'body of light' was lost to man in his fall into matter (i.e. incarnation) in the sense that man has become unaware that he once possessed this inner self – this Mithras within – this regenerator.

The cult of Mithras claimed to be able to restore fallen mankind to its former state, not of grace, but of knowledge; and by means of its initiations and teachings the rebirth of the 'Mithras within' was brought about. The initiate was washed in the blood of the sacred bull which was in some way identified with Mithras himself. At times the expression used is 'washed in the blood of the Ram' for both the Taurobolium and the Kriobolium were used for purification.

Throughout the ancient world we find the idea that 'without shedding of blood there is no remission of sin'; an idea that the Protestant cults are fond of placing in their wayside pulpits today. It is worthwhile comparing the ideas of Mithraism with those of Christianity. But two things must be remembered; first, that Christianity is not the older religion, and then, that God has never left Himself without witness, or His world without light.

The religion of Mithras on its westward journey from Persia and Babylonia split into two main streams of emigration when it reached the Syrian shores of the Mediterranean. One of the streams flowed north, and the other turned south into Palestine and Egypt. The northern stream passed through Asia Minor, then across the Black Sea and up the Danube; later it turned off into northern Italy, Spain and England. This branch of the Mithraic Church had for its chief devotees the officers and soldiers of the Roman army. It was essentially the cult of a healthy religious mind in a healthy fighting body.

A brief, clear and very vivid summary of its teachings and ethics is given in Kipling's poem 'The Hymn of the Thirtieth Legion: c. AD 350'. A verse of this is quoted at the beginning of this chapter because this great modern poet has conveyed to us, in a flash of genius, a religious teaching that ponderous theological tomes could never have given, however learned their authors. Even the excellent technical works of the great Cumont have not got to the heart of the Mithraic religious teachings as this poet has.

In these few lines there is summed up the religious and ethical code of the soldiers of Mithras, the men who formed the bulk of the local Mithraic sodality, or community. Each community when it grew to about 150 members split and formed a new one. These communities were 'churches', guided by well-instructed priests, who knew how to work with power the secret rituals, and they were administered as regards their property by lay officers who were independent of the priests. Each church was a religious family – slave, soldier, officer and general were all equal in Mithras while celebrating their Mysteries in the little underground chapel or cave, and in this respect they resembled the Freemasons, for inside the Lodge each is a brother, no matter what his standing is in ordinary life.

The Egyptian Mithraic stream seems to have furnished the thinkers, the philosophers, and the teachers. Of course, it must be remembered that, here, one is speaking in very general terms, for all members could progress, if suitable, to the highest rank.

So far, we know that there were seven grades in the Mithraic Mystery. Three in the Lesser Mysteries and four in the Greater Mysteries. The three lower grades of the Lesser Mysteries were: the Raven, the Griffin or Occultus, and the Soldier or Server. Those serving in these grades were non-communicants in the Mithraic Eucharist or holy supper. The four grades of the Higher Mysteries were: the Lion, the Persian, the Courier of the Sun, and, the highest of all, the Fathers, who were also called the Eagles. All these became communicants after reaching the first grade of their Greater Mysteries. At the head of the church hierarchy was a priestly initiate who was called the *Pater Patrum* – or the Father of Fathers.

Now what do we know of the initiation into Mithraism? In many ways, we know very little, but one is permitted to suspect a great deal, if that be of any use. There exists a statement made by a well-known modern writer and lecturer – Mr W. Loftus Hare – in the Journal of the Society for Promoting the Study of Religions. (*Journal of Transactions*, No. 5, June 1932, p. 59) concerning the essential character of these so-called Mysteries: 'The research of generations of scholars has failed to reveal anything more than might be expected from our general knowledge of the external aspect of these mystery religions. They could not keep their secret because, perhaps, there was no real secret to keep...' Now if the explanations already given are clear, it is evident that from one point of view this opinion is correct. There is and was no secret, no great and sudden revelation of dogma and creed, such as the external Christian Churches claim to give in their formularies. The secret wisdom of the West, as concealed in the Mystery traditions, exists, but it is no short cut to knowledge, or to power, or to heaven. There is a secret teaching, and there is an unusual but not supernatural knowledge – and it is still secret. Carved over the doors of the Mystery temples is *Gnothi se auton* – 'Know Thyself'. This was open for all to see and read; and it is a key to much, for the primary secret of each of the ancient Mystery schools was their particular process for 'knowing the self'.

All the schools had a common, and to most of us today, an unusual form of knowledge; and it is the method of using this knowledge that is peculiar to each school, and which constitutes the secrets of the Mysteries. The final aim of all Mystery schools was the same; namely 'apotheosis'. There exists today a Mithraic ritual for this operation, a rite which is often called by other initiates in the technical terms of certain of the Mystery schools – 'The Sacrament of the Birth of Horus'. It is the rite of Athanasia or Immortality. This Mithraic rite is examined and commented on very carefully by G. R. S. Mead in *Echoes from the Gnosis*, Vol. VI. But the more closely one examines this 'ritual' the deeper becomes the obscurity that surrounds it, for it is the final ritual of a long process of 'ritualistic initiation'; a process which must have stretched over many years of careful training, and must have involved much hard mental work as well as the keeping of a very strict discipline. In the Mysteries, the word 'Initiation' means a beginning. The initiate is one who begins to tread the 'Path'. Initiation begins a process; it is not the end of a process.

None of the working rituals of the intermediate grades that lead up to this final ritual are known to us today. We are in the same position that a non-human scientist from, say, the planet Mars would be in, if he got hold of the corpse of a man of eighty and then tried to deduce from it 'ab ovo usque ad mala', the life processes of the (to him) unknown human race of the planet Earth. We have then in this ritual, the method for attaining the final result of a long mental process, but we do not have the intermediate steps.

Still, by the use of analogy, something can be done, for Madame David-Neel's book, *Initiations and Initiates in Tibet* and a trilogy, *The Tibetan Book of the Dead, Tibet's Great Yogi Milarepa* and *Tibetan Yoga and Secret Doctrines*, by Dr Evans-Wentz, can help us considerably in these studies, because Buddhism, Hinduism and Mithraism all spring from a common root religion which is Aryan. The Tibetan initiates claim to be very ancient, and evidently are extremely primitive in form. As they have an immense age behind them, and have changed but little, they can throw much light on the preliminary methods of mind culture which were used in the early initiatory processes of Mithraism.

It is well-known that the Egyptian and Chaldean Mystery schools functioning in Europe, combined with a meditation system a strong appeal, through gorgeous ritual, to the emotions and to that sense of beauty, majesty and fitness which seems to be inherent in southern European races. Further, we know that the Greeks, Egyptians and Syrians made a strong appeal to the senses by means of rhythmic ritualistic dances and dramatic representations (see the Chorus Song, p. 121). Also, the cults from Asia Minor strove to raise their initiates, by meditation and fasting, into such a state of ecstasy, that the would-be initiate, like St Paul, was literally beside himself.

Then, too, it is known that the initiates of Mithras carefully avoided the extravagances and excesses of some of the Semitic cults. Their ritual was conspicuous for its collective silent meditation (like the Quakers) as well as for its austerity. Its rituals were carried out in small caves or in tiny underground chapels. It is known that they laid particular stress on daily meditation, on physical tests of endurance, and on solitary, ritualistic contemplation of the Mystery symbols, using for their purpose the symbolic reliefs behind the altars of the cave or the shrine. The pupil, so the Mysteries taught, became the godchild (literally) of his spiritual teacher and initiator, being bound to him by a tie which was then considered to be closer than that of a physical parent; for it is well-known that an extremely strong psychic tie grows up between a Mystery teacher and his god-children.

All these points are emphasized in these books on the modern Mystic of Tibet. Again, Paul Brunton in his book, *In Search of Secret India*, describes much the same type of phenomena as Madame David-Neel and Dr Evans-Wentz.

Reference is here made to the inner teachings, and not to that vulgar commercial clap-trap that so often passes for yoga in America and Europe and elsewhere; here one is talking of mystics, not of pathological fakirs in India, or dollar-snatching religious sects from across the Atlantic.

In India and Tibet, the inner teaching of mysticism is usually given by the teacher to his pupils in one of three different ways:

1. By telepathy, without the aid of speech. Only the very highest type of teaching is thus given. It is rare, for trained teachers in

this method are few, as are the seekers who are sufficiently advanced to profit by such a method. Brunton gives several descriptions of this method.

2.   Then there is a teaching by gestures and signs (*mudras*) – in silence, and without words; a sort of ritualistic meditation by a trained group, working in a sanctuary. This also is rare, though far more common than the first type. This method may throw light on Aristotle's statement (Angus, *Mystery Religions and Christianity*, p. 60) that in the Mysteries it was not necessary for the initiated to learn but to have their emotions stirred. And Apuleius' remark that 'certain secrets too holy for utterance were imparted by the priest', may be literally accurate. It is possible – though far from easy – to teach Europeans by means of collective meditation.

3.   Ordinary oral teaching.

Now the religious and mental background against which both the Tibetan Lama and the initiate of Mithras set their processes of meditation and their symbolic teaching is widely different from that of the ordinary Christian thinking of this century. And although 2,000 years lie between them, the modern Tibetan Lama and the ancient initiate of Mithras both seem to think in terms of a very similar religious background, and of a similar type of 'unseen world'.

The genuine Protestant Christian of today, however, allows no one and nothing, except perhaps the devil(!) to stand between himself and God, as the Absolute. This idea is, apparently, equally true of a Dean Inge or a Salvation Army lass. Jesus, of course, is the Mediator – but 'Jesus is God' – says the modern Protestant theologian.

The ancient worshippers of Mithras did not, and the genuine modern yogi or lama of today does not, bother much about an Absolute. They both, however, recognize various grades of conscious beings or forces, which are at present superior to man and which function 'beyond this physical world'.

Professor Murray, in his *Ancient Greek Literature*, p. 272, writes:

Reason is great, but it is not everything. There are in the world things, not of reason, but both below and above it, causes of emotion which we cannot express, which we tend to worship, which we feel perhaps to be precious things in life. These things are God or forms of God, not fabulous immortal men, but 'Things which are', things utterly non-human and non-moral which bring man bliss or tear his life to shreds without a break in their own serenity.

Both the Lamas and the initiates of Mithras sought and seek, by meditation, by ritual and by service, to attach themselves psychically to one or more of these beings, 'Things which are', whose disciples and servants they become. In return, they receive the protection of that being in this physical world, as well as when travelling in the 'World to come', both before death and after death. Thus it is clear that the silent rituals and the solitary rites of initiation in Mithraism have a parallel in the silent rites that today accompany not only the teaching of, but also the initiations into, some of the higher degrees in Tibet.

Now the Mysteries were not driven underground by persecution in the East, as was the case in the West; also these Eastern (Aryan) initiations claim to go back to a Hinduism which is long before the time of Buddha. And as we find hints in Mithraism – an ancient Aryan faith which has a common root with Hinduism – of practices similar to those found today in India and Tibet, there is at least a *prima facie* reason for studying these two methods together. It is not claimed that they are identical; these religions are not even similar in their outlook on life; but a study of the training methods of the one that still exists in the East may help, for the Tibetan methods are now over 2,000 years old, and they were once contemporary with the Mithraic methods.

The former have remained apparently almost unchanged and undamaged by religious ignorance, bigotry and intolerance, and they may throw much light on the lost teachings and methods of the Ayran religion of Mithras, which was destroyed by that intolerant Semitic religion, Christianity; and for this reason the books of Madame David-Neel and Dr Evans-Wentz are recommended to the earnest enquirer.

Part 9: General Conclusions and Summary

One God there is, greatest of gods and mortals;
Not like to man is he in mind and body
All of him sees, all of him thinks and hearkens ...
But mortal man made gods in his own image

Like to himself in vesture, voice and body.
Had they but hands, methinks, oxen and lions
And horses would have made them gods like-fashioned,
Horse-gods for horses, oxen-gods for oxen.

(Xenophanes)

Let us now try to recapitulate that which the Mystery Traditions of Chaldea, Greece and Egypt sought to do and teach during the thousand years they held sway over the world of the Mediterranean.

They came at a time when the beautiful myths of the gods of Hellas were being ridiculed by the sceptics and cynics of Greece. In Egypt the might of the Pharoah had crumbled. Life was insecure for the ordinary man, and sorrow and suffering were the lot of the poor. In Asia Minor the conquering armies of Assyria had destroyed civilizations older and more refined than that of the city of the winged bulls. Outwardly it would seem that the gods were powerless against the gibes of their scorners and were impotent to protect right from might.

From the gods without, man was turning to the god which is within – the Unmanifest and the Most-Manifest, the One and the Many, the Objective and the Subjective, the Transcendent and Immanent, the 'All'.

This is the great redemptive work of the Ancient Mysteries. They taught man to turn from the Without to the Within; from the bloodstained sacrifice upon the altar to the stainless sacrifice which is made only within the human heart. They taught that no person can stand between the god who is within and the human who is without. Priests, however, have their functions and their uses, for they act as a restraining influence upon the folly of the totally blind.

The Initiates of the Ancient Mysteries, priestly or lay, made no attempt to bring the teaching of the Mysteries to the masses. Then, as now, the masses have to be spoon-fed by paid teachers with religious pap. And such diet, for the tranquillity of the State, is better than nothing.

Once the restless questing human intellect has tasted the pleasures of religious destruction, it is apt to turn its attention and slake its appetite on the decalogues of social life. Its desire for destruction becomes dangerous to the organized life of nations. Hence the value of State priesthoods and great conservative bodies such as rich churches; hence also the danger of dynamic teachers such as the Master, Jesus – King of the Elements, and the crown and flower of pagan civilizations. Christianity, as a state institution, muzzled the Master, Jesus, and turned attention from his teachings by making Him 'God'.

The Mysteries stood between the humanity of their time and the dangers which are run by civilization when organized religions fail to meet the needs of their worshippers. True, they taught the educated man to see the folly of the organized religion of his time, but they did not give this teaching to the unprepared masses; hence the necessity for secrecy and oaths. They had a constructive side to their work, for they taught the discontented and potentially destructive intellectuals to see in man a miniature of the cosmos, in man's daily life and progress an epitome of the evolution of worlds.

By means of personal experience they taught man to see himself as an individual portion of a great evolving scheme of things, to feel himself to be a conscious part of a great, living, conscious Whole. They taught man that as there are orders of creatures whose minds are more lowly than the mind of man, so there are orders of creatures whose minds vastly transcend in their powers the mind of man, and the trained mind can commune with both strata of evolution.

In the cosmic background of the Mysteries there was no place for a god who was fabled by his priesthood to be at one moment a bloodthirsty tyrant, at another a sentimental parent. The god of the Mysteries required no sacrifice of his only begotten son to appease him for the crimes with which man, born in sin and apparently only for the purpose of committing more sin, annoyed him.

The God of the Mysteries was no person at all; and man could not make, without error, any conception of him. The most they could say symbolically of him was that he is Infinite Being in which all things living have their becoming. In, through, and from this Being, (which they sometimes symbolized as the thrice-greatest Darkness, the Abyss beyond all Abysses, the Light beyond all Lights, and the Life beyond all Life) they conceived by way of imagery, a pouring forth of a tremendous life power which built all worlds, visible and invisible. Within this infinite life which they called the primal mind, they postulated the existence of other stupendous minds whose lives and powers sustained the worlds that we know, as well as worlds that are as yet unknown to us. Within these minds again there existed hierarchies of subordinate beings in an ever-descending progression ending in man.

By means of a sacerdotal theurgy the ancient Mystery schools taught their neophytes to realize – that is, to make real through experience – these hierarchies of beings which are evolving in states of consciousness more subtle than man's physical one. They also instructed them how to enter into conscious communion with superhuman minds and to draw into their own human nature that life and power that radiates from the cosmos into every crack and cranny of this universe.

They pictured this great cosmic life welling up from a state of being into a state of becoming, and in its progress passing through spheres of becoming which are more subtle and refined than that of matter. So far as man is concerned this physical sphere is the end result of this progression; but they did not teach that this endless descent of power stopped short at the physical world as we know it; for there may be worlds of becoming, so to speak, still lower in the scale of progress than is this world.

All through this endless scheme of becoming there is life, order, and definite purpose. The ordinary man sees in life a disorder which appears to exist solely for the purpose of testing his powers of clinging to life and eventually of destroying him in death. For the initiate this view of life was replaced by the idea of divine life pressing into manifestation, working to an ordered plan, bringing order out of chaos; man in this scheme of things is a conscious partner of the divine mind. Man is, as it were, a junior partner in a great firm whose head – i.e. guiding mind – is symbolized by the term 'God'.

The training given in the Mysteries was physical, mental and spiritual. To the initiate, the physical body was a valuable tool whose powers had to be kept at their highest pitch of development. Man's mind is part and parcel of that great mind which directs this universe. His conscious mind was trained by the study of the arts, and of science as then known, so as to make it a keen instrument in the search for truth. His unconscious mind was given special training, by means of meditation and ritual, to enable it to apprehend abstract truth; and for the ancient initiate, the apprehension of abstract truth was conceived to be the work of a faculty which lay beyond the borderline of conscious sense perception.

The whole theory of that magical training which is so prominent a part of the Ancient Mystery systems is based upon the idea that man in body, soul and spirit is an integral part of the body, soul and spirit of a being greater than himself. Apprehension of the divine was the aim and object of the training given in the Lesser Mysteries, and the method by which it was achieved was the uniting of the higher and the lower self, of the man without and the god within, of the neophyte and his vision of the goddess, Isis, of Osiris or of Iacchus. By means of this blending and mixing, as it was called, the initiate, while still living on earth, was able to reach out to those super-essences or cosmic beings whom the vulgar called the gods of the Mystery religions.

The student who has persevered so far is entitled to ask how all this information about the technical training of the Ancient Mysteries is going to assist him in this search for practical religious experience. How is he to get away from authority and secure that personal conviction which is the result of personal experience?

Someone has said that the roads to God are as many as the breaths of the sons of men, and the student must first realize that a method which may suit one man may not suit another. Also that there are many sound methods, and most of them are of value to the student who gets hold of the one that suits him.

The following method has been tried out with a number of students and a large percentage have found it successful. If the student will spend ten minutes every morning in meditation on certain subjects – such as, for example, the goddess Isis if he is attracted to the Egyptian Mysteries, or Demeter if he prefers the Greek Mysteries, then he will find that a change will slowly come over his own attitude towards that aspect of divine power which man has personified under the names of Isis and Demeter. A mutual sympathy will begin to develop. An example of this method of training is given in Dion Fortune's novel, *The Winged Bull*.

If he will also go to the British Museum or to neighbouring shops and buy, for a few pence, reproductions of these gods and goddesses (coloured in the case of the Egyptian), and before meditation study them carefully, he will find that these god-forms tend to build up automatically in his imagination.

If he will further collect and note all the information he can get with regard to these gods, their history, religions and social attributes, and, above all, their symbols, he will make the discovery that at the back of the idolatrous tendencies of the ancients there is a sound system of mental and religious training.

This method sounds childishly simple. In fact its very simplicity is its chief difficulty. Commenting on *The Tao Teh King*, a modern translator has written: 'The Simple Way; but so marvellous is its immaculate simplicity that those who find it, being like little children, oftentimes know it not, while those who seek it but are not child-like, find it not.'

The student should note, especially, that in connection with this system, meditation does not mean sitting passively and warming a chair seat. This meditation is hard thinking. It involves the processes of analysis, synthesis, and above all, comparison with other things of a similar nature.

The student may ask how long he should persevere. The answer to that question is: some students obtain results very quickly, in a few weeks; others spend years apparently without tangible results. Quite a large number never get any results at all, because they get fed up with the hard work which clear thinking involves; they find the daily discipline of concentrated thinking, at a special time, in a special place, and the immediate and accurate recording of results, if any, to be too irksome for them.

Success in the attainment of religious experience demands from the student a wholehearted and regular application of the best of his mental, moral and spiritual qualities. If the student is not prepared to undertake this long continued drudgery then he must give up his quest for gaining – through the Ancient Mysteries – that personal inward authority which can come only from convictions born from experience. The 'adventure' of personal religion, as understood by the initiates of the Western Tradition, is not for him.

June 1935 to September 1936

4.

Meditations for Temple Novices

The following article is one of the best introductions to meditation as an art and as a training within the magical curriculum written within the last fifty years. It has been reprinted in *Round Merlin's Table*, the house magazine of the Servants of the Light, and has been of great value to its students.

In this essay he speaks of the freedom of man in this New Age to choose his own experience, for he says, '... Man is his own Saviour ... no one else can save him ...' I for one will not argue with that, though there will be many who will disagree!

Foreword
This work aims at inducing a hidden knowledge from the deeper strata of the subconscious minds of certain of its readers rather than giving a definite teaching on the subject of meditation. There are in existence scores of excellent books on meditation by competent teachers. These will be referred to as necessary.

Many who are now once again in incarnation were formerly initiates of the Ancient Mystery religions. The vital symbols of these Mysteries are able, even today, to stimulate the memories of a past that has long been forgotten by most of us. Thus they can summon back to the Temple those who were once 'Knowers'. These can resume labours that were interrupted by the fire and sword of ignorance and bigotry.

OMMA THEIS EISO PEPLON

Part 1
In the Wisdom Religion emphasis was laid not so much upon dogma and knowledge as upon a kind of uniqueness of understanding which showed itself in those individuals who had

developed certain inner experiences which are made possible by
the use of a genuine system of meditation. The search for
uniqueness in matters religious is thus described by a modern
philosopher and mystic, and apostle of the 'unique':

> In all respects, 'being' is more important than 'efficiency': in all
> respects, depth of life is more valuable than external riches: in all
> respects, understanding alone and not exterior knowledge leads to
> real progress as opposed to success. I, personally, never meant to do
> more than create a symbol for meditation. Those who meditate upon
> it in the right way will find out for themselves what they can do.
> This depends on them, not on me. (Keyserling, *Creative
> Understanding*, Introduction, p. 24.)

In any genuine system of cult meditation the symbolic images
are, for us, always more important than the exoteric religious and
philosophical teaching given out by the officials of the Cultus;
because, if the system is genuine, each symbol acts as a creative
spiritual source of life. The system only works when the symbols
become alive and replete with spiritual power, and when the
devotee feels within his own personal being the life forces that
they represent. In this lies the uniqueness of each meditation
system, for every student must learn first of all to 'turn the eyes
within the outer covering of her personality'. The inner kingdoms
are within you.

Modern education, as Keyserling points out, 'imparts
knowledge, but it does not inspire personal understanding; it
develops efficiency, but it does not create a higher plane of being.'
Meditation should be a sort of personal postgraduate course for
the mature. It is a self-education, a learning to use symbols in the
right way, for each 'self' symbol is unique in the way that it acts.

A very common question from beginners is: what system of
meditation do you recommend? Naturally one recommends one's
own system. Trying to work two systems at once invariably ends
in failure. There are many systems, some good, some not so good,
and some extremely dangerous, especially those which are
Western adaptations of Eastern methods. Again, systems
involving Eastern breathing exercises are best avoided, as it is so
easy to disorganize one's system, and very hard to put it right
again.

The sole criterion of any system is, does it or does it not
adequately meet your needs? If not, then no matter how good it
may be for others, it is not the one for you. Give it up and make a

fresh start elsewhere. The methods used must vary with the objectives which you are aiming at. You must ask yourself again and again until you are certain, what is your object in taking up meditation as a system of self-education? After all, most of our experiences and skills still come to us from repeated personal experiments.

Meditation has been defined as a methodical and scientific process for consciously uniting the human and the divine. It is like a school and college education, an integral and natural part of human evolution. But speaking generally, and for novices only, it may be said that meditation is the act of turning the attention upon some subject or object for the purpose of gaining a better understanding of its nature. Now, attention is the faculty of mental concentration which leads to close continued thought or consistently sustained reflection. So before it is possible to meditate efficiently it is necessary to learn to concentrate, not always an easy matter.

It is with the learning of concentration that the weeding-out process begins. It is doubtful if more than a third of students on average complete their first year's training. Most leave because they do not find the work sufficiently exciting. They are indignant because there are no psychic thrills, because they are expected to work hard, and pass tests instead of decorating the seats of a weekly lecture session.* How many would go to church if quarterly examinations on the sermons were compulsory?

The key to concentration is interest, for you have only to develop enough interest to secure attention. If interest does not come naturally then one must learn to develop it by artificial means. Lack of interest is usually due to a poor imagination and a lack of perseverance. But if one has sufficient imagination to see the goal and the way to it clearly, then interest can be quickly developed. Imagination is the royal faculty of the human mind, as perhaps it may be of that all-pervading Divine Mind in which we live, move and have our being.

The easiest way to teach oneself to concentrate is to do one thing at a time, and to think about it carefully while it is being done. Then the concentration exercises which are taught in any Mystery school will become not only easy and interesting, but also exciting.

There is a science of meditation with its own definite laws

---

* Forty years later this is still a problem with many students.

based on immutable first principles, but it must not be forgotten that it is also an art, and as such, it must be expressed, like music or painting. Also, it demands for success, a long apprenticeship and honest, steady, daily work. Concentration exercises especially demand great care and a high degree of self-observant honesty in their performance. Self-honesty is the first test a novice has to pass.

From the point of view of one who is preparing for work in the temple, there are three main stages in the art of meditation. These are meditation, concentration and contemplation. Contemplation is the art of identifying oneself with the object or subject being meditated upon; it is not, as a rule, for beginners. It is mentioned here because, if the interest is strong, an ordinary meditation is apt to pass unperceived into contemplation, which is a less positive form of mind work. So without noticing it the novice will have identified himself with the subject or object of his meditation. This is often the explanation of the strikingly successful meditations that come unexpectedly to some students in their early lessons, but which fail to repeat themselves in later stages, when eagerly sought. Early enthusiasm and intense interest have temporarily lifted the student beyond his natural limitations.

In any system of magical training which is based upon the Ancient Mysteries there are two main objectives which should eventually be reached. The first is personal and psychological, the second is cosmic and should be impersonal. The first pertains to the Lesser Mysteries of ancient Egypt and Chaldea, and the second to the Greater Mysteries.

Over the doorway of many of the ancient temples was written *Gnothi Se Auton* or, *Nosce Te Ipsum,* Know Thyself. This psychological process is sometimes called 'the unveiling of the self', sometimes 'the knowledge and conversation of one's holy guardian angel', or higher self. This is the first great goal. Its essential symbols are to be found on the Qabalistic Tree of Life, and in the Pythagorean Tetractys, important symbols for the trained mind.

The second objective, higher up on the path, is the unveiling of the Goddess Net of Sais. She who is the parent of all things, the mistress of the elements, the primordial offspring of time, and first among the celestials. Sometimes called Diana Dictynnia (Diana of the Net), Queen Isis herself. She is the world self, and the unveiling of this world self pertains to the Greater Mysteries of the ancients.

Isis of Sais is held among initiates to have said, 'I am all that was, is and is yet to come, and no man hath lifted my veil.' Of Athene it was carved upon her statue, 'No mortal hath ever lifted my cloak.' Yet, this same Great Goddess says to those who serve her, '*Omma theis eiso peplon*', 'Look within the coverings'.

The Great Temple of Thoth, the Lord of Khemmennu (Hermopolis), one of the great centres of Egyptian priestly learning, was called *Het Abtit*, 'The House of the Net' or Veil. Thoth was the Master of Divine Wisdom, the Lord of Meditation. He was also the teacher of Isis, the Moon-Goddess of Wisdom and Nature Magic, she who is veiled on earth, but who unveils for those who have been 'commanded' at each full moon.

The net in the Temple of Thoth, the peplum, the veil, web, robe, mantle of the Goddess, are Mystery symbols which have many grades of meaning. There are deeps beyond deeps to be explored until the pole of supreme immanence as contrasted with the pole of supreme transcendence is reached. From the point of view of the novice these terms stand for the veil of the universe, the many-coloured veil of the Temple of Nature.

The scholar and teacher G. R. S. Mead tells us that the famous veil or robe of Isis was the spiritual nature of man himself. No mortal man has raised that veil, for to raise it man has to transcend the limits of individuality, to break the bonds of death, and so become conscious of immortality. To raise the veil is to see Nature as she *is*, and not as she appears to be.

The symbol of Isis is the *Ankh* and it symbolizes the forces of life contained within the form of matter. Behind the individualized life form that is man there is the Great Sea of Life. Isis is the star that rises from the Twilight Sea, the star that itself is the symbol of the divine spark in man. The Egyptians called it Sothis, we call it Sirius. When that star is unveiled and brightly burning within the human soul, then conscious touch with the Isis of Nature becomes fully possible.

One of the objects of meditation is the gaining of such a conscious touch with the Great Sea Mother, as opposed to the ordinary subconscious contact. This contact results in an integral consciousness of personal immortality (*not* the immortality of the personality as a form). This is the initiation of Isis, of the divine form emerging from the sea as described by Apuleius in Book 11 of his *Metamorphoses*. This is the second unveiling of the Mysteries. There is yet a third unveiling, that of the Great Silence in the Mysteries of Chaldea, for the Great Silence and the Great Sea are the Divine Syzygy.

If the novice has understood the Foreword, he should now begin to see why so many ancient symbols and references to ancient myths have been given long before the elementary technique of the art of meditation has been set forth. The explanation is simple. The new recruit does not understand and so does not realize the pitfalls and difficulties that lie before him. Neither does he understand that man learns through the exciting of his curiosity, and the stimulating of his interest. Interest is the starting handle of the mind's apparatus.

Seated in your most comfortable armchair with your back straight, and the body well and firmly fixed, spend ten minutes each day brooding upon any one of the symbols given to you. Do not lounge either physically or mentally. Read, and re-read each paragraph until the meaning becomes part of your own mental make-up. Gently and interestedly brood day after day over these symbols and word pictures without any strenuous effort or feeling of strain. After each meditation make a note of the ideas and feelings, especially the latter, that these symbols call up from your subconscious mind. This should be done as soon as possible after the meditation for the record to be accurate.

Stop the moment you are tired or lose interest. When you have finished your meditation, imagine its contents to be rolled up like a parcel and dropped through a trap door into your subconscious mind. Picture it being digested there until the next day when it will be handed to you neatly sorted out and ready for your further examination. Symbols dropped thus into the subconsious will incubate and realization will hatch out from the depths of the unconscious as surely as a chicken, given the proper conditions, will hatch from an egg.

This may seem a childishly simple method. As a matter of experience it may prove to be less simple than it appears to be. As a method, it works best with much honest practice. Try it and see what the mental 'Brownies' of your subconscious mind can do for you if only you will trust them and visualize carefully what it is that you want them to do.

This is the first and to my mind the most interesting stage of learning the art of concentration, i.e. the art of picturing clearly and appositely; for it will suggest to you subtle ways of working up an interest in any subject that you may have to consider.

Concentration when the interest is aroused is easy, for it is automatic. Concentration without interest is slow and inefficient, so learn to arouse interest at will.

Omar Khayyam complained: 'There was a door to which I found no Key.' Had he only realized it, the key was already in his possession. For the key to that door is interest, just concentrated interest.

Part 2: The Tools of the Mind

> In the centre of the Temple is the Hall of the Altar, with entrances opening East and West. Beyond it lies the great Hall of the temple entitled the Hall of the Child in his Cradle. From here access is obtained to the secret and concealed Shrine entered once a year by the high priest, on the night of mid-summer.
>
> (G.R.S. Mead, *Thrice Greatest Hermes*, Vol. I, p. 74)

For meditation the ancients had drawn up a very clear and easy schema which in its broad outlines is common to almost all Mediterranean Mystery systems. Plato used a form of it some 500 years before Christ, Proclus used it nearly 1,000 years later.

It is not advisable for novices to try to fit this ancient schema into modern systems of psychology, because until practical experience has been gained in its use, this is not easy. Also a mixing of terms that have contradictory meanings, and an ignoring of what one system considers to be fundamental principles, can only lead to confusion. In addition, meditation, as understood by the ancients, had as its field of action the planes of worlds more subtle than our own and invisible to us. Now, modern psychologists, and most modern philosophers and religious teachers, are rationalists in their outlook on life, and rationalism denies the validity of these ancient concepts of unseen worlds where the gods, greater and lesser, have their field of action.

Later the student can profitably compare both the ancient and modern concepts with regard to the nature of reality. At present he is advised to study carefully and use the following schema which has served the mystics and initiates of Europe for several thousand years.

For the purposes of meditation the ancients classified all knowledge and experience, objective and subjective, under the general headings of the divine, the cosmic and the human. These are explained below.

The Divine Unity was considered to have three methods of functioning, which were called *mone, proodos* and *epistrophe,* i.e. the abiding, the proceeding and the returning; or the static, the dynamic and the rhythmic; Brahma, Vishnu and Shiva.

The cosmos was seen as a duality and symbolized by pairs of opposites: the spiritual and the corporeal; the natural and the supernatural; the intelligible and the sensible; the noumenal and the phenomenal; the eternal and the transient.

Man was looked on as a trinity consisting of body, soul and spirit. The spirit was symbolized as the indwelling spark of divine fire; the incarnations of a man were thought of as being strung like pearls upon the thread of his spirit. The instrument for the manifestation of the unmanifested spirit was the soul of man.

The soul, with its many faculties, was considered to be the principle that makes of man an independent self-conscious unit. It is man's normal consciousness, and it is this principle that manifests as a trinity of mind, heart and will. As will be shown later, it can only be described by a series of paradoxes; its real nature is disputed and its very existence often denied by many. The propositions of Proclus with regard to the soul will be discussed later by way of an exercise in meditation.

The body was looked upon as the instrument by means of which the soul of man gains experience in this physical world and realizes its potentialities.

The mind, according to Platonic tradition, had five faculties for knowing: *aithesis, eikasia, pistis, dianoia* and *noesis.* These are dealt with under their respective headings below.

Aithesis

This faculty has its source in the nervous system of the physical senses. These are almost passive in their function, which is that of receiving vibrations from the external world. The nervous system is the medium through which all knowledge of the outside world enters the mind. It is the mind, not the senses, that turns vibrations into colour.*

You will now see the reason for the bodily temperance which is so strongly insisted upon in all systems of meditation. If the nervous system is out of order, the knowledge that enters from the outside world will be defective. It is best therefore not to eat,

---

* I think here the Colonel is confusing the physical brain and its functions with the phenomena we now refer to as the mind and which we have yet to 'find'.

drink or sleep too much if you want to get results from meditation. Above all see that bodily intake is balanced by an adequate bodily output. Take as your motto 'A Healthy Mind in a Healthy Body' if you wish to climb the steep slopes of the Hill of Vision.

Eikasia

In Greek this meant image, likeness or conjecture. It comes from the Greek verb *eikadzo,* to represent by a likeness, to infer from comparison, to conjecture or guess. *Eikasia* to the philosophers of that time meant the active aspect of the functioning of the senses. It was looked on as an irrational faculty that men held in common with animals, and concerned entirely with the apparent nature of things. It takes effects for granted and does not possess the capacity to estimate the cause of the effect. Today we call it instinct. For example to act upon instinct is looked on as acting without first using reason. When a gun is levelled at you, you do not stop to reason, instinctively you jump for cover.

Pistis

This third faculty by which man 'knows' is usually translated as belief or trust in others. It comes from the verb *peidomai,* meaning to be won over, or persuaded to believe in a thing or a person. As its derivations show, *pistis* is a belief which is not based on reason as a process, but adopted from the opinions of others. Often such belief is grounded upon the testimony of the instincts and senses, and not upon reason. For example the old belief that the sun revolved around the earth was based upon the evidence of the senses, and not upon reason. Today this is called the 'estimative faculty'. This faculty can know that a thing *is,* but cannot explain why. One often meets with people who are very sure of certain facts but cannot tell you why they are so sure, but they are often right. When highly developed this faculty can lead to worldly success, but it cannot usually apprehend things of a very abstract nature. It is a lower form of *dianoia,* or pure reasoning, and often mistaken for it.*

The ancients considered these three faculties to be the instruments of the personality as such, developing as the result of concrete experience. The two that follow find their highest expression in the individuality as the unit of evolution.

* In other words it is the 'hunch' that leads the broker to a correct prediction on the stock market, or the detective to his arrest.

Dianoia

This is Plato's fourth knowing faculty of the soul; it means thought, intellect or the sense of meaning of a thing. Its verb is *dianoemai*, to think over. The Latin equivalent is *meditari*, and its adjective, *dianoetikos*, had the special meaning of intellectual.* In meditation it was thought to be the key faculty for knowing. All these words have quite a different meaning to *pistis*, which implies a trust in others. *Dianoia* conveys the idea of knowledge arrived at through understanding the meaning of a thing. *Pistis* knows that a thing is. *Dianoia* understands *why* it is. This faculty is the result of the highest form of self-education. It is superior to all the lower faculties and is sometimes referred to as pure reason. It is not only able to comprehend concrete things, but also abstract ideas and principles. It is the faculty most used by the philosopher, the metaphysician and the theologian in their search for truth, beauty and harmony. When raised to its highest degree it imperceptibly merges into, and becomes, *noesis*.

Noesis

This fifth and last faculty is generally translated as intuition. Psellus calls it the Intelligible or Divine Soul. In the Platonic schools this was a word that denoted a mode of being, power or perception that transcended intellectual comprehension in the way that *dianoia* transcended *pistis*.

The Platonists considered intuition to be wholly distinct from and superior to rationalization. For them it meant direct understanding of universal and abstract ideas, and this as an activity of the soul is very rare.

The novice is unlikely to be called upon to develop his neotic abilities as yet. However, if he wishes to understand his instruments and not work blindly to some rule of thumb process, he must be able to distinguish between the respective functions pertaining to those faculties used in meditation. If he cannot do this he is likely to be deceived as to the nature of what is coming through.

In every meditation the student must clearly recall the difference between the knower, the subject to be known and the process of knowing. The description of these five faculties, i.e. the senses, instincts, estimative faculty, pure reason and intuition, is intended to analyse this process, and correlate the

* The word 'Dianetics' used by L. Ron Hubbard to describe his method of teaching is derived from the same base.

results obtained. In a normal person they are thoroughly reliable, although man often errs in his use of them.

Now to practical work, meditation as an art. The first things you need to develop and use in meditation are the senses (passive) and the instincts (active). These two in function form a pair, or syzygy, and you cannot separate them in practical work.

The Mysteries taught the first step of meditation as being 'to see God made manifest in Nature'. If you do not like the word God change it to whatever means the same thing to *you*. In nearly all the great religions there is the idea of the indwelling spirit of the divine being seen in the visible universe. 'In Him/Her we live, move and have our being,' taught the Greek pagan Aratus,* and St Paul quoted him deliberately. See also Romans 1:20. Yet another great thinker, Xenophon, wrote 'The Supreme God holds Himself invisible and it is only in his works that we are capable of admiring Him,' and this long before Christianity.

The early stages of meditation should be stages of development where the seeker learns to see and realize more than was formerly the case. He seats himself in the 'Hall of the Child in his Cradle' and like a child opens wondering eyes. With the opening of the inner eyes, this familiar world expands its 'becoming' to him, and he also expands and is able to grasp more of the deeper being behind our everyday world.

As an exercise in meditation, think over the sentences given above and extract the inner significance of these ideas. Find out more phrases, and there are plenty, that express the same ideas. Soak yourself in the cosmic ideas of Being, Life and Intelligence substanding all the Becoming that lies before you when you look through the window onto the world at large. Picture yourself as bathing in the warm sea of cosmic life and realize the rhythm of the cosmic light that vibrates as Mone, Proodos and Epistrophe. Above all feel yourself to be one with the ancient initiates who knew these things.

Now estimate the value of all this to your own being, life and intelligence. Picture your own consciousness as an integral part of the wider consciousness of nature and place yourself deliberately in rapport with Mother Nature. See yourself standing in the Temple of Hidden Wisdom, wait and watch. Consider this quotation from *The Gospel of Eve:*

---

* This is the first meditation sentence given in the SOL course.

I stood upon a high mountain, and saw a giant and a dwarf, I heard as it were a voice of thunder and drew nigh to hear. He spake unto me and said, 'I am thou and art I and wheresoever thou mayest be, I am there. In all am I scattered, and whencesoever thou willest, thou gatherest me, and in gathering me, thou gatherest Thyself.'

The mountain is a symbol for deep meditation. The Greater Self is seen by the Lesser Self, and the Gnosis of Nature. The Great Mother and the Great Father of all worlds are within reach. (See *Thrice Greatest Hermes*, Vol. II, p. 2.)

Build this picture with care, filling in the details, and see what it can teach you. Its meaning is far from obvious and there are at least three planes of being upon which the student can exercise his knowing faculties in order to grasp the inner meanings. In the temple of the Hidden Wisdom of Hermes Trismegistus there are the Halls of the Altar and the Child in His Cradle, and beyond them is the sealed and secret shrine where you should see yourself.

Part 3: The Universal Soul and the Soul of Man

> I sent my soul through the Invisible,
>   some letter of that after life to spell:
> And after many days my soul returned
>   and said, 'Behold, myself am Heaven and Hell'.
>
>   (Omar Khayyam)

One of the first things the neophyte has to realize is that he himself, and no other, is responsible for what he is. Reference is not made to environment. The point being stressed is that we are entirely responsible for the nature of our reactions to the circumstances of life. What we are today is the result of the way that we have managed, or mismanaged, our thinking in the past. What we will be in the future will be the result of our present method of thinking, and his holds good not just for this incarnation, but also for those in the future.

Man is his own saviour. No one else can save him, for the method of salvation is right thought followed by right action, and right thought is the result of right reaction to the circumstances of life; all this should be the result of knowledge. Sin is the result only of ignorance.

Today we are living in a new age, the age of the man who is freeing himself from the fetters of superstition, a free man who carries his own burden. In the past Piscean age when the average man was savage and uneducated, and unused to depending upon his own reason, it was better for mankind as a whole to be in leading strings and dependent for religious welfare upon those who made a profession of shepherding the untrained flock. It was to the State's advantage to exercise close control over religion, the government being, as it was, based largely upon vested interests, for a strong religious tie binds the tribe or nation together and so prevents splitting or divergent social interests. It gives peace to the many even if this be done at the expense of the few who are born before their time, pioneers for the future. That era, however, is nearly past. In the age opening before us the cry is raised by the younger generation, 'From authority lead us to experience; we will not be driven to God, nor even to No-God.

There is one great way to the obtaining of religious experience which all may take, and that is the inner way, the way that is to be found in the Inner Chamber concerning which Jesus spoke. The Mysteries taught: man, know thyself, the kingdoms of the world are within you, look within the outer covering. Most of the great teachers have proclaimed this way, among them Plato, Lao-tzu, Buddha, Jesus and Emerson.

If the saying, 'Look within', be analysed it will be discovered that as a process, it is far from easy. At first it seems so obvious that boredom sets in. Then begins the real struggle, which is to re-arouse and maintain interest. This can only be done by practical experiments. But if carried out faithfully and with reasonable intelligence they should have the desired effect of arousing and maintaining the interest.

For example when the mind has been trained to hold itself steady to a particular line of thought, the student will discover that he, the thinker, is where he thinks he is. That is to say, if you have a trained mind well-filled with the appropriate knowledge, you can, for a while, live in the scenes of long ago. It is this fact that makes the training system of the Jesuits such a potent one; for this system enables one to 'conquer oneself and to order one's life without being influenced by the vagaries of others', a valuable achievement for anyone who desires to replace authority with personal experience.

Again, 'the mind touches that which it thinks about constantly and with sympathy'. Experiment with these two aphorisms. Sit comfortably in your armchair, and take any scene in history that you know well and can picture clearly. Commence to build it up item by item in your mind. In doing this you are building a representation, that is to say an image of the past is being built within your own consciousness. Remember, it is a personal representation of your own thought; you and you alone are its creator. It exists solely within your mind. If you have built it clearly and without any mind wandering, you, the thinker, are for the time being able to live within your creation.*

In making this statement it is presumed that you are not one of those who identify the human thinker with the physical body. If you are, then the above statement will appear totally absurd to you.

There is a third aphorism that no one can prove to you by means of argument, logical or otherwise, which you can prove to yourself only by much practice, repeated experiments with the same subject, and a careful analysis of the results obtained: 'There subsists an Absolute and Universal Mind which contains within itself all other minds both human and non-human. This Mind, of which the human mind is a faint reflection, is endowed with Memory.'

You cannot prove that this mind is in being any more than you can prove the existence of that medium through which wireless works. But in meditations you *can* get practical results if you will work and experiment *as if it were true.*

In visualizing historical subjects there comes into play the theory that the mind touches that which it thinks about clearly and with sympathy. If you have built your representation consistently, until it is clear and accurate, if you have, as Loyola taught, put yourself thoroughly into your picture, and can act a part in it with full sympathy and strong emotion, then you will find that your meditation is no longer working *within the limits of your imagination.* Instead you will touch the memory of that event that is held within the universal mind and the scene will unfold like a cinema film, independent of your control, and not solely the result of your imagination.†

* This is the basis of many magical acts. They take place within the mind, but are none the less real for that, nor does it render some of them less dangerous!

† This I can vouch for myself. It is also the basis of 'far memory' which enables a highly trained mind to extract information from the distant past. It has other, far deeper levels of use.

You have to go through this experience personally in order to fully understand and realize it. It is impossible to describe it in terms that would make it comprehensible to those who have not been through the same experience. Those who have will recognize it at once, for it carries its own standard of validity. One *knows* that it is real. Such scenes have a life of their own, and appear to the watcher as intensely real. There is a curious sense of power about them, tenseness and emotion. But it is the personal factor that makes it feel so valid, grounded in one's being. Once felt, there is no doubt of its intrinsic reality in one's mind. When it is over, a haunting memory of what has been seen and felt remains for days. The drabness of ordinary life is very hard when one returns from such an expedition into the Memory of Nature.* One has indeed 'looked within the covering'.

In the previous pages a few hints as to methods, and a great many word pictures taken from the Ancient Mysteries have been given. These word pictures are a familiar part of our national system of education, and thus, though foreign, they have become part of the group mind of the English race. Nevertheless there still survives, buried deep in the subconscious of Britain as a whole, this other, non-Christian yet true native strain of mystical experience which can be evoked by those who know something of the ancient technique of our Celtic ancestors, and of the methods of the Orphic and other Mysteries.

Below is given a sample of what a carefully directed group meditation carried out by neophytes can do. It is the record of a student who took part in a Candlemas ritual, the modern name of an ancient festival of Faunus, of him who is Hades, Lord of the Underworld where is Elysium. Hades is the Zeus of the Netherworld, the ruler of the Astral Plane, and he has nothing whatever to do with the Christian idea of the Principle of Evil, i.e. Satan. There is more truth in the conjecture of Baronius that Pope Gelasius changed the pagan festival of the Lupercalia in February into the Purification of the Blessed Virgin than many ardent Christians would care to admit. Also it must not be forgotten that many of these ancient festivals were based upon the

* This is part of the danger of the occult, for sometimes the urge to stay 'within the world of the mind' is very strong and can lead to a complete mental withdrawal in one who is weak-willed. It is essential that such training is done under the guidance of a teacher.

changes in the magnetic tides of the Inner Planes, and that is why throughout the known pagan world of the past, and of the present, the same type of festival, no matter what the name may be, was and is held about the same date.

When the work on the T... began I did not feel oppressed by the power, or heavy. Instead I was keenly excited; but this excitement was without any of the hindering effects on the physical which I used to experience. Formerly, every rush of power threatened to knock me down as if with heart strain. I felt as if I must try to ascend the T... and I started almost at a run, but not up to its shoulder. I chose the spiral path. At the first turn it became a great cloud path round a glass mountain with precipitous sides. The top had four great peaks, whether towers or crags I could not distinguish. Later they took on Archangelic shapes. Through and under the glass mountain I saw a different landscape, the cities of a lower world. All the time the sensations which seemed to me to be almost ecstatic, persisted. I felt tireless and alive, tingling with a life that remains with me, even though I have lost some of the details of the experience.

That experience took place in London physically, yet in the Island of the West in reality. Compare this with the old Celtic romance of Connla of the Golden Hair and the Fairy Maiden. Connla meets a lady, very beautiful and dressed in strange attire, he alone can see her, though his companions can hear her speak. On being asked who she is she replies:

'I have come from the Land of Life [Tir na mbeo], a land where there is neither old age nor death. The inhabitants of earth call us Aes Sidhe, the People of the Shee or Fairy Hills, for we have our dwellings within large pleasant green hills. I have come to take you with me to Moy Mell [The Plain of Pleasure].' And she sings:
'A land of youth, a land of rest,
          a land from sorrow free,
     It lies far off in the Golden West,
          on the verge of an azure sea.
     A swift canoe of crystal bright,
          that never met mortal view,
     We shall reach the land ere fall of night,
          in that strong and swift canoe.
We shall reach the strand of that sunny land,
          from druids and demons free,
     The land of rest in the Golden West,
          on the verge of the azure sea.'

Part 4: Forbidden Marches

> Up from Earth's centre through the Seventh Gate
> I rose, and on the throne of Saturn sate,
> And many knots unravelled by the road.
> But not the knot of human Death and Fate.
>
> And lately, by the tavern door agape,
> Came stealing through the dusk an angel shape
> Bearing a vessel on his shoulder, and
> He bid me taste of it; and 'twas – the Grape.

(Omar Khayyam)

There is one thing that the organized world religions as a general rule very much dislike – trespassing in the 'Forbidden Marches'. Wisely, from their point of view, they forbid all entry into this debatable land under threat of hell, lunacy, loss of reason, etc. Some call such trespassing sorcery, which it is not. Others call it delusion, which it often is. As self-appointed wardens, these professionals do not enter themselves, and try to prevent others from interfering with what they claim to be their own special interests.

There are three roads that lead from the comfortable solid surface of Mother Earth to these Forbidden Marches, and eventually to that which lies beyond them. By the Qabalists these are known as the Road of Elemental Fire, the Path of Saturn, and the Path of the Moon.

To the student of the Western Tradition who has the keys of the ninth and tenth Sephiroth, one meaning of this verse is clear. The maiden comes from Tipareth, where she dwells during each life awaiting every one of us. The strand at the verge of the azure sea leads to the Thirty-Second Path and the swift crystal canoe is prepared within your own soul, for it is the equivalent of the Moon Barque of the Ancient Egyptian Mysteries. To those who are prepared to work and accept discipline, even today it can be truly said:

> There are strange delights for mortal men in the Island of the West;
> The sun comes down each evening in its lovely vales to rest.
> And tho' far and dim
> On the ocean's rim
> It seems to mortal view,

We shall reach its halls
Ere the even falls,
In my strong and swift canoe.

(Joyce, *Old Celtic Romances,* p. 35)

The rulers that have to be satisfied before such a journey can be completed are: Mercury, the Lord of Wisdom; the Moon crowned with silver and ruler of the Hidden Wisdom; and Venus clad in green, the ever virgin ruler of the great nature forces.

These roads, these destinations, and these rulers exist only in your imagination, and you will find them nowhere else. But be sure that you understand what that most royal faculty of man's mind, imagination, really is. It is more real than your body, and it will outlast this solid flesh.

If you can see that four-coloured veil which is stretched across the pylon gate, the veil that divides the known from the unknown, the actual from the real, the phenomenal from the noumenal; if you can steal unchallenged past the throne of grey-haired Saturn who, silent as a stone, sits watching, there will meet you in the darkness, silvered by moonlight and angel shape, yourself. But not your everyday self. It will take you to a mountain land of deep gorges and lofty pointed peaks.

On tree-clad hills, in boulder-strewn gorges, and upon bare windswept wastes and steep-sided peaks dwell the Old Gods, the essential Gods. These are the nature gods that the slum-dwelling children of modern man have forgotten, to their infinite loss. Once you have mastered the technique of a Mystery meditation system you will find that this oldest of lands, the 'Forbidden Marches', is rising into consciousness. You will then have to decide quickly on your course, for indecision is either self-rejection or loss of control. And that angel shape will not offer to one who hesitates or loses control the vessel that is upon his shoulder, and without the divine one you will not taste of that sacred grape juice which is the real wine of life.⋆ For in these 'Forbidden Marches' you can taste the fruit of that life-giving vine which thrills and exalts the inner self as not even the best of earthly wine can do. And it will leave no aftermath like earthly wine, unless it be the forbidden wine of sorcery.

⋆ The Colonel is speaking here of man as a dweller in the Age of Aquarius, one who carries his own water jar.

The technique of a Mystery meditation system is simple once you have achieved concentration, and understood what it is that you are trying to do. Then there is no fear of your losing the gods. You may neglect them, but you cannot lose them, for there is no part of you that is not of the gods.

The poet Aratus, quoted by Paul, wrote: 'in him we live, move and have our being.' If you can realize this in the same way that you realize the need for an overcoat on a cold day, then you have mastered the first great difficulty met with in the practical work of meditation. We are not speaking here of ethical meditation upon good works or good thoughts, but of meditation as a means of enjoying that fullness of life which is offered by the Divine One to those who can partake. And this partaking means to take a share in something with a person or being.

This means that the basic laws that govern thought (in meditation) apply to man *and* to the gods. You must be consciously aware of this fact, making allowances of course for respective differences in capacity. Man's mind bears the same relation to the divine mind that a wave bears to the waters of the earth; each drop is a part of the whole. But here the analogy must stop. Man's mind is individualized and not even the high gods can take away this divine gift of the Great Unmanifest.

It is an extremely useful exercise to get fairly deep into meditation and then to examine the contents of your own mind. Strange as this statement may sound to a bustling, practical, modern citizen, you will find in your own mind only the internal creations of your own thoughts. In it you will find only the images of objects produced by your own consciousness, they are merely representations, an awareness of the present plus memory. The external world produces sensations which are merely the raw material upon which the mind works. It is the mind grasping sensation that first leads to perception, then on to conception. The actual images that your thought creates are not directly the results of an external reality acting upon you, just the result of your mental faculties acting upon your present sensations or upon recollections. You see a red door. Ordinary man says the red is in the paint. The psychologist knows that the colour is not in the paint but in the mind of the beholder. Outside the mind colours are merely differences in the rate of vibration.

Your mental bias will determine your reaction to such sensations or recollections. Take this extreme case. Suppose you meet a spectre in a haunted house, your reaction will be determined by the attitude of your mind towards these peculiar and specialized sensations called 'ghosts'. As a strong-minded sceptic, you may blame your liver for such untoward sensations. If you are an experienced Spiritualist you may be mildly interested and unawed. As a devout member of certain European sects you might be inclined to blame poor old Diabolus. Note that the minds of these three types do not consciously create their respective representations and their reactions to these sensations. The action of mind in creating perceptions is usually subconscious; yet it is possible to create these representations and these reactions by a conscious process when the mind is trained by means of a certain type of meditation used in the Mysteries.

All sensations come to the mind via the senses, but not always the physical senses. The Doctrine of Sensation as understood in the Mystery schools covers much that is unrecognized by academic psychology. Further, it is possible to polarize one's own sphere of sensation with the sphere of sensation of the world soul.

The mind works upon the material brought in by all the senses and much of its action is subconscious for a time at least. So sensation is really feeling and not cognition. There are more worlds than this physical one, which can, and do, act upon our feelings and ultimately upon cognition, that faculty by which the raw material is made over into true knowledge. So it may be said that a man's personality depends upon the type of his sensations and recollections. It is *mind,* not manners that maketh man.

In meditation let the neophyte call to mind first of all that in the Mysteries consciousness, human and divine, has grades other than those affected by physical sensations, then let him remember that a specialized system of training will enable him to become conscious of the creative action of his own mind. When thus conscious you can deliberately modify the contents of your consciousness, and by changing the methods of sensation you can also change the planes or levels of consciousness. Remember, in the terminology of the Mysteries a change of consciousness means a change from the physical level to levels far more subtle than this one. We term this 'rising on the planes'.

We now turn from theory to practical work in the art of meditation. One of the greatest of the ancient teachers was Proclus. He has been described as 'a systemizer who carried the ideal of one comprehensive philosophy to its utmost limits'. The works of Proclus, especially his *Elements of Theology,* are a gold-mine for the mystic and those who seek for the practical part of the techniques of meditation as used by the initiates of old. His is a symbol system designed to help the human mind to change levels during meditation. He uses these mystical symbols to explain the time and space of these levels of consciousness other than the physical one. The gods, he maintains, have no existence outside the minds of men. They are fashioned by the mind of man alone.

All Mystery and religious systems that are more than just an expression of herd law, are systems of props whose sole object is to support and steady the human mind as it prepares itself for the final plunge into the Thrice Greatest Darkness, that is, the Ineffable Light. Bearing this in mind let us make use of Proclus and through his propositions seek a point of contact with those entities which the ancient initiates built up by means of their specialized techniques.

For example, meditate by means of visualization of such symbols as are known upon the following nine propositions:

Prop. 1.   Every manifold in some way participates [the verb is used transitively] unity. The symbols are: the Deeps of Interstellar Space; the Void; the Plenum.

Prop. 2.   All that participates unity is both one, and not one. Symbols are: the Unmanifest; the Cosmos; Man.

Prop. 3.   All that becomes one, does so by participation of unity. Symbols: the Immanent; the Transcendent; and the Many.

Prop. 4.   All that is unified is other than the *one* itself. Symbols: Nirvana; Night of the Gods.

Prop. 113.   The whole number of the Gods has the Character of Unity. Egyptian Theology is an example.

Prop. 114.   Every God is a self-complete henad or unit, and every complete henad is a God. Iamblichus explains this very clearly.

Prop. 115.   Every God is above Being, Life and Intelligence. Analyse this in terms of your inner self.

Prop. 116.   Every God is participable except the One. Try this as an experiment in metaphysics.

Prop. 117   Every God is a measure of Things existent. Consider the Solar Logos and his sphere of manifestation.

These nine propositions contain keys that will unlock some of the deepest secrets of the Mystery systems. All that is needed is perseverance, concentration and imagination. These qualities when fully developed will lead to Nirvana where you and your 'angel shape' are one, a unity that is one and not one. This road to Nirvana (not the Cosmic Nirvana) is a long one with many stages. Each stage is marked by the advent of a new phase of personality in the seeker, a new set of sensations and recollections, and the birth of these new 'selves' can be painful.

The ancient initiates built up the personalities they needed by deliberate mental action and detailed daily meditations on set subjects. In the Mysteries this is called Re-generation from above (*Anothen*) and the term *Hoi Anothen* means technically 'The Living'.

But when at least you become *Hoi Anothen* you will have passed far beyond the grade of temple novice. You have drained the Sacred Vessel, and tasted the Wine of Life, and left the Forbidden Marches far behind you. Like the Gods, you will be, temporarily, beyond consciousness of Good and Evil, that is, beyond this human existence in the sphere of manifested duality.

Part 5: Summary and Retrospect

> But when I woke I was murmuring to myself, as if in interpretation..., and I knew there were many at that mystery who would wake up again outcasts of Heaven and the God of this world would obliterate memory so that they would never know they had kept tryst with the Kabiri.
>
> Once before, not in dreams but in meditation, there had broken in upon me such a light from the secret places; and I saw through earth as through a transparency to one of those centres of power, 'fountains out of Hecate' as they are called in the Chaldaic Oracles, and which are in the being of earth, even as in ourselves there are fiery centres undiscovered by the anatomist, where thought is born or the will leaps up in flame.

(A.E., *The Candle of Vision*, p. 80)

In this last chapter will be given in place of mystic symbols, three short tales from life in which will be summed up the essence of this system of meditation. I have stressed the fact that the aim of all Mystery training systems, present as well as past, should be the knowing of the self. It was also pointed out that this was a long process, sometimes called the Unveiling of the Self. When you have done this you have opened a road into a realm more fascinating than that of the Arabian Knights.

In *The Mystic Rose,* by F. Cartwright, there is the following tale.

> When I was in the Holy City of Kerbela it seemed to me to be a smelly, dirty, hot, dried up Arab town, remarkable only for the number of its flies and the fanaticism of its inhabitants. But it is extraordinary how the imagination, when properly trained, can transform things and places. For while meditating on the imagery of the Mystic Rose, Kerbela suddenly became, for me, fragrant and green, the garden city of Wisdom.
>
> I learned much from this vision as told by the Sheikh Hadji Ibrahim about the art of meditation, and the use of imagery when forming analogies, that is the description of the things of one plane in terms of another and lower plane. For example there is the suggestion put forward by the Govenor's Barber, one Hadji Mahmud, for a better way of retaining the fidelity of women than the guardianship of eunuchs. [p. 17]
>
> Commenting on the normal Eastern system of guarding women in harems, the barber said that 'No better system hath been devised for securing the fidelity of their bodies and the infidelity of their minds.' He then explained his methods by saying, 'O excellent Governor, make the interior of thy house so pleasant to thy wives that they will not desire to look out of the windows, for when a woman looketh through a window, Satan entereth through the door.'

Let the novice using these articles imagine himself to be the Governor, and by doing his part thoroughly he will find that he like the Governor has also suffered from an 'infidelity of the imagination'. If he will remember the teaching already given, that the inner self is anima and feminine, he will appreciate the analogy of keeping a lively harem from getting discontented, and keeping one's thoughts from wandering during the practice of meditation. For in silence the mind looks through the windows of her house, and Satan, in the guise of unwanted thoughts, enters through the door. So follow the advice of the barber and train the imagination in pleasant ways so that it will have no need to look out of the window with eyes filled with desire. *Quod superius, sicut quod inferius!*

Then do not be a killjoy, but enjoy life and be reasonable. Seek virtue in moderation as did the Greeks, and seek physical well-being as a preliminary to mental and spiritual happiness. Asceticism can become a pathology. As A.E. pointed out, 'there are fiery centres' in the soul of the Great Mother and these have their analogue in the soul of man. Experience will soon teach that the unloosing of these centres within man, and their linking to the centres within nature cannot be safely carried out under pathological conditions.*

Much can be done by mental preparation just before sleep. For in a deep sleep man returns to rest in the soul of the Great Mother, and She is the source of genius. As a man thinks, so he is, especially when he takes notes on the thoughts that come in the night.

If your life is governed by a fear of hell, you will meet the devil in your imagination, in a hell of your own creating, and you will live in it with the utmost contentment, imagining that you are pleasing God by being uncomfortable and scared. Then, when the beautiful things in life come your way, you will hold up your hands in horror and dive back into your cosy hell.

Without realizing it the ascetic inverts life's values. Beauty has for him the ugliness of sin, joy displeases his beetle-browed God, love, even in its highest aspect, is for him nothing but lust. For such a man, a sickly body, a maimed mind and a mutilated emotional nature are things of holiness.

Sheikh Ibrahim illustrates this in *The Mystic Rose*. A disciple came to this Sheikh seeking 'the Path', and complaining of his passions. The holy man told him to go for a walk in the city. Here he fell for the wiles of a very unattractive woman and returned weeping to his master. The latter instead of being angry sent him forth again. This time the student got gloriously drunk and again returned to his teacher in the usual state of maudlin repentance. Once again, in a fresh robe, the holy man with a kindly smile sent him into the city. On the way he met a girl, young and beautiful, and she spoke to him thus: 'Friend, what seekest thou?' and he replied, 'Peace.' Then exclaimed the lovely damsel, 'I am that peace which thou seekest, in my bosom wilt thou find rest, for I am what thou art not, and in the merging of opposites alone is absolute rest obtained. Gaze into my eyes and see the things thou dost not know, from my lips take the wisdom thou wouldst have, in my embrace know the security for which thou longest. I alone can soothe thee, comfort thee and be thy torch bearer.'

* This is the reason for the searching questionnaires issued by genuine occult schools. Certain types of people are at risk in occult work, no matter how well-intentioned they are.

Long the disciple gazed at the vision, then he fled. In a quiet garden he composed himself and later, calm and proud of withstanding such a temptation, he returned and told the teacher. The latter rent his clothes and wept saying, 'O wretched man, what hast thou done...? Thou hast committed the sin of sins... Go from my presence, I can do nothing more for thee.' And he drove him away.

In the previous sections, mystic symbols have been given as subjects for meditation. Here you have scenes from life such as anyone might encounter. The story contains a series of teachings. It is a subject for meditation, as is the quotation from A.E.'s *Candle of Vision*. There is also the barber's advice to the Governor to be considered. All three tales can teach you much, even when treated as purely mythical, if you will re-present them to the inner eye. Then they will reveal their meanings, for you are no outcast of heaven, and never will be once you fully understand the meaning of that ancient magical phrase: *Omma Theis Eiso Peplon*.

March 1936 to September 1937

5.

The Old Gods

In this article the Colonel is at his best, writing about something dear to his heart, soul and spirit. It speaks for itself in words used by one for whom the Pagan Heart of the World Soul was a living and loving entity, one, moreover, to whom he had full access gained by trial and error and suffering.

I like to think that the Gates of Horn and Ivory swung open softly for him at the end, and that waiting to welcome him home were 'the Old Gods' in whom he believed with such passion.

Part 1

Who or what were the Old Gods? Pause for a moment and reflect on this, then note what pictures float up from memory's storehouse as the conscious mind focuses attention on the question. The answer will show, to some extent, what religion you hold. An atheist might well dismiss the whole question as meaningless, holding that there is no God and no gods. He is probably right and certainly not altogether wrong.

The Westerner brought up in an atmosphere of so-called Christianity will usually dismiss the gods of pagan religions as nonsense, or, he may admit to their existence, in the past of course, and attribute them to Satan.

It has been written that: 'An honest God is the noblest work of man.' Turning over the sacred books of mankind and considering their claims, it would appear that man is not yet an expert craftsman. The student is here recommended to read J. M. Robertson's book *A Short History of Christianity*, published by the Thinker's Library. It is widely read and to meet this type of thinker on his own territory one should have a sound knowledge of this type of literature. Do hold in mind, however, that the Church historians start with the assumption that the pagan religions were false, and on this basis they exalt the Christian religion as being the only true faith. Robertson starts with the same assumption and shows clearly that there is nothing in the theology or rites of Christianity that was not in the various pagan religions, and on this he bases his conclusion that Christianity is also a false religion.

Both these outlooks are false for they ignore the fact that all theology and all rites are of human fabrication. All religions contain some small portion of the truth mixed with much error for they are all the result of man's inner and personal religious experience. Paul, not Jesus, is the founder of modern Christianity, for it is a religion *about* Jesus and not the religion *of* Jesus.

It is often forgotten that religion, *per se*, is a matter of personal experience which is valid only for the person experiencing it. Since this is so, religions should be systems for the obtaining of that experience. They would then avoid the dogma which has crippled modern Christianity, and the need for a privileged class of priests claiming to be mediators between man and God would disappear. Naturally this will antagonize vested interests.

It is a universal principle that to appreciate a thing one must share the mental attitude of its creator. Once able to enter into its spirit we can reproduce in our own souls the same quality of life which called that thing into existence. To understand paganism we must enter into the spirit of paganism. What answer then can be given to the question asked at the beginning? Let us see what the pagans themselves had to say. Seneca wrote:

> The wisest among men understand him whom we call Jove to be the Guardian and ruler, spirit and soul of the universe, the Lord and Maker of this mundane sphere, to whom every name is applicable. Dost wish to call him Fate? Thou wilt not err. He it is on whom all things are dependent ... Dost wish to call him Providence, rightly wilt thou do so; for by his counsel ... provision is made for this world so that it may proceed in an orderly fashion, and unfold his deeds to our view. Dost thou wish to call him Nature? Thou wilt commit no sin; for he it is from whom all things are sprung and by whose spirit we breathe life. Dost wish to call him the World? Thou wilt not be mistaken, for he ... is all infused in its parts.

Over a temple at Sais in nothern Egypt was the inscription, 'I am all that was, and is, and is to come.' An Orphic teaching runs,

'One is the Self Begotten, and all things were derived from this same one.' The Egyptians called God *Ua Neter*, the One God, they were as much monotheists as the Jews, the Arabs and the Christians who officially believe in saints, archangels and jinnee.

Proclus in his *Elements of Theology* gives the same teachings, as the following will show, related to the Qabalistic Tree of Life.

(A) The One Originative Principle of the Universe — The Qabalistic Unmanifest, called by Proclus The One and the Good. The First Principle. It is 'Unparticipated, and is Unparticipable.

(B) The Many or High Gods — The Qabalistic Manifest. The ten Sephiroth in Atziluth

The high gods are the 'Participated' and the 'Participable' as well as the source of all that participates. They are above being, life and intelligence. These gods are divine henads or unities, the outshinings of the One and the Good. They are the Ten Holy Sephiroth, and are derivative terms proceeding from the first principle. Their attributes pre-subsist them in a unitary and supra-existential mode.

In connection with the above and with the aid of the Tree of Life consider the implications which are contained in the following propositions of Proclus.

Prop. 126. A God is more universal as he is nearer to the One, more specific in proportion to His remoteness from it.

Prop. 128. Every God, when participated by beings of an order relatively near to Him, is participated directly; when participated by those more remote, indirectly, through a varying number of intermediate principles.

These propositions when studied in the light of the descent of life force through the Four Worlds of the Qabalists give a clue to the use of god-forms, and to the varying functions of certain gods, like Osiris, Thoth and Isis.

To the uninitiated the pagan systems look chaotic, but there is a clue. It goes by function and not by name. So to answer the question posed at the opening of this chapter we may say that for an initiated pagan, the gods, as distinguished from God, represented divine intelligences and hierarchies of intelligences who were, and are, living out a form of experience which is other than man's experience. They were, and are, undergoing this experience of living on the various planes of consciousness in this universe in much the same way that man undergoes the experience of living on this earth.

The atheist believes he is the highest type of intelligence the universe can produce, which conceit explains why he is an atheist. The average Christian is little better, for he usually repudiates all the unseen that stands between God and man. He may give lip-service via the prayer book to the angels and archangels, but he is secretly ashamed of them as being ancient and unscientific. The Catholics are a little wiser, they at least acknowledge the existence of the archangels, angels and saints, and teach their followers how to get in touch with them.

We can divide these intelligences and hierarchies into three main classes, which in turn have many subdivisions. There are the high gods which correspond largely with the Qabalistic names of God, the archangels and lesser gods corresponding to the great devas, jinnee and angels, and the humanized gods such as Osiris, Orpheus, Im-hotep, etc., which are somewhat similar in conception to the Christian saints.

Behind these high gods are unmanifested divine aspects which are not usually personalized, and are named as the Unmanifest, Chaos, Old Night, etc. They could be said to correspond to the Unmanifest and the Three Veils of Negative Existence as used in the Mystery schools of the Western Tradition.

Within the above classification there is another and smaller one: that of the sun-gods, the underworld- and moon-gods, the earth-gods and the mind-gods. This last is important for it contains the 'principles' which were and are used by the pagans for the practical working of their rites and for meditation work.

The first classification gives us the broad background of paganism. The second gives us the foreground of the stage on which the action takes place in the pagan Mystery dramas. Therefore, for the pagan both past and present the gods as a class represent the type of experience of which it has been said, 'I do not believe that our experience is the highest form extant in the universe.'

The gods were personalized and named by the initiates in the same way, and for the same reason, that modern science names certain types of experience as electromagnetic, radioactive, etc. The Old God names are labels for certain types of divine experience which the initiates of old met up with in the course of their researches into the nature of the unseen. To sum up we may say, by using methods similar to those used centuries ago we can get similar experiences of the divine, for the old classifications still hold good. This again means the message which the Egyptian Thamus gave to the islanders of Palodes is false.

Part 2
In the study of religions it soon becomes evident that each one has its inner and its outer section. Christianity denies this and protests that all its goods are in the shop window. At first sight this appears to be so. But even a perfunctory glance at Roman Catholicism shows that its priesthood forms an inner section and the laity its outer. The priesthood, too, has the same inner and outer sections, and this division rests not upon the secret dogmatic teachings which the 'inner' keeps from the 'outer', but upon the use of secret methods of spiritual, mental and emotional training.

The Roman Church says that it has no secret dogmas which are kept from the faithful that support it with money and votes. This is probably correct. But the priesthood, the monastic orders, the enclosed orders and the higher grades of the hierarchy have methods of training which are not readily available to the general public. The expression 'religious vocation' had for the highly trained Roman priesthood a meaning of which the Protestant laity has little suspicion. The highly trained priest bothers little about dogmas, for he knows it is the method not the dogma that really matters.

The great difference between the Church of England and the Church of Rome is that the former base their faith on a regard for the Thirty-Nine Articles, and the latter upon that special religious experience that Mother Church provides for those who are capable of using it.

The intent of celibacy and monasticism is, *au fond*, magical, and their community life prevents worry about the earning of their daily bread. With no financial worry, discipline, celibacy and a highly developed system of mental training, the efficacious evocation of the 'real presence' becomes an easy matter of daily religious routine. This explains why almost all the Roman Catholic churches are centres of magical power, and those of the Protestant have all the charm and warmth of an empty lecture hall. The Roman Catholic is said to call Protestant churches temples. This is the one thing they are not.

The reason why the Roman Church has this magical power is that it works, in a modified form, the old magical system that it took over from paganism. The Protestant divine is in most cases totally ignorant of, and hostile to, magic, which is why the spiritual and devotional atmosphere is lacking in his church. Such churches are not temples, for a temple is the dwelling place of the god and is ensouled by him. Instead they are places for the teaching of an ethic tinged with a decorous emotionalism. The magical element is absent from their rituals, the ministers are teachers, not priestly magicians as are the Roman Catholic clergy.

The Mystery schools based their training methods on the maxim, 'As above, so below.' They taught that man is a replica of the Great Cosmos, he is the little cosmos. The ancient teaching of Hermes is the method to be followed in this exposition of paganism, and it takes 'mind' in its various forms as the working basis of its training methods.

It postulates that mind is everywhere and directs everything. For example: the earth is the outward symbol of an indwelling intelligence in a manner analogous to a man's body, which should also be the outer symbol of an indwelling intelligence. This intelligence incarnates to gain experience as does man.

All upon the earth lives, moves and has its being and is dependent upon this intelligence, called the Earth Soul or Earth Mother. These indwelling cosmic intelligences are graded. The grade above that which controls the earth, is that of the sun. This intelligence controls the whole solar system, which in its outer spatial form is its body. The planets and all they contain live, move and have their being within the all-inclusive being of this solar intelligence, considered to be the Great Father and giver of life to the Earth Mother.

The same idea holds good with regard to these vast transcendental intelligences which control the systems of solar intelligences and even the cosmos itself. Each god lives, moves and has its being within the vaster intelligence of the grade above it, the grade above fertilizing the grade below it. If you wish to study this more deeply you will find the ideas developed more fully in Proclus, *The Elements of Theology*, Propositions 113–17.

These ideas are worth bringing into the sphere of everyday life. For example think of the multitude of little lives that have their being within the vaster life, being and intelligence of a man. Study the living contents of your next boil with a microscope, then meditate by analogy on man and the gods, and the cosmos, keeping in mind the axiom, 'As above, so below.'

Compared with man these cosmic gods are superior and perfect, while man is inferior and imperfect. The object of the initiated pagan was to gain conscious touch with these superior beings in whom he had his own beingness. He based his methods on the psychological maxim, 'As a man thinks, so he becomes.'

The second great hypothesis on which they based their training was, 'The mind gains conscious touch with that upon which it broods.' The method of Loyola depends upon this, and his system is one of the most successful that Christianity has produced and is essentially magical in its methods and results.

It now becomes necessary to define the word 'pagan'. According to the *Oxford Dictionary*, it means 'heathen, unenlightened person', yet Socrates, Plato and all the great intellects of the ancient world were pagans. Jesus ben Joseph was the flower of a pagan civilization. The word comes from the Latin, *paganus*, meaning in, or of, the country. When Christianity came to power it was used to denote those who worshipped the old gods at their shrines on the hills and in the vales, in contradistinction to the Christians, who were mainly town-dwellers.

The modern pagan, too, is a lover of open air, one who worships God made manifest in nature. In Qabalistic terminology he worships Adonai Ha Atretz, the Lord of the Earth. He sees God most clearly in the countryside and finds Him in the open spaces. He knows that God is just as present in the stuffy chapel, and the slum dwellings, and in the public houses as He is in the wooded vale and the dim forest glade.

For him the approach is not via a priesthood for every pagan is his own priest or priestess, he is the master of his own soul, and his own saviour, he has no belief in a supreme personal God. He denies all that the Church holds dear, including bishops, priests and even deacons. However, he remembers gratefully the great pagan mystic who walked and taught in Galilee, a man who, when he was tired of working in the towns and slums, went out into the hills to commune with his Father, Adonai, to obtain by meditation refreshment for body and soul from the open spaces and night skies. He learned to draw near to the Great Mother and to be at One with Her.

Jesus was essentially a pagan whose home was the *paganus*. It was the city-dwelling Saul who founded that which we call Christianity. The communism of the Galilean pagan was put to one side and its place filled with a teaching *about* Jesus, which made of him a God to be worshipped. Thus the very real dangers of communism were averted by deifying this Arch Communist and turning attention from an inconvenient teaching to the person of the teacher.

It has been said that *real* Christianity has never been tried. It might equally be said that the supposed founder of Christianity was the greatest of the ancient pagans.

As with Jesus, so with the modern pagan; communion with nature is his means of worship and of rest, of refreshment for body and soul and spirit. Religion is for him a conscious linking of phenomenon with noumenon. Once this has been mastered the pagan is his own high priest, and he is independent of the priesthood as Jesus was independent of the Temple and the priests in Jerusalem. The third great hypothesis upon which modern initiation bases its system of training is, every man can become his own priest by right of *function*.

Part 3: The Background of Paganism

> The mind of Man is this world's true dimension,
> And knowledge is the measure of the mind:
> And as the mind, in her vast comprehension,
> Contains more worlds than all the world can find,
> So knowledge doth itself far more extend
> Than all the minds of man can comprehend.

> Rupert Brooke

The cosmic background to pagan religious thought is formed by the idea of the 'oversoul' or 'world soul', which Plotinus calls the Divine Creative World Soul, and which he describes thus:

> First let every soul consider that it is the World Soul which created all things, breathing into them the breath of life – into all living things which are on Earth, in the air, and in the sea, and the stars in heaven, the Sun, and the great heaven itself. The Creative World Soul sets them in their order and directs their motions, keeping *itself* apart from the things which it orders and moves and causes to *live*.

It will be seen from this quotation (*Enneads*) that the Divine Creative World Soul is the ultimate form of creative energy to which the mind of man can reach. The other great and divine souls, such as that of the solar logos, our sun, of the great Earth Mother, of the various stellar logoi, are born and persist as this Oversoul grants them life ... but this oversoul lives for ever and ever and never ceases to be *itself*. This is not the Earth Soul, which is of a lesser grade.

To use the terminology of the Qabalah, in its first manifestation this creative over soul is the Supernal Triad of Kether, Chokmah and Binah, and *as such*, it is the primal manifestation of that Unmanifest which the Qabalists call the Ain, the One, the Absolute; that which has its own mode of being behind that purely human convention which is called the Three Veils of the Unmanifest. The Ain thus corresponds to the *itself* of the passage quoted above.

Emerson, as the prophet of modern paganism, in his work *Oversoul*, writes with regard to man, the microcosm: 'The Soul of man is not an organ, but animates, and exercises all the organs: it is not a function like the power of memory, of calculation ... it is not a faculty ... it is the background of our being in which all faculties lie.'

'As above so below.' The ancient initiates, recognizing the limitations of human thinking and of human methods for expressing their thinking, postulated as a working hypothesis the theory of the Divine Oversoul, analogous to the Soul of man. And this theory of a Divine Creative Oversoul which is analogous in its working to the Soul of man, and with which the human soul can get conscious communion, is the backgroud of both ancient and modern Mystery school training.

We can divide up the Mystery systems of the Western Esoteric Tradition of today into six groups – Qabalistic, Chaldean, Egyptian, Greek, Celtic and Norse. It is not easy to decide which of these is the oldest. When educated people thought of human history as beginning in about 5,000 BC, it was generally considered that the Egyptian system was the oldest and that Egypt was the Mother of civilized religions. Today this assumption is considered a doubtful one. There are schools which think that the Druidic branch of the Celtic religion and the Egyptian Mystery systems are both offshoots from a common and still more primitive religion which they call Iberian, a system which was in vogue between 10,000 and 5,000 BC. If this theory is true it will explain the likeness as well as the curious differences between the British Druidic systems and the Mystery religions of ancient

Egypt. The Celts themselves are not Iberians, but in their wanderings conquered or displaced the more ancient Iberian tribes and added their predecessors' religious practices to their own.

It must here be remembered that these ancient religious systems were not collections of dogmatic teachings which are supposed to be capable of demonstration by, and to, reasoning minds. They were practical systems for obtaining 'religious experience', in its widest sense; and as most of them were based upon a technique for using the subconscious mind, they could not be rationalized or made reasonable in the modern sense of that term.

The ancient initiates found these systems reasonable because their sole religious criterion was that of utility. A system was valid if it produced religious experiences. If it did, all well and good – if not, the priest died! Invaders coming into a new country found that the old power centres were easier to work, and the old and local methods often gave more satisfactory results than their own. This is why so many of the old centres have remained in use for religious purposes down to the present day. Many Christian churches are sited upon old pagan centres that have been in use from time immemorial.

From a practical point of view it is far easier to open up, and gradually modify an ancient centre of religious power, than to start a new centre and a new system that is alien to the country, to the oversoul of the place and to the race. Looked at from the pagan initiate's point of view the key idea is this: that man can get into intimate touch – almost at will – with the world soul once he has realized that the mind touches that which it constantly and sympathetically thinks about.

Part 4: General Classification of the Gods

The object of this section is to classify the gods of the pagan initiates from the practical point of view. This classification may not recommend itself to the historian or to the scholar. In the first place it is limited. In the second place it deals with deities which are unlike those of the classical religions and philosophies. And, finally, it is according neither to popular historical importance nor to the conventions of esoteric religion, but to the efficiency of gods when they are used in accordance with a certain technique.

The reader may say here: 'What does this mean? Can I for example see, hear and touch the Great God Pan?' Certainly. You can make Pan your constant companion and you can bring the 'Pan within' to life in exactly the same way that the orthodox Christian saint by a certain technique brings to birth the 'Christ within'. But you are not recommended to do this without safeguards, for the pagan who has called into over-activity the 'Pan within' can be as unbalanced a person as the Christian saint who has roused into undue activity those forces which are sometimes called the Christ Within.

If you are a monotheist, and not that much-abused person, the dualist, you must, logically, recognize that Pan and Christ are but two aspects of the same thing, which temporarily, for the sake of convenience, will be called God. Both aspects are good – in the right place and in the right proportions. Both are harmful when misplaced in time, or space, or both. Spiritual adultery is just as common as physical and in the long run it is even more undesirable.

In *The Mystical Qabalah* by Dion Fortune there is given the system for the classification of the pagan gods which is used by the initiates of a number of modern schools. Briefly, it divides all the gods of the pantheons into ten classes, called the Sephiroth, and presupposes that they emanate from an unmanifested state of being which is the source of all that has been, is, or will be. The Neo-Platonists call it the One, as opposed to the Many. These ten classes are:

1.	The space – time-gods	— Kether
2.	The all-fathers	— Chokmah
3.	The great mothers	— Binah
4.	The builders	— Chesed
5.	The destroyers	— Geburah
6.	The sun-gods	— Tipareth
7.	The virgin nature-gods	— Netzach
8.	The wisdom-gods	— Hod
9.	The underworld- and the moon-gods	— Yesod
10.	The earth-gods	— Malkuth

From the practical point of view the student need, for the present, concentrate only upon numbers 1, 6, 9, 10 and 8, which reduces his classification to the space- or time-gods, sun-gods, moon- and underworld-gods, earth-gods and the gods of wisdom.

The more common types of symbols for these cosmic
intelligences are:

1. The space-gods.   The point within the circle. 'The Serpent
                       that devoured his tail.'   ,
                       and occasionally   .
                       The signs   and   are also used
                       for Chokmah and Binah respectively as
                       the positive and negative functions of the
                       Kether space – time gods.
                       The zodiac is also a symbol for
                       Chokmah.

2. The sun-gods: .
3. The moon-gods: .
4. The signs of the Four Elements are used for various
    elemental deities:
         fire;   air;   water;   earth.
5. The sign   for the gods of wisdom.

A short comparative list of the more common forms is:

1. Space-gods:

Qabalah	– – Eheieh.
Greek	– – Chaos, Nox and Eros. Zeus, Jupiter as sky-gods.
Egyptian	– – The Eight Gods of Hermopolis with Thoth at their head; Amen and Ptah; Nu and Nun.
Chaldean	– – Apsu, Mommu and Tiamath. Anu as the All-Father.
Celtic	– – Lir and Beli.
Nordic	– – Odin or Tiwaz or Tyr.

2. Sun-gods:

Qabalah	– – Aloah va Daath.
Greek	– – Apollo and Helios.
Egyptian	– – Ra, Horus and Osiris.
Chaldean	– – Shamash. Asshur, Enlil, Merodach or Bel.
Celtic	– – Lugh or Angus Og, Dagda, Bile and Hu.
Norse	– – Balder.

3. Moon-gods and the underworld-gods.

Qabalah	– –	Shaddai El Hai.
Greek	– –	Semele, Pluto, Persephone.
Egyptian	– –	Isis of the Moon and Thoth as Tehuti, Khensu and Osiris.
Chaldean	– –	Nin-gal and Sin. Ishtar. Allatu and Nergal.
Celtic	– –	Celi as the husband of Keredwen. Midir and Etain of the Fairies. Bile, Manannan Manawyddan Mab Llyr the Welsh Lord of Hades. Brigid and Gwynn ap Nudd.
Nordic	– –	Mani the moon-god. Ran and Hel the Goddesses of Death.

4. Earth-gods:

Qabalah	– –	Adonai.
Greek	– –	Demeter, Gaea as Earth Mother and Ceres.
Egyptian	– –	Isis.
Chaldean	– –	Ishtar. Tiamath as Earth Mother.
Celtic	– –	Keridwen and Dana (Irish), Brigantia. Cernunnos.
Nordic	– –	Rinda. Thor and Sif, the God and Goddess of Crops.

5. Gods of wisdom:

Qabalah	– –	Hermes, Thoth.
Greek	– –	Hermes. Pallas Athene.
Egyptian	– –	Thoth.
Chaldean	– –	Nabu or Nebo, and Sin.
Celtic	– –	Ogmios and Briganda. Ogma (Irish), Myrddin (English). Dagda ('The Lord of Great Knowledge').

Nordic   – – Odin, with Loki as the
                God of Evil Wisdom.

This list is a brief one, and it refers only to the cosmic intelligences, i.e. to the type of beings that Iamblichus in his book *The Egyptian Mysteries* calls 'the gods'.

In the Mystery schools of Egypt and the Gnostic schools at Alexandria, the 'many' gods were considered to be the emanations or the 'outshinings' of the 'One' God who was the super-essential deity, or, as we should say, the Unmanifest Cause of All. Iamblichus divides the divine hierarchy into the gods and the superior races, and it is clear that he considered the former as representing or personifying qualities in the Divine Mind rather than as personalities or individuals.

For the ancient initiate, mind was 'the leader and King of the things that actually are'. Thus we can best understand these pagan gods by thinking about them as the great directing minds of this universe.

When studying these deities, the student, in the course of meditations made with some degree of proficiency in the technique of the Mystery school method, is bound to come across certain curious phenomena which have been described as the Memory of the Earth. A.E. in *The Candle of Vision* (p. 56) has dealt with this subject and the student is advised to study this great writer's theories. But for the present we may take the 'Memory of the Earth' as a working hypothesis. The *modus operandi* will be discussed later, and if the student will tentatively accept this theory, he will save himself a good deal of worry about details, and this will result in accelerated progress.

The student is advised to read and re-read these classifications of the gods. He may not agree with them. If he has been educated in what is called the classical tradition he will probably disagree heartily. But it must be called to mind that we are not dealing with the classical pantheons. The criteria of the classical records are not the same as the criteria that are applied to results obtained from the recovery of Earth Memories. The latter are empirical; the former are not. The main object is to get a working process that can be relied upon to give adequate results when recovering the past.

The more these gods are reflected upon in solitary meditations the more such meditations pass inwards into sympathetic contemplation and the easier it becomes to develop, from latent existence in the subconscious mind, the long-hidden memories of the ancient Wisdom religions.

Part 5: The Gods and their Functions

> The souls came hither * not by sending, and not of their own will; or at least their will is no deliberate choice, but a prompting of nature ... The Intelligence which is before the World contains the destiny of our abiding yonder † no less than of our sending forth; the individual is 'sent' forth as falling under the general ordinance. For the universal is implicit in each, and not by authority from without does the ordinance enforce itself; it is inherent in those who shall obey it and they carry it always within them. And when their season is come, that which it will is brought to pass by those in whom it resides; bearing it within them, they fulfil it of their own accord; the ordinance prevails because the ordinance has its seat in them, as it were pressing upon them weightily, awakening in them an impulse, a yearning, to go to that place whither the indwelling voice seems to bid them go.

(Dodds, *Select Passages Illustrating Neoplatonism*)

When striving to unravel the complexities of the numerous pantheons it is necessary to call to mind the fact that the gods are but symbols for certain manifestations of divine force. Their names are the X, Y and Z which enable the theurgist to work out this system of divine algebra and to function as a priest.

Isis, for example, is a man-made personification of a certain type of divine force. Again X may stand for many things which are not of this physical plane. Isis too stands for many non-material things. There is Isis as the Earth Mother, as the Virgin Lady of Nature, as the Queen of Heaven, as the Moon, as the Cosmic Mother, and so on.

There are many forms in which electricity can be used – as a motor agent, as light, as heat, as a curative agent, or as a means for executing a criminal. What electricity is *per se* we do not know, but we do know how to make use of it in various particular ways. What the gods are *per se* we do not know, but the theurgist does

---

*   'Hither' is a technical term for the material world. (Seymour)

†   'Yonder' is a technical term for the unseen world. (Seymour)

know how to bring into function a god-form, i.e. a divine symbol – in many particularized ways.

From a practical point of view this is all that really matters. The divine within reaches out to the divine that is without, the contact is made, and the divine machinery is set in motion upon the plane of consciousness that is required. But if there is no Isis within your own soul, you will call in vain to this goddess. You must seek within yourself for the starting-handle.

To understand what the pagan was trying to do one must imagine, as he did, that divine all-embracing power which welling up under pressure from the unmanifest is ever seeking to express itself more and more fully, more and more perfectly. It has been well said that 'God is pressure.'

This pressure is often called Spirit, or Life. In reality it is all these things, and more, for there is the transcendent aspect to this power which the Chaldeans called the Great Silence, as well as the imminent aspect which is the Great Sea. In order to exist – this universal power must differentiate itself into particular units. The One must become the many – the High Gods.

The Qabalists use the system of the Tree of Life to explain the process by which the One becomes the Many. They divide divine manifestation into four worlds or states of consciousness. The most subtle of these worlds is Atziloth, which might be called the world of pure spirit, the Archetypal World, the sphere of the divine archetypal ideas, the plane of the High Gods, or the world of the ten Divine Names. All these things, and many others, it has been called, but it must be remembered that in itself the world of Atziloth is beyond our comprehension. It can be described only by means of analogy and by the use of symbols. Neo-Platonism, as a system, gives a full and very vivid teaching concerning this sphere of the divine activity. But the modern student must not forget that these ancient initiates were carefully trained in the pure dialectical method, a subject little studied today.

The best line of intellectual approach to the comprehension of ideas concerning the world of Atziloth is a study of mystical theology. This art reaches out to the supreme goal by the use of analogy and paradox, by blending the *Via Affirmativa* and the *Via Negativa*, until the super-essential Darkness which is the Ultimate Light of Light is reached in a contemplation that ends in *Agnosia*. One can study these methods even if one cannot use them. A study of Neo-Platonism can take the competently taught student by an ancient, well-trodden road to identification with the

'One and the Many'. But competently taught students are
extremely rare for the world has seen few such teachers as
Plotinus, Ammonius Saccas or Lao-tzu. These teachers are
themselves living embodiments of the divine wisdom-gods. By
sympathy they have become 'at one' with the divine wisdom. By
their 'at-one-ment' they are able, at least temporarily, to lift the
prepared student up to the metaphysical heights of the Light
beyond all Lights – the Transcendental One, or to take him down
to that abyss beyond all abysses.

The experiences which these teachers produce in the student's
soul are evanescent. Yet something remains in memory for the
hand of the Initiator has been laid upon the neophyte. When
Height has challenged Height, and Deep has called to Deep, one
is never quite the same.

The second sphere of the divine outpouring is called the world
of Briah, a word derived from the Hebrew verb meaning to create,
to produce. The divine ideals have, as it were, become the divine
ideas. In Qabalistic terminology this is the world of the
archangels, of the creating gods and the all-mothers of the ancient
pantheons. It is the world of the great devas of the Eastern
systems. In modern language we might call it the sphere of the
abstract mind, or the world of abstract thought and ideas.

The third world is called Yetzirah. Now the Hebrew word
Yatzar (Yod, Tzaddi, Resh) has several significant (from our point
of view) meanings. It means to form in the mind, to plan, to
fashion as an artist, and in certain cases to destine for a particular
purpose. Now the initiates conceive the physical world to be
crystallized astral matter, the astral world to be crystallized mind-
stuff, and mind-stuff to be crystallized spirit. The same thing but
varying in, shall we say, density.

In this third sphere of being, ideas take form, and the etheric
moulds that hold dense matter in its physical form as we know it
are fashioned by the divine artists; for Yetzirah is the sphere of
the greater localized divinities, and the student will find a good
deal given in Chapters 3–6 of *The Egyptian Mysteries* by
Iamblichus. In modern terminology Yetzirah may be called the
astro-mental world, though one must remember that there is no
hard and fast line between the various spheres of being; they
shade off imperceptibly one into the other. Dividing them up is
like dividing the human mind into the descriptive sections that
are used by psychologists. This is convenient for teaching and
description, but these hard and fast lines of distinction exist only
in textbooks.

The fourth sphere or world is that of Assiah. It corresponds to the physical world in its most subtle form. It is the densest form of the etheric world. In this sphere of the subtle pre-matter of existence are to be found the nature spirits, elementals, and the children of Dana, of the Great Earth Mother, the divinities of mountains, streams and woods.

If we bear in mind the ancient Mystery teaching that 'all the gods are one god, all the goddesses are one goddess, and there is one Initiator', it will be seen that in the system of the Tree of Life as expounded in *The Mystical Qabalah* there is developed a perfectly logical sequence of cause and effect. From the human point of view the Tree of Life works as a system for enabling a human being to obtain contact with divine things, and again using the analogy of electricity, to put himself in circuit with the power-house of the universe.

Once more the student is warned that he must distinguish between 'the order of that which is' and 'the order of ideas concerning that which is'. One is not now trying to describe a chemical experiment. How these things that have just been described by analogy and by symbol may appear to minds superior to our human minds, we have no idea. To such minds our explanations are certainly childishly inadequate even if they are not entirely inaccurate. But this Qabalistic system of describing and using the mind fulfils the following fundamental conditions for obtaining results. First there is the power. Then there are individuals of various grades in all four worlds of manifestation who understand how to use this (divine) power. And, lastly, there is a method , or rather methods, for using this power in so far as mankind can become aware of it.

The divine life or power – like electricity – is not generated by the individual. The individual uses power which is already existing and the specializing of the divine energy which alone leads to manifestation must take place through individuals, human or otherwise. In theurgy this is a matter of experience as well as of common sense.

The pagans taught that every man is a distributor of this all-embracing, originating divine spirit or power. The initiate, however, was a trained man who, understanding the nature of the divine power, was able to transform it at will. He was a well-trained engineer, and he got his training in the same way that an electrical engineer gets his today – by working practically in an electrical power station. The initiate worked in the power-house of nature after having been taught the theory of his craft in a Mystery school. Then he took his practical training in the sphere of Yesod, which is the unmanifested element of the Four Elements of the physical world, the aether of the wise, the astral light of the ancients.

Thus it will be clear that the pagan initiate looked upon life from a rather different point of view from that of the ordinary man. The ambitious self-reliant man of the world strives to make himself a forceful personality and to get things done by his own driving power. He is his own power-house, and he supplies – or thinks he does – his own energy. The pagan, however, grasped the idea of 'Spirit' as the fountain head of a great 'forming power' which he received into himself. Then he proceeded to manifest it in accordance with the Law of Harmony and by means of a technique that he had been taught.

The various gods and their hierarchies are specialized functional types of this omnipresent divine energy. For example, Venus is the personification of the divine activity that is called attraction; Mars is that of repulsion, the divine destructive force; and Jupiter is a constructive mode of action. Again the religions of the mother and the daughter – Demeter and Persephone for example – are not so much family relationships as psychological stages in the life of the soul. From this point of view, the doctrine of the identity of Kore the Maid and her mother is obvious. The Maid is the psychological parent of the mother, and so the confusion of the persons disappears – the mother is the virgin and vice versa. The One God has become many gods, and each god functions as the head of a divine hierarchy with aspects that are spiritual, mental and astral. Each hierarchy in its turn carries further into manifestation the cosmic principle of the One, which becomes the Many. And each plane of manifestation has its own standard of truth and its own ethic, and these standards are by no means identical.

Cosmically, every man is a unit, but he is also a multiplicity, a hierarchy of divine lives, and in his activities proper to himself he manifests the same principles as the One and the Many. The virgin is the parent of the mother(!) psychologically if not physically. The virgin goddess renews her virginity every winter solstice. This becomes clear if we study the Babylonian Ishtar, who is called 'the Virgin', 'the Holy Virgin' and 'the Virgin Mother' by her worshippers. Yet this virgin goddess says of herself, 'A harlot compassionate am I.' Among the ancient Jews and Babylonians a veil was the mark of both virgins and prostitutes – Ishtar in certain aspects wears the veil. And Genesis 38: 14–15 throws a curious light on this custom. Also, the word *Parthenos*, upon which so much theology has been founded, is worth looking up in a *modern* Greek dictionary, for in ancient days bastards were called *Parthenioi*, virgin-born.

To sum up we may say that in this universe there is an ever-descending stream of divine power and life welling up under pressure from an unmanifested state of being and pouring down into manifestation. The various gods, each on their own plane and functioning according to their own degree, manifest and specialize this life force on planes of being which are more subtle than the plane of physical matter. The pagan by taking conscious thought of the gods can draw through himself the specialized life force of the gods or god with whom he is most in sympathy. Thus by a conscious effort man can forward evolution by increasing his capacity to distribute and to specialize this divine life power.

Again, by the study of the inner aspects of man's existence before conception draws him back into the realms of matter, the identity of Kore becomes manifest, for Kore is the Virgin Mother, the higher self in man; and every man – in terms of his lower self, and excluding the physical body – is one of the *parthenioi*. For the ancients, the moon-mother is a virgin, yet Demeter, curiously enough is the goddess who presides over divorce. (Harding, *Women's Mysteries*, p. 78.) The doctrines of the virgin who has a child, of the perpetual virginity of the mother, of the renewal of the mother's virginity with the death of the child, will yield much spiritual food for thoughtful meditation.

There are many curious paradoxes to be found in the psychological teachings of these ancient myths when once we begin to study the 'Great Silence'. For, as the 'Great Sea' is the root of things that are in matter, so the 'Great Silence' is the root of thoughts that are in mind – divine mind. As the Chaldeans taught, the 'Great Silence' and the 'Great Sea' are cosmic yoke-fellows. They are the duad of the monad which, on each plane of being, forms a divine triad – such as woman, saint, butterfly; Zeus, Apollo, Dionysius; Chaos, Erebus, Nox. Does not the picture of Nox, crowned with poppies or stars, with large dark wings and flying robes, riding in a chariot drawn by two black horses, touch the very depths of your being with a feeling that is subtle and mysterious?

The key to 'understanding' is sympathy, which is strong feeling carefully directed. Once sympathy has been aroused, the soul feels the truth of a 'mythos', not because it is in any way reasonable, but because something in the depths of one's innermost being has been touched. Pre-natal memories of a divine knowledge that the soul once had long ago – a knowledge temporarily lost while wandering in the realms of mortal generation – begin to stir. By meditation these memories of a lost understanding can be recovered; for in the long dead past, perhaps, one may have known something of the Egyptian, Chaldean, Orphic and Pythagorean systems.

Part 6: The Earth Mother

26

Oh, come with old Khayyam and leave the Wise
To talk; one thing is certain that life flies:
One thing is certain and the rest is lies;
The flower that once has blown for ever dies.

27

Myself when young did eagerly frequent
Doctor and Saint and heard great argument
About it and about: but ever more
Came out by the same Door as in I went.

(*Roses of Parnassus*, Number One)

The modern man with his childhood mind shaped by the dogmas of Christianity, his youthful mind filled with the facts of modern science, and his mature mind discarding both, is often apt to let religion slide. If there is life after death he just hopes for the best. And so we find that among the more thoughtful men of this type an intense pleasure is sometimes taken in Fitzgerald's 'Omar Khayyam'. Consider the first verse just quoted. Can, so far as human experience goes, anything be more certain than these facts and this conclusion? Can anything be more satisfying to the average logically trained mind than stanza 26?

Christianity and science alike consider that the earth is a soulless ball of mud, following natural laws which condemn it to float for aeons through apparently boundless space. Man's body is part of it, man's mind is – and here please read stanza 27, for it describes the situation as regards this last point perfectly.

The greatest of the Masters told us much about that inner reality which lies just beyond appearances. He called it the Kingdom of the Heavens. It is within man himself; men have got to become as little children to enter it; it is possible to know the hidden things of this inner kingdom of the heavens, and that those who think that they are 'learned' and the 'sanctimonious' cannot enter it themselves, and will even try to prevent others from entering.

The pagan initiates who lived at the time of Jesus knew that the earth is not soulless. They knew of the greater reality that underlies the actuality of outward physical manifestation. They could enter this Kingdom of the Heavens at will. They would not have contradicted any of these statements of Jesus.

There is no reason why the student of this ancient paganism should not follow in the footsteps of these initiated pagans if he wants to do so, and if he knows what to do. And the knowing what to do is perfectly simple; all that is required is to get in touch with the earth soul consciously instead of subconsciously. For the subconscious mind in always in touch with the earth soul, even when the conscious mind denies the earth soul's existence.

There is an ancient proverb which runs: 'Any fool can tell you what to do: only a wise man can tell you how to do it.' Having, I hope, achieved the first of these things, let me try so far as lies in my power to do the second.

Speaking generally, it is unwise to try to take the Kingdom of the Heavens, i.e. the inner worlds of nature, by force. For the average man, the only safe and reasonable way is to train under a competent teacher in a Mystery school which is functioning under a duly authorized authority. There he will be taught, and guarded, and later on, guided. The difficulty does not lie in opening the gates – that is easy – but in closing them after your return, which is quite another matter.

There are many who are by temperament what is called nature mystics. These persons seem to have an innate right of entry into those kingdoms of nature that substand the outer form of the Great Mother Nature. The process comes so easily to them that they are almost unaware of the fact that a technique is needed. And the very facility with which they are able to function makes them unsafe as teachers. They are unaware of the many and dangerous pitfalls which await persons less gifted than themselves; and so they can do little to help or guide their pupils in time of trouble.

The number of desirable students who can attend a Mystery school is limited. The number of schools which can teach under duly constituted authority is exceedingly limited. What then can be done by the would-be enquirer who cannot, as yet, attend a school in order to learn the 'How' to which reference has just been made?

He can do a great deal in safety if he sets about the long preliminary preparation methodically. If he determines to get in touch with an authorized school, it is curious how the way will open for a really determined student.

In the preliminary stage one can get in touch with the Earth Mother by taking a pre-determined line of thought and sticking to it. Also, it helps to store the mind with ancient symbols, and with the myths and folklore of the pagans, studying their pantheons as a record of psychological processes which are both human and cosmic. Here the Tree of Life makes a good filing system, and it is an aid to their analysis, classification and synthesis.

There are two distinct aspects to this method of study, and for convenience we will call then the 'out of doors' and the 'indoors' methods. The student must remember that unless he is a nature mystic of a very high type, one who has recovered from his subconscious mind the knowledge that we once had before the darkness of the Middle Ages fell upon Europe, he must work these two methods in a harmonized proportion while waiting for the opportunity of joining a Mystery school, an opportunity which will come fairly quickly *when* he is ready.

The minor details of this out of doors method for regaining touch with the soul of the Great Mother must vary widely. No two individuals are alike, no one method will completely suit all comers. But the following generalized methods are suggested, not because they are specially valuable, but because they have been tried out and found to be adequate even if elementary.

Next time you are alone in the country or by the seaside, get into a quiet place and note carefully all that you can see, hear and *feel* of the nature happenings that occur within a hundred yards of where you are sitting. Be sure to limit your awareness strictly to the things that happen within this circle, and do not go outside it. Later, with practice, you will be able to limit your sphere of sensation further, to, say, a single tree or a bed of flowers.

Below is an example of how the method works. Remember that

in actual practice you make the experience intensely personal until you find that your consciousness of yourself is merging into something that is wider, greater, and more intense than you are: also it is of a beauty more vivid than that of your own imaginings at their best. This sensation of merging is the test of success; by it you can tell whether or not you are at heart a pagan, i.e. a member by right of function of the *paganus,* of the countryside.

Example of the Method

You are lying on a cliff face on the coast of Devon; the sun is hot and bright, and the cliffs are covered with sea-pinks and small yellow flowers. The sea, a hundred feet below, is blue and very still. It is late spring or early summer, and the young gulls in their brown plumage keep the old ones busy. They scream and mew. It is lovely and warm lying on the red-brown earth, and no one is near. A large gull floats up, balances for a moment, looks at you seriously out of bright, intelligent, but soulless eyes and then slides swiftly to the left and out of sight. The warm air, the warm earth, the soft murmur of the summery waves, produce a feeling as of sleep, and slowly one begins to slide down that slope that leads to unconsciousness and to slumber.

Now comes the critical moment if you want to gain touch with the earth soul. You must slide down until you come almost to the slumber line. Then by an effort you bring your focus of consciousness to a fixed point and watch in an active and yet detached manner, the impressions that are coming in upon the inner senses and recording themselves in your mind. And here the student had better note that this is much easier said than done.

This last stage must not be allowed to develop into passivity. It is a simple form of semi-physical contemplation. The mind and the inner senses are intensely active, while the bodily functions have passed out of the focus of consciousness. The soul of man can then consciously draw nearer to the soul of the Earth Mother. What this exercise tries to do is turn a subconscious into a conscious contact: and this takes time and much earnest practice. Constant *daily* practice is necessary. This need not be always in the same place, though it undoubtedly helps to have one favourite spot for this type of meditation. What may we expect to get from this exercise? At first very little. In any event the conscious result is small even when a careful daily record is kept. But the object is not factual knowledge; instead, it is the conscious opening up of latent powers within the soul itself that is aimed at. And this slowly leads to a heightening of some inner sense of awareness, to some inner sensing of the beauty and harmony of the unseen side of nature. The focus of consciousness is very carefully being transferred from the Malkuth of Earth to that inner kingdom of life and strength and beauty which lies just beyond this visible physical plane. And in times of weakness and weariness the trained soul can draw consciously on the life forces of these 'inner kingdoms' for renewed health and strength.

The next stage in this process comes when the holiday is ended. Suppose one is back in town and that the noise, and smells, and asphalt have cut one off from earth contacts, then indeed the Earth Mother can seem very far away. The past is as a dream, vague, distorted and lifeless. The initiated pagan, however, does not let this worry him. He settles comfortably in the easy chair he uses for his daily meditation in the privacy of his own room. His thoughts turn inwards and he seeks the Kingdom of the Heavens that is within himself. He goes into that inner chamber as that great man Jesus ben Joseph told his disciples to do. By means of the technique that his school teaches he is, in thought, *in feeling* and in action, back in Devon. Again he is lying on that cliff, he sees the sea-pinks, he hears the sea-birds; once more the big gull with its bright eyes floats up, hovers for a moment, and then slides away. More and more the focus of consciousness turns within until suddenly a contact is clearly *felt* between the soul of the initiate and the living earth soul. Then once more he is in the loving arms of the great Earth Mother. Her life flows into him until every cell and nerve is bathed in it. The joy becomes almost an agony of ecstasy. The Chalice of the Soul is full to overflowing. Later the contact is cut deliberately. Grateful thanks are given, and the pagan initiate returns to his daily round, rested, strengthened and refreshed with the Elixir of Life.

Heidrun supplied Odin with the heavenly mead, the drink of the gods of the Norsemen; this supply is still available for those who can earn it; for the high gods never die. It is man who foolishly forgets that they are powers immanent within his own soul.

But one must have understanding if one is to earn this sacred drink of the gods, be it called Soma, Haomo or the Heavenly Mead; and the indoor training of the nature mystic aims at producing this understanding. For few educated persons today are content with 'rule of thumb' methods for attaining to glimpses of that Truth, Harmony and Beauty which are aspects of that

Infinite Unity which we know as Nature, the Earth Mother.

The first question that has to be answered is 'What is nature?' It has been said by modern philosophers that, as a man sees things, nature is 'a concept of order', also that nature is 'an empirical reality in space'. The nature mystic would say that these concepts are undoubtedly true, and they are useful so far as they go. But they do not go far enough; for, from the mystical point of view, they do not cover the whole of man's experience, even though they may cover the whole of some men's experience. It can fairly truthfully be said that many people regard the existence of nature as a self-evident fact, and say 'why worry about asking "What is nature?" Is it not obvious that nature is just naturally nature? Why bother about the obvious?'

Looking at this question solely from the point of view of the nature mystic, there are three ways of approaching the study of nature: the way of materialism; the way that some philosophers call spiritualism (this way has nothing to do with ghosts and mediums, but refers to ideas and not to so-called psychical manifestations); and the way of the initiates of the Ancient Mysteries. The wise student will study all three with strict impartiality, for all are true, none is all the truth, and one learns most by combining them in that harmonized proportion which suits your own mental make-up. Study most the aspect you like least in order to obtain balance.

Some of the most modern materialists deal only with nature as an 'empirical reality in space and time'. The late Professor J. B. S. Haldane describes this attitude of mind thus:

To many persons in modern times, it seems that the only reality is what can be interpreted in terms of the physical sciences, with the addition, however, that certain physical processes occurring in the brain are mysteriously accompanied by consciousness, the quality of which depends on the nature of these processes. This belief is known as materialism, and for those holding it, religion is necessarily no more than an illusion based on ignorance ...

For traditional physical science the visible and tangible world of our experience is interpreted as consisting of self-existent material units reacting in space and time with one another in such a way that the energy represented in mutual movements and reactions remains constant. Any apparent co-ordination or unity which exists in the physical world is regarded as accidental to the unit of which it consists, and ultimately a mere matter of chance as far as our knowledge goes ...

If we disregard the fact of life, and of our own relations to the universe around us, it undoubtedly seems to behave in such a manner as physical science assumes ... If we assume this interpretation then anything that we can really be conscious of can only consist of isolated impressions in our brains, these impressions being somehow put together to form a picture which is really subjective, and only simulating a surrounding universe.

These extracts from one of Professor Haldane's last lectures are worthy of close attention. Materialism from the nature mystic's point of view is a true and very valuable belief so long as it is remembered that here is a partial and not an integral or complete view of nature as the mystic apprehends it. For him Nature is more than her physical manifestation in time and space.

As regards philosophical spiritualism, which is the foundation of all religions, Professor Hocking in his extremely useful book *Types of Philosophy* (p. 28) has summarized it as follows:

There exists another world than this world shown us by the senses. This other world is somehow veiled from our ordinary perceptions; and yet is is continuous with Nature; and of easy access in either direction if one has the right path. It is the residence of powers or agencies which we distinguish as divine; they always know how to get at us; we are not so clear as to how to get at them.

In these seven short statements there is given us a very different conception of nature; and yet it is one which is the complement and not the contradiction of materialism. For when both are taken together, a more complete and satisfactory view of Nature and man's relationship to Nature is obtained than when either is taken singly and the importance of the other ignored or decried, or denied.

Now let us turn to the third way – that of the initiates of the Ancient Mysteries. How did they touch the inner realms over which rules Rhea, the Tower-Crowned Phrygian Mother of All?

One way is shown in the celebrated romance of *The Golden Ass* by Lucius Apuleius, a well-known writer and philosopher who lived in the early part of the second century. This book, while suited to grave students, advanced in years and learning and above all in understanding, should not be left lying around indiscreetly, lest a prudish and priggish ignorance mock at that which it cannot understand.

Some 400 years ago, Apuleius was familiar to classical students and was used by discerning theologians. The student of the Mysteries will remember that the 'ass' is the symbol of the Typhonic aspect of human nature. This is the key to the inner meaning of the first ten books, for nature mysticism may, in an ill-balanced soul, stir up that aspect of human nature which is here depicted in the adventures of the 'ass'.

In the eleventh book Apuleius turns to the Goddess of Nature, to Isis of the Sea, of the Moon, and of the Earth, imploring her to save him from himself; for the forces that he has, by mistaken methods, evoked from within himself threaten to destroy him. In this, the last book, we have in carefully veiled language the story of his initiation into the Lesser Mysteries. The scene by the seashore depicts, in the curious symbolism of 2,000 years ago, the first step that must be taken by those who seek this ancient way into the adytum of Pessinuntia, who is the mother of the gods. With the coming of this divine vision that, star-crowned and moon-girt, rises from the hushed sea of man's subconscious nature, the great adventure of religion begins, for this is the inner way to vision.

Without this vision, and without the direct summons of that Tower-Crowned One whom the ancients adored under many forms as Aphrodite Pandemos (seeing her veiled in the symbols of the Moon, of the Star that rises from the twilight sea, and of the 'Rosa Mystica') there is for the would-be initiate no road to those unseen realms that are concealed within the soul of the great and fruitful Earth Mother, Queen Isis.

Part 7: The Door and the Bowl

Stanza XXXII

There was a door to which I found no Key:
There was a Veil past which I could not see:
Some little talk awhile of Me and Thee
There seem'd – and then no more of Thee and Me.

Stanza XXXV

Then to this Earthen Bowl did I adjourn
My lip the secret Well of Life to learn:
And lip to lip it murmur'd – 'While you live
Drink – for once dead you never shall return.'

(Omar Khayyam)

Reference has been made to that peculiar phenomenon which A.E. in *The Candle of Vision* calls 'The Memory of the Earth'. He says:

> We experience the romance and delight of voyaging upon uncharted seas when the imagination is released from the foolish notion that the images seen in reverie and dream are merely images of memory refashioned; and in tracking to their originals the forms seen in vision we discover for them a varied ancestry, as that some come from the minds of others, and of some we cannot surmise another origin than that they are portions of the memory of Earth which is accessible to us. We soon grow to think our memory but a portion of that Eternal memory *and that we in our lives are gathering an innumerable experience for a mightier being than our own.* The more vividly we see with the inner eye the more swiftly do we come to this conviction. Those who see vaguely are satisfied with vague explanations which those who see vividly at once reject as inadequate.

This quotation with regard to the earth memory should be carefully studied. It reveals ideas concerning the nature of experience which are much the same as those which William James expressed when he wrote: 'I do not believe that our experience is the highest form of experience extant in the Universe.' It lays stress on seeing vividly with the inner eye, and upon the fact that those who have not this gift strongly developed are really not in a position to offer criticism of a constructive nature. How can you criticize that of which you are ignorant? In order to see, you must visualize the veil until the intentness of your gaze renders it transparent; you must knock long and loud upon the unseen door until an unseen hand presses the key upon you. When your lips touch the bowl that some call the Grail, and some the Cauldron, the Goddess will Herself impart to you the riddle of the secret well of life. Omar Khayyam had the solution of that secret, though Edward Fitzgerald did not.

If the student with aptitude and energy takes up the study of these ancient pagan systems, he is bound, in time, to come across things unpleasant as well as pleasant, and it is well to warn the enquirer that he may, unexpectedly and without any previous preparations, touch pages of the 'Earth Memory' congruous to hidden records buried deep in his own subconscious mind. This experience may leave him badly shaken mentally and physically. By working in a group with trained teachers and obeying the rules, this shock can be minimized and no permanent harm is done; but working alone, groping blindly in the dark, using a half understood technique drawn from the books of those who pretend to have been able to betray the secrets of the Mysteries, is folly. The genuine secrets of the Mysteries cannot be betrayed. Would Judas have betrayed Jesus if he had really understood the source of his Master's power and could have used it himself? Jesus taught nothing new; and even Judas, the intimate companion, the treasurer of the inner group, one of the Twelve, could not betray the secret of the power of Jesus for he could not *realize* it, or use it. Judas only betrays because he does not understand.

The student working alone is advised to read and to ponder deeply on the symbols of the ancient pagan systems, on their gods, on their teachings, on their folklore and myths. This work is preparatory to the real inner work that is developed in a Mystery school. He must not expect from these articles anything except hints as to how he must best prepare himself for the coming of a teacher. When the neophyte is ready, the Master will see that he is called to the Temple. This sentence – an ancient one – is written from personal experience, and from seeing again and again this same experience happen to others.

As the Memory of the Earth is one of the chief clues to the Mysteries of the pagans, it is worthy of examination as a working hypothesis and in order to familiarize oneself with this somewhat unusual concept. Beyond, behind, within and yet without (one has to use spatial terms) transcendent to and yet immanent in man's body, is the soul of man. Man is triune: spirit, soul and body. The soul, as the instrument for gaining experience, has faculties which are called the will, the memory, the imagination, the emotions, the reason, the instincts, etc. If the student will accept the hypothesis that the earth is the body of a great entity whose soul may be thought of as being in certain respects analogous to the soul of man, he can pursue the following methods of study with the prospect of getting a mental and spiritual training that will enable him one day to come prepared to the Temple. If he cannot accept this working hypothesis then he had better go off and play golf, where foozling – even if it leads him into blasphemy, will not take him, and others, into serious trouble.

The Earth Mother has many names. In Egypt the initiates called her Isis, and they thought of her as veiled in green. In Ireland they called her Dana or Danu, and in that country, which was one of the world's greatest spiritual centres, the Tuatha de

Danaan, the Tribe of the Goddess Dana, can be communicated with – given the right conditions – more easily than is usual elsewhere. The veil between the actual and the real, the phenomenal and the noumenal, the seen and the unseen, the sensible and the intelligible, is less dense in Ireland than it is in stolid, bovine England. This fact, probably, is the true explanation of the curious characteristics of the Irish, and of the 'more Irish than the Irish' sentiments of certain Sassenachs that settle there. Ireland can stir strangely the deeper strata of the souls of certain Englishmen. It can charm, it can also annoy. It can produce love and hate, seldom indifference.

In England the Great Mother is Keredwen, and from the Welsh point of view Snowdon is her most sacred district. But the true Englishman can get in touch with the Great Mother at Glastonbury where Christianity has metamorphosed the goddess Brigantia into Saint Brigid. On the Tor and at the Well are nature-worship centres which are inferior to no other. Brigantia is as potent for better or for worse as is the Greek Athene.

The classical tradition has had its effects on the group soul of England, and the gods of Greece and Rome must not be neglected. Demeter was the best-known name of the Earth Mother in Greece, and her chief centre was Eleusis, the centre of the Eleusinian Mysteries. In Asia Minor and Babylonia she was known as Astarte, Ishtar and Astoreth, the Earthly Venus-Aphrodite. The student must never forget that while names seem to divide, functions bind the pantheon into an intelligible religious unity. Here is a valuable clue.

Before we start meditation, it is wise to examine facts and to avoid fancies. So let us take this list of names – Dana, Keredwen, Isis, Demeter, Ishtar, Astarte – and see what we can find out about them when we consider them as symbols of the unknown power which we call the Earth Mother, the great Fertile Mother. Go to the monumental works of Sir James George Frazer. Read if you can the twelve volumes of *The Golden Bough: A Study in Magic and Religion*, and see what is to be found. Dana is not mentioned in the general index, neither is Keredwen, though there is a large number of useful references to the other four names. *The Golden Bough* is supposed to be a study in magic for the English-speaking race, but although Sir James may know much about curious and indecent rites which he thinks are magic, he has not made clear to his readers the elementary principle that true magic, like charity, begins at home, in the group soul of the English race.

There is a very interesting book by Dr M. Harding called *Women's Mysteries Ancient and Modern*. In it is an immense amount of information which should set the reader's subconscious mind questing to and fro on a scent which grows warmer and warmer until Chapter 15 is reached. What Chapter 15 means to you will depend entirely upon what you are. It is true this work deals almost entirely with the Moon Mysteries, but, a man's immediate inner self – his anima – is feminine; also it is well to remember that the ancient initiates believed that the earth and the moon shared one 'etheric', and that in this state of cosmic matrimony the moon is the positive and the senior partner – a situation not altogether unknown in the earthly state of so-called holy matrimony, for woman has an animus (masculine aspect) – not an anima – if Jung is correct.

Let us suppose that you have got your supply of facts from your general reading, and that from meditation upon your reading you have built up in your mind a set of living symbols dealing with that Great Mother aspect of the Inner Worlds with which you wish to get in touch. The next step is to specialize in type. So concentrate on Isis, if that suits you best.

Isis is a goddess that is peculiarly attractive to this race. She was worshipped under her own name for a long period of the Roman occupation of Britain. The adoration of the Virgin Mary is the Christianized adaptation of the Egyptian Isis worship, and its introduction in the fourth century was the cause of bitter strife in the Christian Church; so the intense Mariolatry of medieval England has been a blessing for us pagan moderns, for it has kept alive in the great power centres of England those ancient forces which were once called the goddesses Keredwen, Danu, Isis and Briganda – who as a nature goddess is the Catholic St Bride. The modern English pagan owes the great Christian Church of Rome a deep debt of gratitude for preserving for him in working order these ancient shrines of the pagan power deities. In these places are concentrated centres of pagan power, astral, mental and spiritual, of which the Protestants and agnostics in their ignorance have never suspected the existence. In the ranks of the Church of England are many fine scholars, great social organizers, and great ethical teachers, but genuine priests are few.

In Isis, Keredwen, Dana, Briganda, and in their particular symbols of the Cup, the Grail, the Cauldron, the Sword or Spear, and in the young horned moon, low in the southern sky, are the keys of the Mysteries of the English Earth Mother, the One who is veiled in green; yet first you must solve the mystery of the ever-fruitful virgin mother who dwells in the most secret recesses of man's individuality. The cosmic aphorism 'As above, so below' has its counterpart in the psychological aphorism 'As within, so without.' In all the pagan Mystery systems it is clearly taught that the clue to the forces of Mother Nature is hidden within the soul of the worshipper, and it is there that the search for the key must commence. The veil that was impenetrable to the outward-looking eye of Edward Fitzgerald becomes transparent to the inward-looking eye of the trained mind. The Cauldron of the Earth Mother when raised to the lips of the neophyte gives him that ever-flowing inspiration which is from the Secret Well of Life.

Now let us turn to the particular symbols and see what door to the inner realms the moon symbols will open. What does the term 'Diana's Mirror' convey to you? Anything, or nothing? A memory that is almost a feeling. Have you ever seen it cold and black, still and star-lit? The moon-goddesses are regarded as the guardians of water, rivers, wells and springs. The moon-god is the local divinity that inhabits many of the sacred wells of Ireland and England. You can get some vivid emotional reactions by meditation upon the moon shining in a holy well if you have had personal contact with one of these holy wells.

Ishtar was called the All-Dewy-One; she is the ruler of dewponds and springs. There are some curious superstitions in Celtic countries about seeing the moon in wells and springs – confused remnants of ancient teachings and practices. There are, even in modern England, superstitions about seeing the moon in the crystal bowl of a dewpond; there are even more curious myths about the serpent in these moon-consecrated wells and ponds. Even Oxford has its Child's Well and serpent lore, and the serpent in the well is the man in the moon. Jung has told us of the interacting effect of a man's anima and a woman's animus. New Thought and Christian Science tell us of the powers of the directed will acting upon a vivid imagination. Hence the maiden at the moon-well concentrating on what is hidden in the crystal bowl in her imagination.

To the average exoteric Christian who carefully refrains from using his mind in religion, except in church when he concentrates on the task of keeping awake, these things are unknown, uncanny, and not quite nice. Study, for example, Dr Jung's *Psychology of the Unconscious*. He gives some examples of moon symbols and their effect on the human mind. Why should this be so? Why should the symbols of the ancient religions live in the hidden recesses of the men and women of this twentieth century? Is this due to the convenient explanation – race memory? Is it due to reincarnation and to the recovery of individual lost memories? Has the earth got a memory, and if so can we recover from it these lost memories? No single theory will explain all the factors. Perhaps all three theories are partially true.

The regular and methodical use of symbols such as those just mentioned, can, in some cases, produce results that are to say the least not dull. Sometimes they can be exciting, far too exciting, and occasionally – and this warning is given from personal experience – they can be rather terrible. A very unpleasant death, died some 2,000 years ago, is still unpleasant if you happen to recover it from what shall we call it? – a race memory, a personal subconscious memory, or the earth memory?

As has been said before, the lore of the Mysteries is not for all and sundry.

Part 8: The Priest and the Moon Bowl

LXXIV

> Oh, Moon of my Delight who know'st no wane,
> The Moon of Heav'n is rising once again:
> How oft hereafter rising shall she look
> Through this same Garden after me – in vain!

LXXV

> And when myself with shining Foot shall pass
> Among the Guests star-scatter'd on the Grass
> And in Thy joyous Errand reach the Spot
> Where I made one – turn down an empty Glass!

(Iamad Shud)

In research work it is usually considered to be wiser to hunt up the facts and then think out the implications for oneself. Afterwards one can compare results with the standard authorities, and then decide upon one's attitude. In dealing with the great myths such as those of Isis and Osiris, or with the ancient sun and moon myths, the student cannot as a rule follow this method in its entirety. In all cosmic myths there are at least two aspects to be considered, the sensible and the intelligible meanings. In applying a cosmic myth to the microcosm, man, there are also two aspects which have to be taken into account, the objective and the subjective. One must know something of both these aspects before one can realize the implications of the facts one has collected.

So when the anthropological school takes an ancient myth and explains it in terms of corn and oil and water and fruitful soil, it is giving a true explanation, the type of explanation that might suit a rude unlettered child of the soil, the farmer and his labourers. But there are at least two other explanations which can be given, and all three are partially true, though taken singly each is inadequate, for it is but a partial explanation.

In the Isis myth, for example, Osiris can be taken as the life-giving moisture, he is the Nile-Flood: Isis, his wife, is the fertile soil rendered fruitful by the Nile. Set, his adversary and slayer, is the dry heat of the desert which hems in the Nile valley. Nephthys is the ribbon of soil that marks the edge of the fertile land; sometimes the Nile is high enough to render it fertile for a short time, then it lapses into the condition of wasteland. And so we find in this myth that Nephthys has sometimes as her husband Osiris, though she is usually considered to be the wife of the destructive Set. The child of Osiris and Nephthys is Anubis, the jackal-headed god. A fit symbol when we remember that the home of the Jackal is the desert edge and his hunting grounds are the fertile lands where men and their leavings abound.

Osiris is the moon-god who measures the seasons, and regulates the moisture and dew as well as the rise and fall of the Nile. He reigned twenty-eight years; twenty-eight is the moon period. Set cut his body into fourteen pieces, the fourteen days of the waning moon. Horus the younger is his son and is the new moon that reigns in place of the old moon, and so on. Divine numbers and god-names were sometimes keys to the 'inner tides' and their festivals, as are the Christian Golden Number and Dominical Letter.

Isis as the moon-goddess plays a role which can be explained by the growth of plants, fertility, etc. Again, up to a point this explanation is true for she is the Lady of Nature, and hers are the moon-powers which influence the physical life of the mothering sex. These ideas may be considered satisfactory when looked at from the point of view of the farmyard, but there were minds in the olden days which had progressed beyond the rather rustic level of modern anthropologists; not that their views are either new or modern. Plutarch, an initiate who lived at the time when St Paul was laying the foundations of Christianity, writes (LXV.):

> And we shall also get our hands on the dull crowd who take pleasure in associating the mystic recitals about these Gods either with changes of the atmosphere according to the seasons, or the generation of corn and sowings and ploughings, and in saying that Osiris is buried when the sown corn is hidden by the earth, and comes to life and shows himself again when the corn begins to sprout.

Plutarch, as one who was initiated into the Osiriaca at Delphi, knew that the true initiate of Isis is one who must for ever look for hidden reasons that substand the things said and done 'in the sacred rites' (III.5). But a true Isiac is one who, when he by law receives them, searches out by reason (Logos) the Mysteries shown and done concerning these gods and meditates upon the truth in them. This last sentence tells us where to look for the cosmic solutions of these ancient myths. For meditation is the process that links the microcosmic mind of man with the cosmos through the mind side of nature, that is with Isis, the Lady of Nature, the teacher, the nurse, the mother, the slayer of all.

Another solution of these problems of the ancient myths is psychological. It deals with the relationship between the subjective in man and the objective mind side of nature. The priest must look within the brimming circle of his moon bowl, for this solution is a matter of interpreting symbols that have an effect on the subconscious mind of man. It is not merely a matter of ancient history of kings and queens, nor of natural phenomena.

Psychologically, Isis is within the soul of man, and from one aspect we may call her the subconscious mind. Osiris, too, has his place in man's soul; he is focused consciousness. Both the Isis within and the Osiris within have a relationship to the Isis without and the Osiris without – that is, with the objective, mind side of nature, the dual-natured world – Isis and the world Osiris. Or in terms of the Chaldean myths, with Ishtar and Sin, the moon-god.

Isis had many names and so too have Osiris and Sin. The initiate of the Ancient Mysteries selected the aspect of Isis or of Sin that he intended to meditate upon with exactly the same care with which a watchmaker selects the tools that he is going to use. Also, a thing that is often forgotten today, the initiate of that day had to know his times and his seasons. It is no good seeking the Black Isis when it is the rising tide of the Lady that is veiled in green. When the silver moon rides high in the blue-black night sky, and when she is seen shining brightly in the crystal vase, waste not a tide that is flowing strongly in your favour.

Osiris too has his black and green and golden moments, and Sin also is a triune god; but it is only within the pylon gates that this detailed knowledge is given to the student. Still, the methodical worker who is able to measure the rise and fall of the tides within his own psyche, and who is prepared to note the times and seasons at the head of his daily meditation record and to analyse and synthesize and correlate results, can work out a practical table for himself. It will not take him very far, but it will save him quite a lot of time that would otherwise be wasted. For how many novices remember that in the Ancient Mysteries the moon is not only the sphere of generation, but it also the place of the dead, and the sphere of regeneration?

Again, the moon-man ever attends upon the moon goddess who sails in the 'Ship of Life'. It is often forgotten that it takes two to make a pair, for the sphere of manifestation is the sphere of duality, and while we are in these realms of duality it takes two to complete the functional unit, whether that unit is in the sphere of generation or in the sphere of intellection. There is always the subject and the object, the within and the without, the subjective and the objective, the worshipper and his deity. Nine-tenths of students' failures are due to neglect of these commonplace hackneyed truisms. How many keep in their daily record a note of their inner states and feelings during meditations? There is a direct relationship between these inner feelings and the so-called superstitions of the myths, for both have reference to the impalpable, immaterial substance which has been well called 'the plastic material of life'.

There is an ancient saying that a goddess cannot indwell her shrine unless there is a priest to offer the acceptable sacrifice. This is true of the cosmos, and it is also true in psychology. 'As above, so below.' All women are Isis; and a woman is most feminine and most like her true self when the priest invokes the inner nature of the goddess. But, whether it be Great Isis above, or one of her human incarnations here below, the priest has to be acceptable by right of function. So waste not 'here' or 'yonder' the propitious seasons; be true to 'instinct' when working in the realms of the moon deities.

When in solitary meditation a man sits in the Temple of the Goddess who nurses, mothers, slays and gives life, if he is to win through to that inner sanctuary where sits Isis, Astarte, Aphrodite or the Great Mountain Mother – the names matter not, for all the goddesses are one goddess – and to find his own regeneration, he must see himself as the priest who bears the sacrifice. That sacrifice is himself. He must face himself, his own instincts; and above all his own emotions. He must experience the latter to the utmost. There is no need for him, today, to become one of the Galloi, but there must be no mental reservations. It is 'all or nothing'. *Do ut des* is a fundamental principle when one is seeking to evoke the appearance of the Goddess.

Isis will come only to the favoured few. Always she, and she only, selects her own priest; and she will come only when the postulant for the ordeal of the priestly initiations has reached his limit.

It is here that the role of Typhon or Set, as the story is told by Plutarch, rounds off and completes the dual role of Isis and Osiris. The great gods of the cosmos and of the souls of men are always triune in their nature. Osiris is the brother of Set, neither is complete and neither can function without the other, as Apuleius shows in the story of the 'Golden Ass'. It is after the Typhonic ordeal that the postulant is given the 'Roses of Isis', and attains to the power of a moon initiate. But a moon priest the initiate cannot become until he has been called yet again by the goddess of Perfect Intelligence.

Sin as the moon-god is triune, and we know from the cuneiform inscriptions, as translated by Rawlinson, that Sin is Three Persons but one god; and these Persons are Anu, En-lil and Ea. As the inscription runs: 'The moon is during the period of his visibility, in the first five days, the god Anu; from the sixth to the tenth day, the god Ea; from the eleventh to the fifteenth day, the god En-lil.'

Look up in a mythological dictionary the essential natures of these three gods, the God of Heaven, the God of the Primeval Deep, and the Lord of the Golden Age. Then you will understand, through your meditations, why the moon priest has to undergo three initiations and has to make three sacrifices before he can drink from the moon bowl the draft of conscious immortality that will make him a priest of Isis or Ishtar, the Lord of the Three Worlds; for the moon-goddess is 'Goddess of Heaven, Goddess of Earth, and Goddess of the Underworld'.

Always there are these three moon initiations, whether the rites are those of Isis, of Sin and Ishtar, or of the Celtic Briganda. In terms of psychology this means that the initiate has gained the knowledge of the subconscious mind as the past, as the source, as the origin of things that are and that will be. 'I am all that has been and is and shall be, And no mortal has ever revealed my robe!' said Great Isis.

When the moon priest has drunk from the moon bowl, the mortal has become immortal, and that which the robe hides is revealed; the Veil has been parted, and the goddess within leaves the shadows of the sanctuary and becomes the regnatrix that dwells within the soul of that man. The Light of the Goddess is rising once again and is enwombed in the psyche of the moon priest.

The moon priest and the moon priestess become one, for the man has found his anima. And once the moon that lights the inner life has risen there is no need to seek in the garden of psyche in vain! There is no need to 'turn down an empty glass'! The bowl is filled with a living water and those who drink of it shall thirst no more – for it is ever flowing, and it is within – for ever. The goddess, incarnation after incarnation, will call her own back to her temple.

Part 9: The Moon Virgin and the Snake of Wisdom

'The Maiden's First Love Song'

What can I do, what can I begin?
That shuddering thing:
There it crackles within
And coils in a ring.
It must be poisoned.
Here it crawls around
Blissfully I feel as it worms
Itself into my Soul
And kills me finally.

(Mörike, quoted in Jung, *Psychology of the Unconscious*, p. 5.)

The snake was a symbol for the divine wisdom. It was a dual symbol, the White Serpent of Yetsirah and the Dark Serpent of the World of Assiah, two aspects of the same principle.

If one thinks for a few moments on the nature of human wisdom it can be divided into three main divisions or faculties. There is first of all that which has been called the estimative faculty, or the wisdom of the children of this world. It deals chiefly with the mundane business of living well, and with that type of concept and opinion which man's mind formulates as the result of experiences met with in what the ancient mystics called the 'sensible' world. Plato calls this faculty *pistis* (see page 126),* faith in the aspect of trust. He considered it to be a non-reasoning faculty because it depends upon the opinions of others and on the testimony of the senses. It is a faculty that when highly developed leads to success in things mundane. It can always be distinguished from reason because though it knows that a thing *is*, it cannot explain *why* it is. Many of those who take their opinions ready-made mistake this particular faculty of the mind for reason. But when the student has begun to study 'religion', then he commences to suspect that much of his supposed religious and philosophical knowledge is based upon an authority external to himself and not upon that personal reasoning faculty which Mother Nature has implanted in every man's mind. Meditation upon the fundamentals of the estimative faculty will lead man to the next main division – reason.

In the Ancient Mysteries each of the moon-goddesses was looked upon as the giver of wisdom, as man's protectress during life upon earth, and as offering worldly success to diligent devotees.

In terms of modern psychology it may be said that the moon deities rule over the estimative faculty of the human soul. They were the goddesses of instinct and of instinctive reaction, and they were the rulers of the powerful subconscious mind. In terms of the Qabalah, they function in the sphere of Yesod. Again, if we study these ancient myths, we shall find that these moon-goddesses were taught by the cosmic wisdom-gods. For example Thoth as the Logos or Divine Reason taught Isis, and there are somewhat similar myths in most of the other great religions.

In the Neo-Platonic system of psychology, reason, which Plato called *dianoia*, is that faculty of the soul which addresses itself to those intelligible principles upon which all sensible nature depends. In the mysteries based upon Plato's teachings, pure

---

* As to Plato's five faculties of knowing, see page 125.

reason was described as the faculty that enables the *mystae* to know and to apply those abstract and divine ideas which the ancient form of 'Idealism', as a philosophy, holds to be innate in the human soul. Their Mystery initiations aimed rather at educing these innate divine ideals by means of the cult's meditation technique than at teaching a special and novel kind of concrete knowledge. Reason is innate in the human soul, though often it appears to be almost completely dormant, as is clearly shown by the difficulty some people have in following an argument when put formally as logic, or in comprehending abstract ideas. How many people can study with pleasure the science of logic?

Thoth, Nabu or Nebo, Hermes, Sin (or Enzu) as the 'Lord of Wisdom', the Celtic Dagda and Myrddin, all are, to a greater or lesser degree, gods of that Divine Wisdom which is typified by the White Snake. As such they are the teachers of the moon-goddesses, who represent that type of divine wisdom which some of the Gnostics called the fallen Sophia. As moon-gods they gave their 'syzygy' the divine knowledge which ensures power over the creations of the great creator-gods such as Ra.

'As above, so below'; and turning to the microcosm and to psychology we find reason as the positive mental faculty controlling, organizing and often repressing those power-supplying instincts that lie behind and energize the somewhat feminine and less positive estimative faculty. In the Egyptian Mysteries Thoth's syzygy is Maat, who is a form of Isis. Nabu's wife was Tashmetu – 'she who hears', an exact description of the rather negative faculty, that is, the lower reason.

Thoth as the god of reason guides the 'Ship of Life', that is to say, Isis, who is psychologically the subconscious mind of man and of Nature, according to the teaching of these Ancient Mystery systems.

In addition to *pistis* and *dianoia* there was also a third faculty – intuition. This Plato called *noesis*, and it was thought of as the highest expression of all the human mental faculties when working as a well-trained team. It is often confused with instinct and with feeling. We all know the person who says: 'I have an intuition; I feel it in my bones.' But the *noesis* of the Ancient Mysteries was something much more than this for it was a faculty of comprehending those 'great universal ideas of which the manifested universe is a differentiated and objective expression'. It is the unfallen Sophia; it is a wisdom that is beyond all earthly wisdom.

Bearing in mind this psychological background, which may seem strange to us moderns, one can comprehend the importance of understanding clearly the use of the snake as an explanatory symbol. Some of the goddesses are shown holding snakes or attended by snakes; to the initiated this explained the phase of the goddess that he was expected to concentrate upon. The snake, or pair of snakes, stood for a particular aspect of sacred knowledge; and there were many special kinds of this knowledge that the ancient gods and goddesses could impart to their devotees through meditation, contemplation and ritual. They knew that one must focus and restrict if power is to be generated in mental work.

Man's greatest task is the finding of himself and his purpose in life. And man can only find these two things by using himself for the conscious and concentrated expression of life (Isis with the Ankh) according to his own personal potentialities. In this lies the dual wisdom of the divine snakes as they climb the sacred rod of Hermes, or the Paths of the Tree of Life. In finding himself man is working in the sphere ruled by the cosmic gods of wisdom, the realm of ideals. He becomes an initiate, or better, a devotee of the Great Hermes Trismegistus. But for the expression of his life purpose, man must serve the moon-goddess, for she and not a male god rules in the realm of actuality. The dark snake rules in Assiah, the sphere of the form-giving mother, Mut of ancient Thebes.

Wisdom, like most other things in cosmic manifestation, is dual in its nature. There is the wisdom of the Ibis-headed Thoth, who has been described as the Logos of Plato. There is also the wisdom of Isis of the throne, and of dark Nephthys of the Cup. Always there is the Wisdom of the Inner and the Outer, of the Sensible and the Intelligible.

The parable of the unjust steward, who was, we are often told, an unworldly visionary and not really a thief, explains this; and the steward's lord commends him for learning the earthly wisdom before trying to master the Wisdom of the Children of Light. In terms of the Mystery initiations, you must serve Isis before you can ascend to the eight steps that lead to the Throne of Khemennu in the House of the Net. For in ancient Egypt there were the Lesser Mysteries and the Greater Mysteries. There was also the Mystery that was taught in 'the House of the Net' at Hermopolis.

For those who care to seek it, there is divine as well as human symbolism in that love song of Mörike which begins:

What is in the net?
Behold,
But I am afraid,
Do I grasp a sweet eel,
Do I seize a snake?

In this section the reader has been given a series of mental pictures, a number of mythological images which have to be meditated upon frequently in order to get at their inner meaning. They are not meant to teach the conscious mind anything. The hard-headed man of the world will find them incoherent and unreasonable. Up to a point he is right. They are incoherent, that is to say, they are not easily followed. But their meanings can be grasped if you will follow the example of Theseus and carry Ariadne's thread with you when, in meditation, you enter the labyrinth that is your own subconscious mind. Again they are, of course, unreasonable! 'Love', that seizes a snake, 'is a blind fisherwoman'. But these mythic images are most certainly not untrue to your own inner nature. Try them and see what comes to you in the still moments of deep meditation; or better still, try to dream about them at night.

Have you ever read 'The Song of Solomon' translated accurately into modern English? Moffat's translation is as good as any other. Try reading the verse given below, and see what comes. Your conscious mind may seek to give you one set of meanings, and they are reasonable. But the pictures that will rise from the depths of your subconscious mind when it is stilled in meditation on this jewel of ancient wisdom may not be reasonable, yet they may not be the less true. For 'The Song of Solomon' deals with the snakes of wisdom and it pertains to a moon-virgin and to the moon-goddess. Get at the subconscious meaning of the following:

5. I am dark, but I am a beauty,
    Maidens of Jerusalem,
    Dark as the tents of the Blackmen,
    Beautiful as curtains of a Solomon.

6. Scorn me not for being dark ...

When the subconscious mind is as still as the dark windless surface of the high-flying, star-lit mountain lake that is at the foot of the five white glaciers, you may enter in safety the labyrinth and rely on the thread that Ariadne (intuition) has given Theseus (yourself).

As Adam and Solomon discovered long ago, there is a close connection between 'the Woman' and the Snake of Wisdom. Today Jung teaches that a man's inner self is an anima not an animus. Here is your Ariadne's thread – if you can use it.

October 1936 to September 1937

6.

The Ancient Nature-Worship

This rather scathing little article is the Colonel at his ascerbic best. As always, he takes up the cudgels against the 'killjoy' outlook he saw as being present in the Church's (though not necessarily the Christian) view of life, and presents in its place the joy and freedom he found expressed by the *pagani* in their nature-worship.

Some 3,000 years ago, two great religious reformers, both adepts of the Ancient Egyptian Mysteries, completed their twenty or more years of training and then took up the lifework for which they had been sent into incarnation. One of them, Moses, went to train the semitic races of the Arabian Peninsula. The other, Orpheus, went to Greece. The former produced a religion of fanaticism and harshness, and wove it around a God who became a sort of national policeman with a heavy hand. Orpheus taught a religion of joy and beauty, and wove it around a God who made Himself manifest in nature. Jesus came to relax the burdens that a wealthy and powerful priesthood had laid upon the common people, and they killed him, for he threatened vested interests.

Orpheus was slain for much the same reason by his own maddened followers. These two Great Ones stand, as it were, for the two poles of religious expression. The pole of the artist, and the pole of the moralist. There has always been conflict between those that belong to the pole of joy and beauty which delights the artistic soul, and followers of the pathological killjoy spirit which sees goodness only in unhappiness and looks upon lightheartedness as the sign of a sinful nature.

Today the conflict between these two poles of thought still exists, but with this difference. The artistic soul has abandoned, as a rule, all religion as a childish survival from the unhappy past. He is not irreligious but a-religious.

The idea of a God who is known through beauty and joy, and understood as the divine life immanent in Mother Nature, has never been quite lost to Western Europe and to England in particular. The English, it is said abroad, like to take their pleasures sadly, and to a certain extent this is true; but it is far more correct to say that the average Englishman likes to take his religion sadly, even when he has not any ... to use an Irishism.

Yet side by side with this killjoy outlook, there has existed in England and Scotland a light-hearted nature-worship. There is historical evidence to show that the old Aryan concept of religion as the joyous worship of the great Father/Mother God who is manifested in nature has never been altogether absent from these Islands. It is not intended to imply that paganism is a perfect religion, or even a better religion than Christianity. The point is this: that the all too common middle-class attitude that God is best served by giving up all that makes life worth living is utterly foreign to the ancient European Tradition. It is the Jewish, oriental strain in Christianity that makes pessimistic asceticism a virtue instead of a pathology. The lice-covered beggars and sore-infested mendicants of medieval Europe are of the same type as the muck-covered modern fanatics and boil-smitten fakirs of Asia. It seems a queer idea to honour God as the Supreme Goodness, Truth and Beauty by a public exhibition of the worst ills of suffering flesh. To serve Him by making a living at His holy places out of dirt, ugliness, and often blatant fraud is an Asiatic trait foreign to ancient European religions.

Modern study of the historical documents of religion, folklore and myth, when carried out by the comparative method, has now led to certain new theories being raised by expert researchers, whose competency in their own line of work cannot easily be set aside. They say, for example, that 'heathen' rites of nature-worship were widespread in France, Spain and England at the end of the seventh century. This we know from the records of the Councils of Arles, Tours, Nantes and Toledo, as well as from the 'Liber Penitentialis' of Archbishop Theodore (died 690). Christianity at that time had hardly touched the life of the country people. It was confined very largely to the upper, middle, and governing classes in the towns. Again, in 1282 the priest of Inverkeithing 'was presented before his Bishop for leading a fertility dance at Easter round the phallic figure of a god'. He was allowed to retain his benefice!

How many realize that in 1303 a Bishop of Coventry was

accused in Rome of a number of crimes, amongst them ... 'quod diablo homagium fererat, et eum fuerit osculatus in tergo'. Again, in 1453, Guillaume Edeline, a Doctor of Theology and Prior of St Germain-en-Laye ... 'confessa ledit Sire Guillaume de sa bonne et franche voulente, avoir fait hommage audit ennemy en l'espece et semblence d'ung mouton, en le bas, sant par le fondement en signe de reverence et d'hommage...' (M. Murray, *The Witches in Western Europe*, p. 127).

Human nature has some odd methods of compensation, and some strange ways of straightening out pathological tangles due to the repression of man's natural desire for life in all its fullness. The witch-hunting of the fourteenth to eighteenth centuries was an effort to stamp out an old religion surviving from pre-Christian days. Its sin was that it celebrated with joy and laughter the great nature festivals. Today we know that any god other than the orthodox God was always made into a demon or a devil for the purposes of propaganda.

June 1937

7.

A Study of Self-Initiation

When 'Griff' Seymour got hold of a subject that held his attention, he rarely let it go under five chapters at least. His powers of observation and his perceptive abilities, to say nothing of his scholarship, could wring the last ounce of meaning from the work in hand. This article is almost a rarity in that it is so short. Nevertheless, it carries his characteristic 'bite'.

EHEIEH ASHER EHEIEH

When Moses the Egyptian initiate on the barren, sun-smitten wastes of Horeb, the Holy Mountain of God, asked the Spirit of the Burning Bush for his name, he got the curious reply that is the title of this article. If the Hebrew text is examined it will be found that it is 'Yod, He, Vau, He' – that is, God as the Creator of All – whom Moses supposed the speaker to have been. That it is no mere angel but the great Creator God who speaks is evident from the terms that are used in the Hebrew text.

The title has been variously translated as:

1. I am that I am.
2. I am because I am.
3. I am who I am.
4. I will be that I will be.

Dr Peake has pointed out in his commentary that the modern English rendering which most clearly conveys this abstract metaphysical idea is, 'I will be what I will be.' Another great scholar, Dr Cheyne, in his *Encyclopaedia Biblica* (p. 3322) says bluntly that this explanation is 'simply the product of a religious-philosophical speculation and far too abstract to be by any possibility correct'.

Speaking generally it may be said that most commentators admit that we have no idea what this term meant to the people who first wrote it. It seems to be a play on the verb *hayah*, to be.

As Dr Cheyne and the other commentators may have had no great *practical* knowledge of the Ancient Mysteries in the countries surrounding the Mediterranean Basin some three to four thousand years ago, let us look at the phrase from the point of view of Mystery teaching and ritual practices.

One of the first concessions that modern scholasticism ought to make is to acknowledge that as practical metaphysicians the ancient mystics and initiates were equal to and possibly better than the scholars of today. No modern biblical scholar would care to put himself on a par with the great prophets and writers of the bible, or of the Hermes Trismegistic literature.

Let us consider what may possibly be the explanation of Jehovah, of Elohim, of the god of nature who speaks to man in the flesh via a burning bush.

The records of modern spiritualism, of witchcraft (consider the case of Joan of Arc), and of twentieth-century psychology have made us familiar with phenomena of this nature. It excites little surprise either in the devout or the sceptic of today. In the past, the devout tended to canonize the person who spoke thus with the Deity. In the present, the doctor is inclined to treat him as a candidate for an asylum. Yet many mediums believe (or say they believe) that God speaks through them. The professional priesthoods, of course, explain this as the work of the devil, while the psychologist hints at some pathology, which after all is no more difficult to understand than the presence of his 'Horned Majesty'.

In any case neither priest nor psychologist ever dreams of following the advice of St John – 'Prove the Spirits'. To them it is immaterial whether the saying be true or the advice be good. The Devil appearing as an Angel of Light to deceive the unwary is a useful theological weapon – as Jesus found when fighting the orthodoxy of his time.

To the Ancient Mysteries, the first objective at which the initiate aimed was the awakening of the god within. Today we call this the higher self or the Holy Guardian Angel; in the past it was named as the Osiris, or Isis within. This process of awakening is as well known now as then. It is called Henosis or Identification and has been described at length by Dr Angus in his book *The*

Mystery Religions and Christianity. In one form or another Henosis is the central idea of yoga, both Eastern and Western. It is also the basis of 'New Thought', as taught by Emerson and the other great American leaders who had the inner vision. These men were teachers who were truly in touch with the Great Mother who rules in the empty(!) spaces of the woods, mountains, prairies and deserts of the New World.

Henosis was brought about through knowing the self, that is, through analysing that the self is an integral divine unit, a divine henad, or god (see Proclus, *Props. 113–65*). True realization resulted in the conscious uniting of the divine human henad with the substance of the god (or henad) invoked by means of the secret knowledge of the Mysteries. This henosis gave the worshipper the power of, and the protection of, the deity invoked.

We can turn this teaching into more modern form by saying: initiation confers the realization of a greater self subjective to and behind the ordinary everyday self of a man. At a later stage it also confers the realization of a still greater self in nature which is objective to and infinitely vaster than either the lower or the higher self.

Now the unity of the higher and lower self in man is the Baptism of Water, but the unity of the whole man with the greater self behind nature is the Baptism of Fire. They are, respectively, the initiations of the moon-goddess and the sun-god.

Moses was learned in all the wisdom of the Egyptians, and he had taken his initiation by water in the Temple of Egypt. He took his initiation by fire when alone on the sun-scorched rocks of Mount Horeb. There is nothing unique about Moses' experience except its final result – the escape of the Children of Israel from Egypt.

There is a Mithraic ritual in G. R. S. Mead, *Echoes of the Gnosis*, Vol. 6, which gives a secret and solemn rite for one person only. This is not a ritual for the initiation of a neophyte of the lower grades, but for one who is to initiate himself in the solitary Mystery of apotheosis. It is a fire rite: it is the invocation of the First Fire in nature and the First Fire in the initiate. It is the worship of the Holy Fire, and beholding the Deathless Eyes, by virtue of the Deathless Spirit, the Deathless Aeon, the Master of the Diadems of Fire.

In the language of the bible, Horeb is 'the bright mountain', the mountain of the sun, the mountain of fire, for the word 'Horeb' means literally 'glowing heat'. Sinai is the mountain of Sin, the moon-goddess. In the cosmological theory of the time, these two were the Light and Dark Pillars of Manifestation, the cosmic sun and moon powers, the Yin and Yang.

The result of this supreme initiation on the Mountain of Glowing Heat is a tremendous influx of spiritual power, for fire is the symbol of spirit. And it is well to remember that such an initiation is, from the material point of view, a subjective experience. 'The bush burned with fire, and the bush was not consumed;' which is a very clear hint as to the nature of this experience. Such an influx of spiritual force always brings, at least temporarily, a great expansion of mental power. For the brief moments of vision, the soul forgets its weaknesses, its limitations. It realizes that it was, is and ever will be, divine. And with this realization the superconscious mind casts into the conscious mind the tremendous ideal, EHEIEH ASHER EHEIEH, 'I will be what I will be,' or 'I will be what I will to be.'

It is only when the glory has passed and reaction sets in, that man cries out his despair at being unable to communicate fully the experience to his fellow men. The fiery baptism is passed, the vision fades, the lonely self-initiation is past. Yet the echoes remain even when the halting conscious mind takes charge of the shaken personality.

EHEIEH ASHER EHEIEH

October 1937

8.

The Magna Mater

Part 1

Notwithstanding the scanty nature of the records that have escaped the iconoclastic zeal of past ages, in most of the Mystery systems it is still possible to trace three distinct stages in the training given to initiates. For this we have to thank those modern scholars and archaeologists who have laboured patiently for so many years, and usually with little material gain for themselves.

The comparative study of religion, folklore and myth, as well as the excellent translations of the scriptures of Buddhism, Hinduism and Islam that are now available have considerably changed the tone of the opinions expressed by the non-professional religious writers of Europe and America. The modern Christian, with the exception of those still interested in the support of foreign missions and 'heresy hunts', has begun to recognize, with some surprise, the lofty nature of the teaching given in religions which not long ago were contemptuously called 'pagan' or 'heathen'. To know is to understand with sympathy. Only the wilfully or thoughtlessly ignorant, or those whose pockets are adversely affected, today incline towards intolerance, bigotry and persecution in matters religious.

Clues to the nature of the training formerly given in the Mystery schools of Greece, Syria, Chaldea and Egypt are often found in the rituals and disciplines of those Eastern religions still flourishing today after thousands of years.

A little-known German philosopher, Gustav Fechner, set forth in his speculations the basis upon which the practical training of any Mystery school, ancient or modern, is built. Unfortunately, his books are not, as far as I know, available in English. However, William James, an American philosopher and psychologist, has given us a synopsis of Fechner's work in his book *A Pluralistic*

Universe (Chapter 4). As an introduction to the third stage of Mystery training this book is invaluable, and will be used frequently in the following chapter.

The key to the type of training given in the first stage is to be found in the inscription once seen over the Pylon Gates of the Temple at Sais: 'Know Thyself.' This is the first maxim the student must study, and probably the last his brain will concern itself with when he begins to open up the wider consciousness. Sooner or later, the study of this maxim will involve a long course of mental purgation which can be rather painful. However, it has to be faced if the next step is to be taken; and in an organized school the teacher in charge of the neophytes is one who has himself drunk of this bitter cup several times. Also, let it not be forgotten that this experience has to be repeated before each major grade in initiation is taken. It should be clearly understood that this is purely a mental process and has nothing to do with that purging from sin laid down by the priestly administrators of modern herd law.

When seated in meditation, seek to analyse the contents of your consciousness. Try to discover what your mind really contains, and where its content has come from. Then ask yourself the following questions:

Of all this store of knowledge accumulated during many years of study, self-training and careful observation, how much do I *really know?* How much of this knowledge has come to me unverified from sources outside myself? Have I accepted this knowledge because it appealed to me and fitted in with my scheme of life? In other words, how much knowledge is first-hand, and how much is second-hand?

When used by a trained thinker, this method of self-analysis can cause considerable mental pain. When carrying it out, concentrate your attention upon the great issues of life. Analyse your knowledge of religion and its *authority* for *you.* Consider your philosophy of life, and ask yourself upon what rests its validity; what do you consider your mission in life to be? Again, what do you know of life, death, and their meanings? Why do you hold this belief? How much do you know? How much do you believe? In carrying out this process try always to distinguish what is first-hand knowledge and what is second-hand. If you are impartial, you will get a result that may be totally unexpected.

There are a number of good, sound, well-educated people who will not face this ordeal. Speaking generally, it may be said that it is only a 'rogue soul', one of the lost sheep who has wandered into the desert of the Moon-God who is prepared to do so.* The sheep who are safe, warm and fed seldom pass far into the wilderness. For the Moon-God insists on his followers doing their own thinking.

A popular Irish preacher once complained to me that he feared he was losing his grip on his audiences, and this indeed was the case. He thought that his knowledge had lost its freshness for him. What could he do about it? Answering almost without thinking, I gave him the first thing that came into my head. 'Discover how much of your religious knowledge is your own, and how much is just accepted on "authority".' To my astonishment this – to me, innocent – remark produced the following reply, given under obvious emotional stress: 'But that would mean I might lose my faith.'

This man had subconsciously arrived at the first stage of initiation, but was afraid to leave the fold. He was married with a large family and a good living. His word carried weight. With all this at stake, he was not prepared to venture into the domain of the Moon-God. In the circumstances, I think he was right, for the 'rogue' has to leave the herd.

This is the reasoning behind the Prodigal Son, the reason for the harsh words of Jesus about fathers, mothers and possessions. To find the Moon-God in the wilderness you must be mentally naked. †

I gave the same words, deliberately this time, to a very promising pupil who after rapid progress had come to a full stop. After a little thought she said, 'I dare not.' Within a few months she had returned to the social fold from which she had temporarily emerged.

In the Mysteries, the second stage is really an extension of the first. It too has a seed phrase which has to be meditated on and then acted upon. Up to this point the student has been in leading strings, first in the sect of his choice, and then in the Outer Court of the Temple. But up to the end of the first stage of 'Know Thyself' he is under authority. But when the first great purgation has been successfully carried out, teachers, books and their

---

* Which sheds a new light on the story of the 'scapegoat' symbol.

† All true prophets, mystics, and great Teachers seek this desert at some time of their life. It is there they find their personal truth.

influence should have been assessed at their correct value. Now the initiate is ready for the next stage.

Metaphorically the teacher takes the student back to the Outer Court and points to the inscription above the Pylon Gate, 'Know Thyself'. Then he is led back into the Temple through the closed gates and into the first hypostyle hall reserved only for the initiated. There he is shown: 'Know Thyself through Thyself.' It is at this stage that the fruits of that first painful purgation should become apparent. In the hours of silent meditation that are now spent within the Temple walls, the initiate learns that he alone can initiate himself.

Teachers, systems, books, religions and esoteric doctrines are but props that he has leaned on in the past. As he looks back he sees many signposts, but they all point back along the road by which he has come. Beside him stands a post that tells him to know himself through himself, and he remembers the saying: 'The Kingdoms of the Heavens lie within you.' From now on there will be no more signposts to guide him.*

In front of him lies a narrow cave-like entrance leading into a darkness in which nothing can be seen. Here is the inner chamber, the unlit sanctuary of the Mysteries. Only the candidate can light that sanctuary, only he can fill it from his own inherent divinity, with the power of the god chosen to indwell it. This is the task hinted at in the phrase 'Know Thyself through Thyself'.

No one but the candidate can carry out this task, though a teacher can encourage and fellow initiates can point out that they have been through that entrance and have seen the light dawning in the darkness and have watched the sun at midnight shining in the Temple of the Mysteries.†

This is the stage of seeking within the soul for the kingdom, of realizing the truth that no man, god or devil outside one's own imagination can either help *or* hinder one's progress. At this stage

---

* This is probably the hardest time for the student. Without these props, the prospects look bleak, and it takes a great deal of courage to make your own way. Most return and go through the first stage again, under the impression that they are moving forward.

† Not all Hollywood series are complete rubbish. What you read in this paragraph is seen in the final initiation of Kwai Chang Caine in the Kung Fu series, when his fellow priests line the way to the initiation chamber, their arms bared to show their ritual brands.

you learn that *you* and you alone are your own god or devil, and as that god/devil you have got to light unaided the sanctuary light on the altar. The divine power is free to all who can draw upon it and use it. It is neither theological or ethical.

The lighting of the lamp and the invocation of the divine no-self into the innermost sanctuary of the divine self, which is the initiated you, is the second great purgation. It involves the realization of one's potential divinity. It also leads on to the third stage when the initiate is allowed, if he is able and not afraid, to brush the stardust with his lips from the lotus feet of the Great Isis.

Part 2

> Truth lives for the most part on a credit system. Thoughts and beliefs pass, if nothing challenges them, as banknotes pass, so long as no one refuses them. All this points to direct verification somewhere, without which the fabric of truth collapses like a financial system with no cash basis. You accept my verification for one thing, and I yours for another. We trade on each other's truth. But beliefs verified concretely by *somebody* are the posts of the whole superstructure.
>
> (Professor W. James, *Pragmatism*, p. 207.)

The student standing before the Pylon Gate leading to the closely guarded Temple of Initiation – a temple that exists in reality within his own soul – must understand that the principle put out by Professor James above is the foundation of all his training. For every Mystery school it must be possible to verify the truth and adequacy of the system used.

A student accepts the teaching given, as a shopkeeper accepts a five pound note. These teachings do not pretend to be *the truth*. They are a token of the truth. A five pound note has behind it the Bank of England; the genuine Mystery teachings have behind them the experiences of the initiated gained by the labours of many minds during many a millennium.

But here the analogy ends; for the shopkeeper accepts his note and there is no further need for action on his part. The student, however, as soon as he is qualified, must proceed to verify through *personal experience* all that he has been taught. For that is the only way of realizing initiation.

The student must become a pragmatist in the sense that William James was one. It is useless to become one by way of philosophical conviction, like a college don. The neophyte is like a motorist passing his test to get a licence ... a practising pragmatist.

A Mystery school issues (or should be able to!) a driving licence which will enable the student to fare forth upon the roads that lead to the unseen. A genuine school is not a place for the issuing of weak tea to pale students, and its students should not expect tea, chatter and uplift to be the chief reason for their enrolment. Let it be said here and now: Mystery training in practical inner plane work is difficult, tedious, and not to be taken lightly.* A question often asked of a teacher is, 'How am I to get this personal experience?' The answer is always the same. The student must have a clear idea of how much he is prepared to sacrifice in order to realize his purpose. He must be prepared to master one system completely, then give a thorough and prolonged testing. He must fill his mind with the imagery he is told to use, and not go wandering off on his own because it looks more fun! He must stick with one system until he is its master. These three things, plus trust in the teacher, and confidence in himself, will take him to that throne on which is seated the star-crowned, moon-girt Queen of the Subtle Planes.

He is now striving to 'know the self through the self'; he is entering upon the third stage of initiation and this has an objective as well as the subjective aspect. He is seeking to suckle at the star-girt breasts of that great entity known to the Egyptians as Nut, Queen of Heaven.

The techniques by which the mystical process above described is attained will be unfolded gradually, given more by implication than by direct assertion. It aims at developing the picture consciousness and the method is by drawing, in vague outline, word pictures taken from ancient myth. These pictures educe long-buried memories and gently draw them out into full consciousness, as the student fills in the details himself.

This system has the advantage that once concentration and meditation have become easy and natural, it is a simple matter to try it out. For example, spend half a dozen meditations in building up in the imagination the Great Mother as she was just

---

* But they *do*, and this is the main reason for lack of suitable potential initiates today. No one wants to work. It has to be 'instant'.

described, and see what your feelings are with regard to her. If this does not appeal to you because it is too vague and shadowy, then try the following.

Think over the symbol of Hermes and see what reaction it will stir within you. Look up just what the symbol stood for in the past, and what it stands for today. What are your emotional reactions? Have you any feeling regarding this caduceus, its history and its meanings? What are your feelings about it and the Lord of Wisdom?

Next examine the symbolism of the Pan, and when you have done that, think upon the Christos in the same way. Notice that if you can personalize these three sets of symbols, or if you can realize that all three are names of and symbols for an office in nature, this will bring you back to Isis, who is Nut the Great Mother, the Bright Fertile Mother of the Qabalists. These things are cosmic aspects of the Soul of the Mother, so they are also aspects of your own soul. They work unseen, and often unrecognized, in your innermost being. When you consider this, consider how you feel about them.

If you cannot manage this, let me suggest a way in which you may start with a clean sheet on your journey to the Great Mother. Picture yourself standing before a dustbin which has its lid closed. See yourself lifting the lid, and throwing into the bin – symbolically – all your preconceived notions and beliefs concerning these four symbols. Make a clean sweep of the past, and remember what Jesus ben Joseph once said: 'Except ye come as little children, in no wise shall ye enter the Kingdom of Heaven.'

In order to travel the inner roads you must shed all prejudice. Shed the burden of your 'settled' convictions. The path is too narrow for such bulky burdens. As a little child you must go to the Bright Mother, or give up for this incarnation the vision of Her as recorded in Revelations, for the fruit of the Tree of Life is not the same as that of the Tree of Knowledge.

So many mistake conscious knowledge for the consciousnes of Life. Conscious knowledge is the fruit of experience in the physical world. To know the life force you must stand beneath the Tree of Life and pluck its fruit. It grows in gardens set in those moonlit purple-shaded mountain lands which form the antechamber of the Great Mother. And you must pass through that chamber if you want to see her as the Woman Clothed with the Sun.

Fechner taught that this planet is a living organism. It is the outward physical body of a cosmic entity that is intelligent and purposive. It has its own collective unconscious which is wider than that of a man. It is one of those vaster orders of mind that go with the vaster orders of body.

'The earth on which we live has its own collective consciousness,' says Fechner. So must each sun, moon and planet. So the whole solar system must have its own wider consciousness, in which that of our earth must play its part. The entire starry system concurs with this idea, thus the whole system, along with whatever else may be, is the body of that totalized consciousness of the universe men call God. (W. James, *A Pluralistic Universe*, p. 152.)

As an exercise designed to open up your inner mind, build this picture every day, time and time again. When you can feel and understand it as life, and when it reacts upon you emotionally, then you have taken that first step on the path that will end when you place your head on the breast of the Great Mother, and taste for yourself the cosmic life that incarnates through Her in this physical world.

We are all familiar with the phrase 'Ashes to ashes, and dust to dust'. It exactly describes the relationship between your body and the body of our Mother the Earth. But go further and see if you are ready to acknowledge that your life force is an integral part of her life forces, that your etheric is part of Her etheric.

This may be difficult until you have learned conscious control of your etheric body. And you learn to control it by thinking about it deliberately and repeatedly over a period of time – a simple but tedious and difficult exercise.

Again, your individualized mind is an integral part of the earth's much wider consciousness. This is the clue to the Earth Memory described by A.E. and the race memory theory of the more prosaic writers on biology and psychology.

Man, along with birds, beasts, reptiles, and the devas that rule over mountains, lakes and storms are, one and all, integral portions of the Earth Mind. We are all part of one another, and each can be made conscious of the other. If you know Greek you will realize what is not apparent in the English translation of the bible – how Jesus personalized when he said to the stormy sea *'Siopa, pephimoso'*, which literally means *'Silence, be thou quiet'*. He used the direct address. For he was a Lord of the Elemental Powers who are, as if men, nurslings at the breast of the Great Mother.

Elementals are not as closely imprisoned in the physical body as are men and animals. They are not, as we are, dust of her dust. But they *are* an integral part of Her Etheric, and Her Soul. They are not without consciousness, and understand a command and fulfil the laws of their being in the wider being of the Mother. Now: close your eyes and open your inner senses; turn your thoughts inwards, and open your inner senses. Do this calmly and trustingly like a child, and in time you will drink consciously of the star milk that flows from the breasts of Nut, who is Isis.

Part 3

The key that opens the door of the Temple of the Magna Mater is imagery, using this term as meaning figurative illustration. If you wish to open this door, you must fashion your own key – it is an ancient teaching that the pupil must fashion his own magical weapons. In this case the key symbolizes a stock of the right kind of images which you must then combine until you have something that is particularly your own. There is no such thing as mass production in the Mysteries. The Mysteries are for the few, something that is often forgotten; for the many there are 'uplifting' societies.

It is unwise in the early stages to concentrate exclusively on one type of imagery, so spread your net wide. The type of image that works best for you depends on the contents of your subconscious mind, and it is usual to spend some time on finding out what these are. Egyptian images suit some, while others prefer Greek or Chaldean. When you are more advanced you can work with almost any system, but there will also be one that will suit you best. At the same time, remember that it takes all kinds to make up a good working system of imagery, and they all tend to explain one another. If you turn to Budge, *The Gods of the Egyptians*, Vol. 1, Chapter 7, you will discover that the primeval gods of the Egyptian priesthood (but not of the common people) are the same as the primeval deities of the Assyrians. Though not much is known about either system when taken by itself, yet when the four pairs of gods belonging to the Assyrian 'Seven Tablets of Creation' are compared with the Paut (eight gods) of the Lord of Thoth of Hermopolis (i.e. Khemmenu), each system will throw light on the other.

The names of these inner realities vary, but the powers touched by meditation and ritual do not. Nut and Nu are used for their

invocation in Egypt; Tiamat and Apzu-Rishtu are the 'calls' by
which the primordial male and female powers of the astro-etheric
planes of cosmic consciousness are awakened first in the psyche of
the invoking worshipper and then in the psyche of the Magna
Mater.

Those who are prepared to seek the inner kingdom of the
Mother must amass their images by creative reading. That inner
kingdom is to be found only in the inner chamber where can be
heard the 'sound of gentle stillness' which is the literal translation
of the Hebrew phrase given as 'the still small voice' in the account
of Elijah's initiation by air, earth and fire on the Holy Mount of
Horeb (Kings 19:12) where Moses took his initiation by fire a
thousand years before.

Creative reading is something different from ordinary reading.
In the former your object is neither reading for pleasure nor for
information. You read with the object of filling the subconscious
mind with selected images which are then built up and dropped
down into the depths of the subconscious. They are placed there
with the intention that after germinating for a while they will re-
emerge when needed or called up.

You must be careful what images you select when using this
method of preparing the mind, because it is very potent. It is a
method for opening the unwritten books of the Lord Thoth. The
knowledge that was once written on the Tablet of Thrice Greatest
Hermes. But you must search for the Thoth within yourself and
say – as did the ancient initiates – 'I know thee, Lord Tahuti, and
Thou knowest me. I am Thou, and Thou art I.'

The seeker will find this Lord of the Mind of Man enthroned in
the deepest abyss of his own essential nature, and in the dark
purple depths of Cosmic Immensity, for Tahuti is the Lord of the
Abyss beyond all Abysses.

This method of revivifying ancient images with one's own
emotions can thoroughly upset the unstable. It is not intended for
the pious sentimentalist or for the Western follower of Bhakti
Yoga. But once this warning has been given we should add that to
those who have counted the cost, there comes a joy and a
fullness of life when using these symbol systems rightly, that
cannot be described. It must be experienced to be fully
understood. Only then can the initiate comprehend the Great Isis
and realize, through Nut, the feminine power of Amen-Ra, the
saying, 'I have truly loved you, and have longed to give you *life.*'

The mind can be stored with suitable images by reading the

sacred books of all races, and studying the composite pictures, or
mandalas, that the priesthoods constructed to enshrine the divine
knowledge collected by personal experience. Also by reading
poetry and novels written by those who know, for many poets
have, through love of beauty, given us fragments of the Mystery
of the Unseen. But few novelists have much real inner
knowledge, and the popular occult novel is usually untrue and
should be avoided.

The Egyptian symbol is the best to start with. Catholic
Christianity has little in common with its supposed parent,
Judaism – and, like its offspring, Protestantism, is a religion of
the herd law. The former enshrines in its devotion to the Queen
of Heaven a little of the ancient Mystery lore that gave to the
Egyptian world its Morning Star. It is the Catholic devotion to
the feminine principle that gives power to its rituals.

The student, in developing and using this method, must not
forget to bring to the ancient teachings any knowledge he may
have of psychology, for without a fair knowledge of esoteric
psychology much of the inner meaning of these Mystery
teachings may be missed. Their whole object was to enable the
microcosm to take its rightful place in the macrocosm.

As an exercise, study Plate 243 in *The Art of Ancient Egypt*
published by Phaidon Press of Vienna. Do not worry about the
hieroglyphs; just take the symbols and let them speak to your
inner mind. The picture is the reproduction of a relief inside the
coffin of a priest. It shows Nut the Goddess of Heaven in the
form of the arched body of a naked woman whose hands and feet
touch the ground. Obviously, it is the sky arching over the limits
of the horizon. On her body are three sun discs with the
double uraeus, the sun at morning, midday and evening. Below
on the horizon is a small man with immense outstretched arms
drawn in the shape of the hieroglyph for the human Ka.

In the psychology of ancient Egypt the Ka stands for the
'genius' or spiritual double of a man. Looking at this picture we
see that the goddess is shown as surrounding the priest's Ka as an
oyster shell surrounds the oyster. The goddess forms a magical
circle around the priest's spiritual body.

Remember that the priests thought of Nu, the invisible celestial
ocean of primordial life essence, as the source of All that Is, the
Father of the Gods, while Nut is his female manifestation. Again,
we have the Hindu idea of Shiva and his Shakti, and the Ka of the
priest is the Shakta worshipping and rejoicing in his new-found

state of relationship with the life-giving influence of the Great
Mother of all life. The two jackals beside the wavy lines that
stand for Nu give us another hint. They are the guardians that
stand by the door of the Temple of the Unseen, the House of
Nut.

On a higher level, this picture represents that inner subtler
world that surrounds and sustains this physical world as the
earth's atmosphere surrounds and sustains a hovering hawk. Nut
is the Ka and soul of this great Universal Mother. Nu is the
unmanifested hidden ego of the Great Entity man calls Nature.

On a lower level, Nut is the inner, more subtle instrument of
consciousness whereby man becomes aware of his own inner
states as well as that of the higher Nut, of which he is an
individual yet integral factor. These are the 'Archai' of the true
Gnostic. Man lives physically, emotionally and mentally within
the higher Nut, as a foetus lives within its mother's womb. But
man as a cosmic ego is in, and with, Nu the Archetype of the
Unmanifest; the Great Temple that is in the Wat guarded by
Anubis of the north and Anubis of the South, is Nut, the Shakti of
Nu; and the priest's Ka is Shakta the initiated worshipper, dead
yet alive in and through Nut.

If a student will take any picture of the ancient gods and use it
in the manner outlined above, that picture will start to live for
him. With constant use, it will become magnetized for and by him,
and thus will become his link with the Unseen Realities of which
Nu and Nut are the Egyptian personifications. But remember
that the magnetizing of such a picture is an emotional experience,
and a mandala is not a mandala until it has become so magnetized.

As you work in this way, try to recapture the spirit of these
Ancient Mysteries by remembering that for the them the universe
– that is, Nut – was alive. This must soak into the mind until it
becomes as real as hunger before a meal.

The stellar universe is *alive*, directed by *will* and controlled by
intelligence. In many ways it is analogous to man's life, will and
intelligence, but on a vaster scale. Within the collective
intelligences of universes are the lesser ones of solar systems, and
within the latter are planetary spirits. Man, beasts, birds and
devas all go towards the making up of the collective intelligence
that is Nut in her role of Magna Mater. This ancient teaching
finds its best modern expression in Fechner's conception of a
great reservoir in which all the consciousnesses of the lesser
entities are pooled and yet remain as individualized portions of
Nut.

Having realized this within your innermost being, construct a hidden and secret mandala embodying the truths faintly and dimly shadowed forth in the last paragraph. Make of it your own magnetizing instrument.

Part 4

In Algernon Blackwood's novel *The Centaur* (Chapter 13), there is the record of an experience gained while standing between the Portals of the Gates of Horn and Ivory, which because it ends in failure is extremely instructive.* Let a student note that failures, constant failures, if carefully meditated upon, can become milestones on the road to success. Some achieve success almost without effort, yet their present success is often the fruit of many failures, and meditation upon the same in lives now long past and forgotten. So never despair. Carry on in faith, for faith means confidence in the technique you are using.

Once you have tasted the freedom of the Proto-world, which the Germans call the *Urwelt*, or – as the Egyptian Initiate would have said – drunk of the star milk that flows from the breasts of Nut, then that nostalgia, which is the lost subconscious knowledge of one's polarity with the Real and Inner, will vanish. Many men and women have rushed into matrimony through mistaking the call of the Proto-world for the natural longings of the senses.

It was the peace of the Magna Mater which they sought, but not being made free of her Temple, they found only the discord of unharmonized wedlock. If you have every cried as did O'Malley in *The Centaur*, 'Oh that I could be with him where he is now, in that place of eternal youth and companionship,' then you know what is meant by nostalgia.

There is a 'Beloved' who is beyond time and space as known to physical consciousness,† and *The Centaur* has been the means of opening the Gate of Horn and Ivory to many who have felt the call of the 'Beloved' in the Urwelt, but did not recognize it at first. But once they passed through that gate which is called 'The Eye of the Needle', they found the gift of Isis which is serenity even in the midst of conflict – a serenity that comes from the

---

* The late W. E. Butler taught this same idea. He said, 'Never underestimate the value of a failure. It's the best way to learn.'

† There were hints in W. E. Butler's private teachings that this inner 'Beloved' was that which overshadowed John the Divine.

depths of man's inner being.* Because it comes from within and not from without, the gift is very potent.

> The terror of a great freedom caught him, a freedom most awfully remote from the small personal existence he knew today ... for it suggested, with awe and wonder, the kind of primitive utterance that was before speech or ... language, when emotions were too vague and mighty to be caught by words, but when beings, close to the heart of their Great Mother, expressed the feelings, enormous and complex, of the greater life they shared with Her, projections of the very Earth herself ... with a crash in his brain, O'Malley stopped. These thoughts, he realised, were not his own. (*The Centaur*, p. 94.)

There are many who know well how nature, when we are in the wild places, comes stealthily nearer with a riot of silent beauty. Through closed eyes in green beechwoods, feelings steal upon us that bring an awareness of some vital essence of the place that discharges itself into the receptive human soul. Something that recharges the human battery that modern town life causes to run down. There is a tingling at the nape and a prickling in the thumbs. Then a glow as from a great inner fire warms one's being. A deep sense of the greatness and goodness of nature's vast life steals over one, and the pagan who knows this feeling says, 'This place is divine. Here the Old Ones are still with us.'

How accurately Blackwood describes the 'crash in the brain', which comes with a sudden and unexpected return from the bright hinterland beyond the inner horizon, where strange roads go down. There is the awful sense of some lost loveliness that comes with the opening of the physical eyes, and how drab and drear are the things that meet the eyes that have been sealed, and then unsealed by the Mystery techniques.

The more one meditates, especially in a place set apart for the purpose, the clearer and stronger becomes the state where shines the sun at midnight. These pitiful attempts to describe things seen and felt in one state of consciousness in terms of another and dimmer state are totally inadequate. There is, however, no other way of conveying the 'things not seen' unless you are prepared to go through the Gate of the Eye of the Needle. It can be done, *is* done, often. But a student who is still a beast of burden cannot

---

* A similar serenity is taught in the Zen Buddhist faith.

pass through this narrow gate that leads to the Inner Planes. One must go through the long period of purgation in order to loose from one's back the immense burden of second-hand knowledge that the blind teachers of blind faiths have slung upon the shoulders of those they are supposed to educate in the essentials of religion.

Jesus as a Lord of the Elemental Powers had much to say about priesthoods that lay burdens upon the laity and lift not a finger to ease them. The modern priest will talk about his 'sure and certain hope' and then persecute all who try to turn this feebleness of hope into the power of certainty.

You have to be able to use your religion for yourself and by yourself in a practical way before you can help those weaker than yourself. Jesus said, 'I am come that they may have life and have it more abundantly.' And he gave the technique of the Upper Chamber to His followers, in order that they might be able to pass the narrow gate into the Greater Light, and on to the slopes of the Hill of Vision. The imagery used by this great teacher who meditated at night in the lonely purple hills above the moon-silvered Lake of Galilee is the same as the pagans of His time and ours.

Use the creative reading technique to educe the meaning of these words: 'But O'Malley rolled into his own berth without undressing, sleep far from his eyes. He had heard the Gates of Horn and Ivory swing softly upon their opening hinges, and the glimpse he caught of the garden beyond made any question of sleep impossible. Again he saw those shapes of cloud and wind flying over the long hills.' (*The Centaur*, p. 88.)

Once this gate is behind you and you stand on the garden-like slopes beyond, there comes a sense of vastness and freedom. You see the vision of life and feel yet more life on the long, blue mountain ranges where the devas and their electromagnetic auras tell of one and the same thing – exhilarating life.

Those who have stood on the extreme tip of a ten thousand foot crag and looked across the blue rain-washed landscape of the monsoon-swept Himalayas will know what is being hinted at here in this halting imagery of the earth plane.

Those who have done so under these conditions and who have then found themselves consciously enfolded within the living etheric body of the deva ruling over such a place will know something that truly *is*, yet can never be fully described. But the genius of Algernon Blackwood has almost caught it in the following lines:

The narrow space of that little cabin was charged already to the brim, filled with some overpowering loveliness of wild and simple things. The beauty of the stars and wind and flowers, the terror of the seas and mountains; strange radiant forms of gods and heroes, nymphs, fauns and satyrs; the fierce sunshine of some unspoilt Golden Age ... it was the *Urwelt* calling. (*The Centaur*, p. 95.)

This is the type of imagery with which the student, by means of creative reading, must fill his mind before he can exchange old images for new. Only after years of teaching does one realize what an extraordinary effect the 'rational' methods of education have had upon the mental make-up of those educated within the last forty years. Thought is almost entirely conducted in words and phrases. This is alright so long as it is just the conscious mind that is being used, though the wide use of memory systems which depend on imagery show that its deficiencies are recognized. But in art and the creative sciences imagery is all-important, for the artist has to create out of the old a new and splendid system of his own.

One quick and easy way to train the image-making faculty is to blindfold yourself and then, trusting to your memory, move about the room changing the position of small articles on shelves, bookcases, etc. Another is to make an image of yourself walking over to a table, then change, in the imagination, the things on the table. If you keep a record of your successes and failures, in a very short time your subconscious mind will become quite expert at image building. It must never be forgotten that the motive power of the subconscious mind is stirred by imagery and not by reason or words.*

It is *imagery* and not conscious reasoning that makes the connection between the objective macrocosmic powers and the subjective microcosmic power that is man. It has been said that the linking of these two types of power cannot be carried out in the heart of a city, but it is necessary to go out into the country to worship the powers of the Great Mother.

This is an erroneous supposition. Provided you have a mind well supplied with the correct imagery it is easier to tune into the elemental powers of nature in the silence of your own room than to touch the same powers in the dim light of a midge-haunted wood. You go to the woods to *collect* the feel and imagery of the place. Then you store it until it is needed.

* It is typical of Seymour to write pages of theoretical material, and then give out important teaching methods in the simplest of terms.

It is, however, the attitude of worship, adoration and devotion for the Great Mother that really links the microcosmic imagery to the macrocosmic reality. To slip into the swiftly flowing tide of ecstasy that comes with the knowledge of the Goddess is an experience best attempted by the beginner in the silence of his own room, working under prepared and protected conditions. In the woods he is at the mercy of the forces that function in that place, unless he is of a high degree of experience.

You can work in the open and reap there a rich harvest by opening the sluice gates of your soul to the ebb and flow of the cosmic tides. But this worship of the outer world should be looked on as a preparation for the moment when the priest and priestess, standing before the empty shrine, deliberately fill that emptiness with the presences that are called forth by invocation and the correct use of the creative imagination from the *Urwelt*, i.e. the antechamber of the great moon deities, Isis, Osiris, Khensu and Tahuti. A sound technique for using the imagery given here is a winged steed or a magic carpet that will bear you far and wide to a realm where time and space as we know them do not exist.

Your body may rest in the comfortable stillness of deep meditation in a dingy flat in some great city. But by the use of such techniques the bonds that bind and fetter the far wandering soul can be eased sufficiently to enable it to range once more through past ages and scenes.

The great civilizations of the past are housed in the wide halls of memory that form the mansions of the Great Moon Mother. You can walk in their temples, and go about the sacred tasks that once were yours.

You can take a broken and dismantled shrine, that has virtually disappeared from the physical world, and by your adoration and loving labour rebuild it. You can go there night after night when the right tides are flowing and as priest and priestess cause the thrown-down double cube to stand upright, the sacred light to burn again upon the altar, the broken pillars and sacred symbols in the temple garden to become whole once more. Even the shrubs and flowers that once bloomed there will return to life as you pour into their inner plane forms your own power of creative imagery. This is union with the Magna Mater.

It is worship in the ancient way of the dedicated priest or priestess that works such miracles. It has been taught that where two or three are gathered together for the worship of a Holy

Name, there the Great Powers are awakened. The solitary mystic can do much to awaken ancient memories, but if he remains solitary he remains barren and his reawakened powers will perish with the body. It takes at least two and really three to bring the living fire back upon the altar. It can be done as Shakti and Shaktas, the goddess and her two priests, one of which is the initiated priest who is permanently on the Inner Levels; the latter directs the power and holds the balance of the scales marked 'Here' and 'Yonder'.

When both priest and priestess are in their earthly sanctuary, then the two halves and four quarters are in polarized function as Shiva, Shakti and the two Shaktas. Thus are the ancient altars served and their lamps kept burning.

Fanatics who think that they honour the One God by defiling another's conception of Him may destroy the walls, break the altar and extinguish the lamp; but those children of the Mother who, in the past, have held the right of entry into Her sanctuary can rebuild it all again. Once Her priest, always Her priest; once Her priestess, always Her priestess. Such, when their memory returns, the Mother will welcome back to the innermost shrine. Service is their right of entry. There are many initiations and many Mysteries, but the road is closed unless you serve Her.

Part 5

'Qui vit sans folie n'est si sage qu'il croit,' said La Rochefoucauld. The ways to the sanctuary of the Great Mother are many, but all have this in common: they lie along roads that wind below the horizon of full working consciousness. So the first task in hand is the crossing of that horizon. This latter, visible to the physical eye, is an imaginary line beyond which sight does not function, and it draws away as you approach it. The invisible line of the horizon of waking consciousness is also an imaginary line that recedes if approached through the reasoning faculties. But by using deep meditation it is as easy to reach and cross that line in the waking state as it is in your nightly sleep.

It takes a long time to learn this technique; some take months and even years to cross it consciously. It took the writer many years to achieve the first conscious crossing. But once mastered, this technique can still the mind at will, and the crossover can be made in moments.

Success or failure depends on the use of your creative

imagination. All horizons are imaginary, be they physical, astral or mental; none can be crossed except by the use of images. But do not confuse imagination with the fantastic. The former is real on its own plane, the latter is not. The human imagination is a divine thing, a Pegasus that can carry you up and through the subtle planes to wherever you wish to go. But uncontrolled fantasy is a disease of the mind. Controlled imagination is a clue to the phenomenon of genius.

Let us use this faculty and make our conscious way along the strange road that lies below the horizon that lies within the soul of each one of us.

Picture clearly a steep, dark limestone cliff in the face of which is a cave. In many religions the source of their power is sought in a cave or dark place such as an underground stable. Mithras, Jesus and Dionysius were all said to have been born in such places. A temple of the Mysteries was also placed below ground whenever possible for good practical reasons.

The entrance to the cave is small, narrow and low. A single stunted tree, a thorn covered with white blossom, rises on a ledge just above the cave mouth. You cannot climb the cliff. You can only advance by way of the cave.

In India, Buddhist sanctuaries are cut into the living rock of certain hills facing west. At sunset, the dark sanctuary is aflame with the light of the setting sun. Every detail of the Buddha's image can be seen by one who sits within and a little to one side. If you stand in a doorway, the shrine will remain dark. You must go right on, and into the darkness, if you are to see the Buddha in the light. Get this picture clear, because it is the symbol of a great truth, and an important step in the preliminary technique of this kind of work. If you are to see the light dawning in the darkness of ths shrine, you yourself must be in the shrine and *in the dark*. You must cross far beyond the threshold to be able to see the divine light that fills what is known as the Moon Cave. The picture is a statement of inner as well as outer phenomena.

The Moon Cave exists only within your own soul and you must sit in the imagination in that cave which is the shrine of the Moon-God, the source of Moon Wisdom, and you must go through it to reach the sanctuary of the Magna Mater. Build this picture often and with care.

In certain lights, generally when there is stormy weather about, and in tropical countries, the moon can appear to change colour, first appearing as a huge green moonstone, one moment white, the next shot through with dull red, blue, green and yellow streaks. It changes so rapidly you may think your eyes are playing you tricks. Now build the second picture. See the moon as an immense globe glowing like a moonstone, changing in hue and brightness. Imagine it growing larger and larger until it seems to fill all space; and see your own tiny figure seated in meditation at its centre. Now only you and the moon exist; all else has vanished. You are now like a moon initiate meditating in the Moon Cave. You are now potential moon wisdom, a potential source of moon power, an image and a likeness of Thoth the Egyptian Lord of Wisdom and the Moon sphere. See yourself in this way, clad as a priest of Thoth wearing the horned moon, carrying the crook and flail, and seated at the centre of a glowing sphere.

When you can do this thoroughly, you will find that much of the instruction given in Chapters 5 and 6 of Iamblichus' *Egyptian Mysteries* will take on a new and more intelligible meaning. If you are persevering and fortunate, the gods themselves may visit you in the Moon Cave.

Do not expect to do all this at once. It means patient work for a long time before the imagery will really live for you. In the early stages, the value of the exercise lies in the concentration it demands and in the exercise it gives to your will-power when you slog at it day after day. These exercises are like those used in physical training. It is the daily grind joyfully done for the sheer love of the task that does the building. Rejoice in the trouble you are taking and see it as progress along the way. Now you are ready for the next part. But not too soon, it is so easy to construct an image that *looks* alright, but which will not hold power without leaking – a dangerous state of affairs.

The next stage is the acquiring of power. Shiva must have his Shakti or the universe will be stillborn. The thinker must have his image clearly formed or his words will be without power. You must now build an instrument for conserving power within yourself. You have built the cave of the Moon-God. This gave you potential wisdom. Now you must build the Cave of Power within that Moon Cave which is the cave of wisdom. Power without wisdom and understanding always brings destruction. Only those who fear power can hope to use it well.

Build a replica of the great Moon Cave of Thoth and place it within your own aura. This replica built around yourself will enable you to capture, hold and concentrate the positive moon powers of the Great Mother and he who serves Her, Thoth, Lord of Wisdom. This image will help you to turn potential into actual. It will also act as a safety valve when you are under pressure. This is the reason why the images must be built again and again with clarity of thought and intensity of will-power. Realization of what this can mean will come quickly when you begin practical work.

By repeatedly building this mental picture in your mind of the cave of power with yourself sitting within, you will slowly build your own instrument for touching the powers of the unseen. And do not forget, it is as necessary to be able to repel unwanted power as to attract that which is wanted.

All this is symbolism, not a statement of fact or physical happening, so you are merely trying to awaken by imagery the powers of your subconscious mind. These inner powers will then put you into contact with the soul of Mother Earth. The vast moonstone that glows in your imagination is a talisman that will persuade your subconscious mind to play its part. Earth and the moon are considered in the Mysteries to share the same etheric. The moon is positive and the earth negative. In man the subconscious mind relates to the moon sphere. It is a vast reservoir of psychic power which must be carefully handled. Hence the imagery of the small moon sphere. You can control the smaller sphere fairly easily once you have personalized it, and made it a living part of your being. If you build it with care you will be able to increase and decrease its power flow with the moon tides. Every force that flows into the aura of the earth sphere from the immensities of outer space directly affects man's aura.

This opalescent globe becomes in time as much your sphere of sensation with regard to the inner planes, as your skin is the sphere of sensation for your physical body. You can train this aura to become aware on all levels. You can open all your inner senses, and by doing so you learn to act consciously in the non-material spheres of this universe. You are trying to gain control of your inner senses, and to aid you in this you have just been given a series of word pictures which to many will appear to be pure fantasy.

For you, these pictures need not remain fantasy. You can 'rise from earth's centre through the Seventh Gate' if you are prepared to spend time and effort in building them until they build themselves within you of their own accord. These exercises are not easy to do, but it is a joy to watch them come alive in your mind with each passing day.

To rise through the Seventh Gate, you must link these exercises as soon as possible to one or other of the Mystery systems. Turn back to page 204, where you will find the description of Nut; re-read this, and if possible look at the picture from which it was taken. Then take another step in your training.

On the portico of the Great Temple of Isis on the Island of Phile, there is a sculpture which can be used to make a link with the Egyptian Mysteries. It can also be used to develop the system hinted at in this chapter. The sculpture consists of two nude figures of Nut with a smaller female figure enclosed within the others.

The first and largest is Nut. She is bent so as to form three sides of a square, and the ground on which she rests her fingers and feet forms the fourth side. On her body are the three winged discs mentioned earlier. The next figure is in the same attitude, but smaller, and she has two tiny female figures holding two boats, one at each end of the torso. It may be that these boats are moon boats. The third figure is within the second figure, and shows a woman (or it could be a man) with the back of her head and neck flat on the ground. The body and legs are curled over the face so that the back of the head touches the toes. The arms are outspread in opposite directions with the fingertips of the left hand touching the feet of the largest figure, and those of the right hand touching the fingers of the second figure.

Notice that the third figure is the reverse of the other two. It is contracted whilst they are extended. It faces up; they look down. Its back touches the earth; theirs forms the sky.

What this symbol meant to the man who designed it we can only guess at. Some think it refers to Osiris and his two mothers; some think it symbolizes the soul of man within the greater soul of the Mother Goddess, which in turn forms part of the still greater soul of the Solar Deity. This latter may be the best explanation for such ideas were widespread at the time. It probably had many meanings, as the priest who used it passed up through the ranks of the priesthood.

So far as the student is concerned, he would do well to take a pencil and attempt to draw this picture, even if just the barest outline. It will then link with the word pictures that have been given and will provide him with a powerful mandala. A mandala built in this manner is the key that Omar Khayyam was unable to find. It will not only unlock the door that barred his way, but it will enable you to see through that veil past which he could not see. That door is within your own soul and you must forge your own key to it.

The veil which blinded Omar, and his translator Fitzgerald, is only opaque for those whose eyes are dulled by excessive devotion to earthly wisdom. The dull clod lying in the winter-sown cornfield is soon covered by the green veil of nature. For the initiate this veil becomes translucent. Pass through it, and you will arrive at the state of consciousness that will enable you to read and understand the following verses.

> But leave the Wise to wrangle, and be with me.
> The quarrel of the Universe let be:
> And, in the corner of some hubbub croucht,
> Make game of that which makes as much of thee.

> For in and out, above, about, below,
> 'Tis nothing but a magic lantern show
> Played in a box whose candle is the Sun,
> Round which we phantom figures come and go.

You begin with the phantom figures it is true, but if you will try, and give time and effort to the tasks that have been set before you, then the Great Ones of the Night of Time will, for you, cause Khephra to rise as Horus of the Horizon, and then the inner horizon will be left behind you.

Part 6

In fancy this tireless child thought of leaping from crest to crest of the long blue waves of hills. Why could he not do it? He imagined the run and the mad gathering of power for the leap, and in the very act of imagining he had left the body behind. What had happened? The air in which he floated was vibrant with timeless melody, a sound as beautiful and universal as the light. Where was he? The Earth was vanishing, swallowed up in a brightness as fiery as the sun; mountains and crags were fading from vision as if consumed by the ecstasy of the fire. A moment more and he would have passed from the illusion of boyhood. He was reaching up to some immeasurable power which was himself when consciousness faded. When he awoke again he heard voices speaking above him.

  'It is time to waken him. The seer cannot be held to the eyes, the being cannot be held to the body.'

  He looked up. He saw a figure thrice the height of mortals, a body gleaming as if made of gold and silver air. It was winged with flame above the brows. The eyes which looked upon him were still as if they had gazed only upon eternities. The boy cried, and knew not why he uttered the words: 'I know you, Shepherd of the Starry Flocks. What soul do you now draw from the Abyss?'

(A.E., *The Avatars*, p. 31,)

Here is an experience with two aspects, not very uncommon. To many come these visions of the Children of the Great Mother. They are real for the seer with a reality that remains long after the actual happenings. The author can remember clearly such a vision and still feels the emotion that it generated many years ago. The lofty Himalayan crag upon which it happened can still be seen, but the happenings of that day have gone. The experience gave a fleeting but potent glimpse of the Great Mother and Her Children, for there are many shepherds and many starry flocks just within the Veil covering more or less densely the earth's surface.

The second aspect is that of leaping the gulf between this world and the next. Always there is the effort and the leap, then a sense of timelessness and stillness as one touches the Beyond. Once you have had such an experience the question of its reality or non-reality will not worry you. It will enable you to project your consciousness from Here to Yonder as did the ancient initiates.

It is important to make clear that no attempt has been made to teach the student anything new, or to give him any fresh knowledge. Many Christian writers have disparagingly pointed out that in the rites of the Ancient Mysteries the appeal was to the eye, the imagination and the emotions, and not to the intellect, which shows how completely the main purpose of the Mysteries and Mystery drama has been misunderstood by non-initiated Christian writers. (See Angus, *The Mystery Religions and Christianity*.)

The main purpose was not, as Angus has stated, to induce the initiate through the substitution of personality (by hallucination or suggestion) to experience his identification with Deity. Angus is making a very wild guess, for he himself has written: 'An awful obligation to perpetual secrecy as to what was said and transacted behind closed doors in the initiation proper was imposed. An obligation so scrupulously carried out that through the centuries not one account of the secrets of the Holy of Holies of the Mysteries has come down to gratify the curiosity of the historian.' (p. 78.)

Many writers build theories upon nescience. This is unwise, for nescience is only the state of not knowing. It can know nothing definite except that it 'knows nothing'. Do not be hypnotized by the authority that enhaloes a great master of ignorance, who in the name of science says: 'I do not know, therefore you cannot know, it does not exist.' Remember the Age of Pisces is past, the fishy age of blind obedience to blind leaders. The new Age is that of Aquarius, the free man. Seek your own freedom by thinking for yourself and refuse to carry the burdens that have come down to us from the past of other people's psychopathologies and repressions.

In developing your imagination and storing your mind with potent imagery, try books written by modern men and women of vision, those who are the prophets of the new age. Quarry from them rough imagery, then refashion it for your own special needs. Let it sink deep into your inner self until it becomes the still small voice of your higher self. Above all, accept no dogmas, and trust no religion or sect that maintains any form of dogma, for such is death to spiritual evolution.

For the purposes of creative reading use above all A.E., the prophet of the Celtic races. His works are of special value, for he goes right to the heart sanctuary of the group minds of these Islands. Like Blackwood he writes from first-hand experience. Neither of these authors gives you a rehash of other men's writings. If they write about the great nature-spirits that can be seen in the valleys of lonely Connemara, or upon the green and purple heather-covered mountains of the Highlands, you may be sure they write about something they have seen with their own eyes.

Both men have seen and felt and experienced the things they describe. Both have the gift of vivid imagery* that enables them to pass on what they have seen, if only in reduced terms. A.E. once told me that he had seen these forms of the Children of the Great Mother long before he wrote about or painted them. He was soaked with their influence. He wrote:

> He had journeyed on and on over an earth rich with lakes and woods, misty with light, over mountains that in the evening sun seemed to ascend in flame. *They* were calling to him to become one with them. It was then that he first felt that their beauty was transparent. Some

* The Colonel seemed not to realize that this same gift of imagery was also his. He was touched by the same genius, the same daemon, that had overshadowed both Blackwood and A.E.

Being, remote yet intimate, peered at him from the depths of Air. The apparitions of light, cloud, mountain and wood underwent a transfiguration into life of a vaster remoter self or overself to his own being. (*The Avatars*, p. 2.)

Here A.E. is writing about that fountain out of Hecate, Ireland. Fechner not many years earlier had touched upon the same sources of power in middle Europe:

On a certain morning I went out for a walk. The fields were green, the birds sang, and here and there a man appeared; a light as of transfiguration lay on all things. It was only a little bit of earth, one moment of her existence, yet my look embraced her more and more. It seemed to me that not only was she beautiful, but that she was an angel in very fact. So rich and flower-like, yet going around in the skies so firmly and at one with herself, turning her whole living face to Heaven and carrying me with her into that Heaven. I asked myself how the opinions of men could ever have spun themselves away from life so far as to deem the earth just a dry clod, and seek for angels in the emptiness in the sky. But such an experience as this passes for fantastic among those who have not felt her kiss. The earth is a globular body that may be found in mineralogical cabinets. (James, *A Pluralistic Universe*, Chapter 4, 'Concerning Fechner'.)

All the world is a fountain out of Hecate for those who have the vision of the Mysteries. The vision may come in a beechwood on the flint-strewn Chilterns, or on the craggy cliffs of Devon and Cornwall, on the Tor at Glastonbury or in foggy London,* no matter. Using what has been taught to you in these chapters you can recover all the power and ecstasy of first experience. With practice you can build in a crowded city a 'fountain out of Hecate' so strong that even modern civilization cannot orphan you out of the Magna Mater. In that fountain you can bathe in the living waters of life.

Much of A.E.'s work was done in dirty Dublin. Yet how many his writings rendered capable of self-initiation into a nature mysticism it is impossible even to guess at. But many drank at his 'fountain' and found the waters pure and clear. For Hecate is the World Soul, the Mother of Souls, the Wheel of Ever Becoming. A study of A.E.'s writing will show that he was well aware of the Chaldean Oracles and drew much of his symbolism from them. In

* This was written long before 'smokeless fuel' made London almost fog-free.

his essay 'The Architecture of Dream' he tells us that he touched memories hidden deep from us mortals in the bosom of the Great Mother, and how he did it: 'Sometimes I even speculate on a world interpenetrating ours where another sun is glowing, and other stars are shining over other woods, mountains, rivers, and another race of beings.' (Ibid, p. 96.) This is a mental picture which brought him much because he knew how to use it. There is no reason why, if you read it with care, you should not use it in a like manner. Or take, as did Elijah, A.E., and many others, the initiation into earth, water, fire and air when you are on the 'High Places'.

Such books as these are worthy of deep study through creative reading. They will throw much light on the subject of imagery, as you read them in the quiet of your room. Close your eyes and try to see those Shining Ones as did A.E. and Blackwood. Feel with them the flaming glories they knew at first hand and strive to realize with your own picture consciousness what this indescribable beauty must have meant to them. Be in sympathy with them, for sympathy in the sense of feeling with is the gate of understanding, which is the seventh gate that leads to the Throne of Binah and Saturn.

Let us return again to *The Centaur:*

> And watching him O'Malley felt that this loosening portion of himself ... began to grow and spread. Within some ancient fold of earth's dream consciousness they both lay caught. In some mighty dream of Her Planetary Spirit, dim, immense, slow-moving, they played their parts of wonder. He was conscious of a sudden wild inclination to use his own arms and legs in a way he had never known before, but which felt familiar. The balance and adjustment of his physical frame sought to shift and alter; neck and shoulders surged forward, there came a prickling in the loins, a rising of the back, a thrusting up and outwards of the chest. He felt that something grew within him with a power that sought to impel or drive him in advance and out across the world at a terrific gait. His hearing became intensely acute. While his body moved ordinarily, he knew that a part of him that was not body moved ... otherwise. That he neither walked nor ran, nor stepped upon two feet, but ... galloped. The motion proclaimed his kin with the flying shapes upon the hill, he cantered ... the experience lasted but a minute, this swift, free motion of the escaping Double.

If Sagittarius is the sign rising on the ascendant at your birth, if you have been haunted by dreams of a glorious galloping freedom, of chasing across wide sweeping purple hills lighted only by a star-crowned darkness, if you have felt in moments of ecstasy that you were not a man on a horse, but a manhorse, then you too have entered the realms of the Soul of the Great Mother.

Blackwood has given many a soul whose waking life is a weary grind, the power to know something of the glory of the silver stars, the winds of night and the fierce joy of galloping free upon the world's wide way.

Build the Mystery sign of Mutable Fire, ruled by Jupiter, the thunderbolt-hurling god of the wide spaces. The gifts of the gods to Sagittarians include high spirits, a love of the outdoors, restlessness, and a love of travelling to far-off places, physically and astrally ...

Such imagery will open for you the gate leading to the Garden of the Temple of the Mother. You may stay in this garden and in it dwell her astral star-bright children. But if you wish to see and serve the gods, then you must push deeper into the centre of the garden until you come to an avenue of ram-headed sphinxes, the roadway of the gods.

In front of you, you will see a high Pylon Gate in which is a narrow door. As you stand in front of it a priest of Horus and a priest of Anpu will appear. They are you, and you are they, for are you not the guardian of your own inner door? Ask these priests for the Word that will admit you to Her Temple. Ask permission to knock upon the door. Here you may wear the sacred dress, and dance the sacred dances, be able to say: 'I have seen the empty sanctuary.'

There is no power outside yourself that can make you stay without the Pylon Gate if you want the Mysteries with all your heart. In his book *Suggestion and Auto-Suggestion* Baudouin writes: 'Still more slowly comes the recognition that in reflective auto-suggestion scientifically applied, we have the faith that can move a mountain.'

In worlds that are mental or even spiritual as well as in this physical world, Baudouin's dictum holds good. Reflective auto-suggestion scientifically applied during the course of your creative reading will take you, guided by Anubis Within who Opens the Way, through the narrow door into the Outer Court of the Temple set within the garden lying deep within an ancient fold of the dream consciousness of the Magna Mater, and also of yourself.

November 1937 to April 1938

9.

The Children of the Great Mother

Part 1: The Gods of the Mysteries

In these articles an attempt will be made to show what the gods of
a Mystery tradition meant to their initiated servers who, being
educated men and women, had a practical working knowledge of
the techniques used by their particular school or schools.

Each of these cycles or systems of gods had their own Mystery
cult, in most of which there were two types of priests. The
ordinary priesthood whose members *performed* the exoteric
rituals, and the initiated priests, selected from the ranks of the
ordinary priesthood, who were taught to *work* both the exoteric
and the esoteric rites. Here the student should appreciate the fact
that the terms to *perform* and to *work* are not synonymous, and
that the difference between them is a clue to the difference that
existed in the past between those priests who served the God in
his earthly temple and the initiated priests who worked the rites
in 'The Temple Not Made With Hands'.

Except in Greece after 600 BC, education was given as a rule
only in connection with a temple. The civil servants of Egypt and
Babylonia, and possibly elsewhere, were almost to a man
educated, as were the governors, princes, priests and queens.
Later when the priesthood fell into disrepute and the temple
Mysteries decayed, the training of initiates in the working of the
rites and ceremonies was carried out in secular schools which
were formed eventually into secret brotherhoods. The school of
Pythagoras is an example of this. The societies formed by the
Orphikoi under cover of the official worship of Dionysius, and
the schools of the Christian and pre-Christian Gnosticism in
Syria and Egypt are examples of hieratic and secular attempts to
supplement the inadequate pabulum given by official and state
religions when in a degenerate condition.

In the widely differing cults of Mithras, Isis and Serapis we have examples of a dying religion taking on a new life, sometimes with a new name and a more up-to-date system of external organization. At the same time it should be noted that these cults as a rule retained much of that inner knowledge and technique which enabled their trained and initiated members to work the rites in their new form, often in a new country.

Mithraism died in its own land with the conquests of Alexander, and then, with Mithras as its divine Saviour with a new role and a new message it flourished in Asia Minor and Europe for nearly a thousand years.

Isis died in Egypt but was reborn in orthodox Christianity as the Virgin Mary, Queen of Heaven. It could be said that the Great Gods never die. Their names may change, the method of using that power which they represent may change, and the new message their priesthoods bring may be different in form and substance, but the Great Gods are eternal. So too, in another way, live on the Lesser Gods, the Heroes, and those earthly teachers who follow in the train of the cosmic gods. Man, even if he follows only in the rear of this great procession, is yet a child of the aeon; he is not ephemeral as some seem to think.

It may be said that the secrets of the Mysteries have been so well kept that little or nothing has come down to us. This objection is a fair one, but it can be explained. The secrecy to which initiates were pledged forbade those who knew to write the inner history of the cults to which they belonged, and rendered it impossible for those who did not know to divulge the inner teachings. Another point is that in addition to destroying the temples and the literature of the Mysteries the Christian writers misrepresented the Mystery cults in such a way that one is sometimes compelled to question how they ever exercised such a potent spell on ancient religious minds.

Consider how great some of these minds were from this hymn of a little-known writer, Cleanthes:

Lead me, Oh Zeus, and lead me, Destiny.
Whither ordained is by your decree.
I'll follow doubting not, or if with will,
Recreant I falter yet I shall follow still.

(Matheson's trans. in Bevan,
Later Greek Religion, p. 15.)

With all the advantages of modern science and education, few could express themselves more clearly or more beautifully.

It is true that the secret of the Mysteries is not known to historians, or even to men of such vast knowledge as the author of *The Golden Bough*. Again, the explanation is simple. History deals with facts, with the things of the age that is under consideration. The secrets of the Mysteries are not concerned with facts, symbols, dogmas or teachings. They cannot be betrayed because they concern a mode of consciousness. This secret has been shouted from the housetops since man became a thinking, tool-using animal, yet it still remains a mystery.

'Behold, I show you a mystery,' said one of the founders of Christianity and his empty hands showed *no thing*. The empty shrine is the Supreme Mystery of the Mysteries; it cannot be betrayed because it is a way of thinking, a *no-thing-ness*.

The acquiring of the technique of *no-thing-ness* is the subject-matter of the Mysteries, yet that technique is not a secret. Pelmanism is a modern adaptation of an ancient Mystery usage which was taught in the Lotus Court of the Mystery Temples of Isis. Yet the Isian Mysteria have not been divulged. Apuleius gives a long account of his initiation and adds, 'Behold, I have told you things of which, although you have heard them, you cannot know the meaning.'

The clue is this: initiation is *no thing*, it is an experience which takes place neither in *time* nor *space*. Consider this saying: 'The Sun is in the macrocosm what Reason is in the microcosm.' This is an ancient word picture of a truth that can be interpreted in a less obvious manner when meditated upon by those who realize the relationship between Macroprosopos and Microprosopos as shown upon the Tree of Life.

Once the principles governing the methods of training used in the Western Tradition have been grasped, it is fairly easy to compare, to analyse and to classify the technique that is used in schools of another tradition. For example, the principles that govern the technique that is used in India, Persia and Thibet are *au fond* the same as those that govern the Yoga of the West, though the techniques are in themselves utterly different.

A highly trained initiate of the West can grasp the core of the technique of almost any Eastern system. This however does not mean that such a one can either practise or use a technique that is foreign to his own. Usually and for good reasons he leaves Eastern Yoga severely alone.

At the back of each of the older Mystery systems is a group mind and behind that group mind is the group soul of the nation or the epoch during which it flourished. If in the past a student has been a member of, say, the cult of Hathor at Denderah in South Egypt, he will be able by means of the technique that is taught him today in a school of the Western Tradition that is working under authority in London, to project himself into the past. His knowledge of the principles taught in this age will enable him to recover from within himself when back in the astral form of The Temple of the Denderah that was built more than three thousand years ago, the principles and the methods that were taught him in that long forgotten past life.

He can then work a ritual of the cult of Hathor for he is still a member of that ancient group mind which is even today a living integral portion of the group soul of Mother Earth. He picks up the trail first within himself, then within Nature's magical memory, and then he very gently draws up from the deeps a forgotten knowledge. This is education in the true sense of drawing forth from within.

But when the initiate strives to pass into a group mind that is alien and into a culture that is also alien he will find that though he may understand it, he can neither practise nor use the technique he is examining. He is not a member of this group mind; he is alien to it; he is one of the profane.

He must as a beginner take his initiation into this, to him, new tradition. This is the reason why so few Europeans are able to use the great Eastern traditions of China, Thibet and India. These do not come naturally to them, and a fresh start has to be made. The would-be initiate has to be vouched for and trained by one who is a competent master in that particular tradition.

Again you will seldom find that foreigners (even Europeans) can take their full training in schools working with the English group soul. They can be trained up to a point in meditation, in psychology, and in the philosophy and comparative methods of the Mysteries. But when it comes to team work in a ritual it will be found -as a rule- that their practical work is weak. There are exceptions to this rule, plenty of them, but it can, by experience, be proved to be a useful practical guide, and it is almost infallible when dealing with the immature.

The rulers of the group minds described above are the gods and the goddesses of the various cults, the divine Children of the Great Mother. And if these results of practical work which have been set forth above are of universal application, as it is thought they are, then it will be wiser – in the case of beginners – to stick to the Divine Formulations that belong to the tradition into which one has been born. One may take it for granted that the Lords of Karma know what is good for each of us, and place us where best we can profit from the experiences that must come from environment.

If you would drink in the Initiatory Rites of the Cold Waters that flow from the Lake of Memory, remember the Guardians thereof, for these are the great Race Angels of the Orphic Tablet. They will know 'who thou art and whence thou art and what thy city is', when thou comest to revive 'the memory of the Beginnings'.

Build clearly the images that rise into your mind as you brood in meditation upon this translation of the Orphic Tablet:

Thou shalt find on the left of the House of Hades a Well-spring,
And by the side thereof standing a white cypress.
To this Well-spring approach not near.
But thou shalt find another by the Lake of Memory,
Cold water flowing forth, and there are Guardians before it.
Say: 'I am a child of Earth and of Starry Heaven;
But my race is of Heaven (alone). This ye know yourselves.
And lo, I am parched with thirst and I perish. Give me quickly
The cold water flowing forth from the Lake of Memory'.
And of themselves they will give thee to drink from the holy Well-spring,
And thereafter among the other Heroes thou shalt have lordship.

(*The Flaming Door*, Merry, p. 159)

The House of Hades is not hell as the untaught of today imagine. It is the bright shining land to which the Celtic heroes voyaged in the *glass* boat of initiation. It is the inner world that lies behind the dark door of the temple sanctuary. The Guardians are the Gods or Race Angels, and the well is in your own soul which is also in the Lake of the Memory of the Earth Mother.

After drinking you may look for the moon in the crystal cup of pure water. Can you build these images in reverie? Try the experiment.

Part 2:   In the Temples of the Gods of Wisdom

'Celui qui a de l'imagination sans érudition a des alles et n'a pas des pieds.'

(Joubert)

In the reformulation of an ancient tradition a great deal of historical research has to be carried out in order to build that bony skeleton upon which all the rest has to fit.

It is often thought that when an adept returns to earth from the unseen realms of Hu (the once all potent Divine Lord of Western Celtic mythology) in order to take up his work in the Temple of Ceridwen – that is, in the realms of the soul of this earth-world, he has merely to open up his own communications with the Masters of Wisdom who are on the Inner Planes, and then a School of Initiation springs into being and also into function as Athene sprang fully armed with a great shout from the head of Zeus.

The Masters of Wisdom from the realms of Hu provide the adept with imagination, and they give him at the same time the winged cup of crystal that contains inspiration. But this is not enough. The adept has to use his own feet in order to crawl among the dusty and forgotten records of the past for the traditional forms into which the contents of the winged crystal cup have to be poured. And the quotation at the head of this Chapter is an exact description of the situation of any leader who, relying on imagination alone, and lacking erudition, gives his group emotional stimuli only.

This type of being is well suited to the pacific and, alas, often soporific atmosphere of an 'uplift' society, where all that is required is a gentle method of consoling old ladies of both sexes.

But an occult society in function, with the terminals of its contacts well plugged home in the realms of both the 'Here' and the 'Yonder', is seldom pacific and even more rarely soporific. Both the society and its members have to be strong in body and soul to stand the strain of the forces that flow through them. There has to be an adequate technique or the force will disrupt both the society and its members. In simple terms this means that such a society must have an outer court for teaching and training, and an inner court to carry on the work of initiation. It is the formation and functioning of the outer court that calls for erudition.

In the Inner Group the members look inward and prepare in silent meditation for the brewing of the 'Three Drops' of wisdom distilled in the seething cauldron of Keredwen. But when the 'Little Gwion' has licked his scalded fingers and become inspired thereby, he must look outwards if he is to escape the furious pursuit of the Goddess and bring his imagination to fruition by means of his hard-won erudition.

In the temples of the Gods of Wisdom there are many books, all with one thing in common: they deal with something that comes from experience, not argument, and this experience comes through nature to man who is her child. The first and most important book of all is the Book of Nature. It lies, ever open, on the altar of the material universe. Its secrets are not written on its golden pages but are hidden so that he who runs may not read. You must take it a little at a time, and visualize in quiet meditation; you must read between the lines to understand.

Plutarch in his *Isis et Osiris* gives a hint of this. He is writing about Anubis, a Prince of the West, the god who leads the dead through the Gates of Death and across the desert to the Halls of Osiris, and who also takes the initiate through the Portal of Initiation, which is always situated in the West. Plutarch goes on to tell us that: 'By Anubis they understand the horizontal circle which divides the invisible [Nephthys] from the visible [Isis]; as the circle touches equally upon the confines of both light and darkness, it may be looked on as common to both.'

Remember here that there is a horizon of consciousness as well as one on the physical level. In terms of the former the titles of Anubis give an explanation of his role. He is called *Up-Uatu* or the Opener of the Ways, and also *Sekhem em Pet* or the Power in Heaven, and he is mentioned as having two faces, one black as night and the other golden as the day.

Plutarch goes on to say that Osiris, the Lord of Initiation, is 'the Common Reason which pervades the superior and inferior regions of the Universe', and adds that another name for it is Anubis or Hermanubis, the first name expressing relationship to the superior, and the latter to the inferior world. Both these worlds exist only in terms of consciousness and have nothing to do with solar light or terrestrial darkness. They become manifest as stages of initiation. (See Budge, *From Fetish to God*, p. 213.)

Turning to the Celtic Mysteries we find that Hu represents the power and the glory of the spiritual world, and is analogous to Osiris. His Shakti was Keredwen, the Soul of this Universe, and she is as the Twin Goddesses Isis and Nephthys. Like Osiris, Hu is the directing principle of the whole universe. Whilst Keredwen in her dual Isis-Nephthys role is the power of the light and dark wisdom or vision. Again these things pertain to planes of consciousness other than the physical.

Anubis is the guide into these dual realms of Isis and Nephthys, but he is also Osiris, and there is a white Osiris and a black Osiris just as there are the Christs of Evil as well as the Christs of Good. Hu, wearing the gold yoke of the sun and the girdle of the Iris of the World, accompanied the human being when he was united with the 'power of vision', out of the Depths and into the Light. (Merry, *The Flaming Door*, p. 150.)

Hu unveils himself gradually just as in the Egyptian Mysteries of initiation and death the Dark Anubis gives way to the Golden Anubis. When the sanctuary is reached the guide Anubis becomes Horus the Child of the Sun. Remember that Anubis was indeed the first-born son of Osiris, it is he who sits upon the throne of the east as his Father, with his Twin Mothers standing behind him.*

Here we have the eternal principle of all things that are in manifestation, a duality that is polarity. We see this clearly shown to us in the symbolism of Osiris/Anubis, Isis/Nephthys and Hu the Golden and the Dark with Keredwen is her aspects of the Fruitful Mother and the Dark Giantess. In the sanctuary the One becomes Two and the Two become Four.

The Law of Polarity is the first thing you learn from the Book of Nature. That which is solitary is barren (as Nephthys was to her husband Set). This is true of Gods and Man alike. It is also true of societies. There must be an outer and an inner, a hidden teaching and a revealed teaching.

Having studied the Book of Nature we may turn to the book that is hidden within the heart of man, and one even more difficult to read than the former. Today we call it the Book of Life, but the ancients knew it as the Book of Thoth. We are told that this book was hidden in the Nile at Coptos in an iron box within which was a succession of boxes of bronze, sycamore, ivory, ebony, gold and silver. Snakes and scorpions guarded it. Where it was, there was Light, where it was not, there was Darkness. This becomes clear only if we remember that for the

---

* This is the meaning of 'All the Gods are one God and all the Goddesses are one Goddess.'

ancients there were earthly, heavenly and human gods. There was
an earthly Nile, a heavenly Nile and a Nile within the human
aura. As will be explained later the ancients had a system of yoga
not unlike that of India. (Griffith, *Stories of the High Priestess of
Memphis*, p. 21.)

All the old Mystery rites are hidden in the Memory of Nature,
that is in the Heavenly Nile. But there is also a Sea of Coptos
deep in the hereditary memory of many alive today. But this kind
of memory pertains to the soul and spirit of man, and has nothing
to do with his physical descent. There are many living today who
have in the past served at the many altars of the ancient world. If
they can discover the hidden box containing the Book as it lies
deep within their subconscious memory, then sooner or later they
will discover the heavenly counterpart of that book. Some have
discovered it already. There is an interesting book by Naomi
Mitchison called *The Corn King and the Spring Queen*.
Obviously it is to a great extent an uprush of subconscious
memories. The author had 'found her box in the Sea of Coptos'
and mankind is the richer for this book. The same can be said for
Joan Grant's *The Winged Pharoah*. Again the prose of A.E. and
the poetry of W. B. Yeats leave one impressed by the fact that
something very old and wise is peeping at us from the pages of
these gifted writers.

Such books have a value for the trained and careful reader.
They set him tugging gently and patiently at the delicate tendrils
of his own subconscious memories, and help him to untangle
those memories from past lives and draw them up into waking
consciousness. They are easy to recognize for it is the great
sorrows and tragedies of life that burn themselves into the soul's
memory, and when they come they often release a flood of
emotion and fear that can be very painful. By this they can be
recognized.

The systems used in the Mysteries for reading the records of
Thoth have come down to us only in fragments, and much has to
be deduced from practical experience. But in some countries the
systems have come down almost uninjured. Tibet, India, Burma
and China have many and varied ways of development that are
coeval with the lost and shattered systems of Egypt, Chaldea and
Syria. Under the generic title of Eastern Yoga the student will
find much that throws light on these lost Mediterranean systems.
For instance a little knowledge of yoga would be enough to give
one a comprehension of the breathing and intoning that must

have been used by the initiate working the Mithraic ritual given in Mead's *Echoes from the Gnosis*, Vol. 6. It may also lead through practical work to a release of knowledge concerning these systems from the subconscious memory of the race. This knowledge is not the same as belief ... it reaches beyond facts and exchanges belief for knowledge. The Gnostic is called by this name because he *knows*, and in knowing he discards believing. He has no *credos* in these matters.

Part 3

The initiate of one system can understand without much difficulty the system of another race. 'All the Gods are one God and all the Goddesses are One Goddess and there is one Illuminator.' The names and methods may vary, but the realities behind the Veil do not vary because they are ageless, timeless and perfect in their way of working; they are always the same. The ever-changing factor is man's conception of these forces and the mental images he builds in order to reach out to them.

Popular ideology after centuries of narrow teaching, misconception and misinterpretation is singularly childish, while the wiser teachings of the modern Greek scholars have been almost unheeded. G. Murray has written in his edition of *Hippolytus of Euripides:* 'The Aphrodite of Euripides' actual belief was almost certainly not what we should call a goddess, but rather a force of Nature. To deny her existence you would have to say "there is no such thing" and that would be a denial of obvious facts.'

Here a great principle had been laid out. But if Professor Murray had also made it clear that in the heart of every man there dwells this potent natural force personified by the ancients as Aphrodite, and that this Aphrodite within forms a link with its parent nature force that is without, by means of the image of a perfect woman, then his statement would have been a lot more comprehensive.

The form which the Aphrodite Force takes in Greece is not the same as that which her counterpart Isis takes in Egypt; nor is the latter the same as that of Isis of Nubia. These varying forms, for their initiates, act as a link between the subjective Aphrodite of the microcosms and the objective Aphrodite of the macrocosm. The forces within and without man do not vary. Only the images that link them vary. Yet the same initiate when trained can get results from all three forms alike when working on the astro-mental plane, or subjectively on the astro-mental sphere of consciousness.

For the trained initiate these forms are not the Goddess any more than the tap which you turn on with your hand is the hot water that fills your bath. The Christian uses the image of Jesus to touch the Cosmic Christ Force, the ancient Egyptian used the image of Osiris to bring him into touch with that same great spiritual being. But though the initiate can understand the techniques of another system, it does not mean that he is competent to *work* that system. To do that he must take initiation into that tradition and become conditioned to its symbolism. This is a point that many junior European initiates of Eastern systems forget.

Each nation has a group soul and a group mind. The group mind is the gateway to the group soul, and that group soul supplies the voltage that lights the altar lamps of that tradition. It is true that there is a Common Group Soul to all humanity; you can, and must, touch it if any system is to work for you with power. But this does not give you the right of entry into the system of another nation. You must be tested, trained, conditioned and vouched for by an initiate of that tradition. This explains why the European Jew is not at home in a Celtic or Nordic system; it is his traditional way of thinking, not the fact that he is a Jew, that isolates him.

Yoga was not unknown to the Egyptians, as the directions given in the tale of Setne Khamuas by the priest to Ne-Nefer-Ka-Ptah clearly show:

The Book of Thoth is in the midst of the Sea of Coptos [near Luxor] in a box of iron. In the box of iron is a box of bronze, in the box of bronze is a box of Kete-wood, in the box of Kete-wood is a box of ivory and ebony, and in the box of ivory and ebony is a box of silver wherein is a box of gold, and in here is the book, there being an endless snake about the box. (Griffith, *Stories of the High Priests of Memphis*, p. 21.)

The following notes by Griffith will show how impossible it is to think of these stories as dealing with physical events.

1. 'The Sea of Coptos.' It takes three days and three nights to row from the shore to the middle of the Sea of Coptos, and the 'Sea' comprised one schoenus (six miles) of ground swarming with reptiles

surrounding the Book of Thoth. Its name and its size suggest the Red Sea which was generally approached from Egypt by the Coptos road; but the identification is impossible since it is evident from the narrative that the shore was close to the city of Coptos, and that a ship could be easily brought to it from the Nile. More probably the 'Sea of Coptos' was a sacred lake, perhaps part of the temple grounds, magically extended when the safety of the book was in question.

2. The endless snake is the snake of Zt, meaning the Snake of Eternity.

3. In Egyptian the order of the boxes is given in reverse of that which appears above.

The geography given here is impossible, but the snake of Zt is a clue, so are the three days and nights spent rowing. In the Temptation in the Wilderness Jesus was taken up to a high mountain and shown all the kingdoms of the world. This is also an impossibility, physically, but psychologically it is possible. The expression 'going up into a high mountain' in the Ancient Mysteries means going into a trance-like state of meditation, another hint which must be taken into consideration with the three days and nights. It is clear that the journey of Ne-Nefer-Ka-Ptah to the Sea of Coptos was a psychological or magical experiment dealing solely with an inner plane journey.

For those conditioned to think in symbols there is more than appears to the eye in this story, for it is about the two most famous magicians in ancient Egypt, Ne-Nefer-Ka-Ptah, and Kha-Em-Uas, and it explains much about clairvoyance and the methods used in that time. It is also a fine example of the misleading methods, used in giving out hidden teachings, of which the ancients were so fond. We have here a direction for finding the lotus centre in the human body that is ruled by the God of Wisdom. The Nile equates with the human spine, and Thoth is the Lord of Daath or Understanding. It was at Coptos that Isis cut off a lock of her hair when she heard that Osiris had been murdered. The Daath centre is at the nape of the neck in the human aura. That was formerly why the priest's stole had a cross at this point.

Kundalini, the coiled serpent, is the guardian of this knowledge in the symbolism and She, the Goddess of cosmic magical knowledge, here appears as the snake of Zt coiled about the box, or the base of the spine, the lotus-like source of magical power within the microcosm.

The story of Kha-Em-Uas can be seen merely as a story, but it is also a mine of information regarding the use made of esoteric knowledge at that time, much of which is still contained in the Book of the Dead. This name is really Pert-Em-Hru, the Coming Forth by Day, or Manifested in the Light. However, the knowledge was also meant for the living as well as the dead. It contains formulae which were intended to enable the deceased to travel where he would. It was by the use of such spells that Ne-Nefer-Ka-Ptah succeeded in bringing the ghosts of his wife and child to his own tomb in Memphis while their bodies remained at Coptos.

In *The Tibetan Book of the Dead* by Dr Evans-Wentz, p. 25, there is this significant remark: 'Such priestly guiding of the deceased spirit is for the laity alone, for the lamas themselves, having been trained in the doctrines of the Bardo Thodol know the right path at death and need no guidance.' The Egyptian Book of the Dead is very similar to the Bardo Thodol and Evans-Wentz remarks that 'both treatises alike [are] no more than guide books for the traveller beyond death'. It is interesting to know that this eminent author studied the ancient funeral lore of Egypt for three years prior to his visit to Tibet. He is looked on as the greatest living authority on this subject and his book is published by the Oxford University Press.

Both these books, the Pert-Em-Hru and the Bardo Thodol, clearly deal with initiation. Now initiation used to be looked upon as being carried out by dramatic rituals rather like the Mystery plays of the medieval Church. In the lesser grades of the Mysteries of Isis, Osiris, Mithras and the pre-Christian Gnosticism of Syria and Babylonia this was probably the case. But is was only in the lower grades of these Mysteries and in the primitive nature-cults that dramatized action was used to induce exaltation of consciousness by means of dancing and sympathetic magic.

In the higher grades and in the more advanced systems this method of ritual action was abandoned. The initiate was taught how to awaken the God within himself. Then in a purely mental drama which was carried out in the 'Temple Not Made With Hands', the Thoth within was connected consciously with the Universal Mind the Ancient Egyptians knew as the Lord Tehuti. Usually these grades were given in a form of very light trance which required only the conscious stilling of bodily senses and the awakening of the initiate's consciousness on the inner levels. But in the higher grades the initiation was given in a very deep trance, a condition so deep it resembled death, and could last up to three days in the tomb, or as long as three days and three nights in the belly of a whale!

In many cases this initiation had to be given by means of the hypnotic power of the presiding hierophant. But if the candidate was sufficiently developed he could cast himself into trance in the same manner. When the candidate was in this condition, those in whose care his body remained checked and followed his experiences in the inner world, the domain of the Anubis Within.

If the student will experiment patiently with the visualizing of these pictures, and the invocation of the ancient names given to him in this chapter, much will become clear and real to him that can only be guessed at by the neophytes. The ordinary and the casual reader will not understand this mass of picture symbolism and the obscure references made to the ancient gods and goddesses, and will deem them to be unreal. So they are, and so they will remain, for him. These things are not real and actual in any sense of those two words for the untrained mind. The initiate has to be conditioned to his symbols through a conscious experience of their powers.

The aim here is the creating within the soul of the untrained a great store of images. These images if brooded on for a few minutes as they are being read will seed the unconscious mind and make of it a rich and fruitful source for future work. The student must tend this richness as if it were a fertile field, which indeed it is, for within each one of us there is a divine husbandman whose task it is to till the soil of the mind and to reap from it a golden harvest.

Let us think back to the Lord Tehuti, the Lord of the Moon Cave, whom the Chaldeans called Zinn, the Lord of the Moon Wisdom. He is also the Lord of the Inner Human Wisdom; he is Merlin in his sea cave by the still waters of the summer sea that flow and ebb over the lost lands of Lyonesse. The blue cloak of this Watcher can still be seen on the hidden shores of the mind. The silver badge of his Shakti, whom men call Morgan Le Fay is the full moon low in the south east, throwing a long bar of silver light across the waves to the feet of the silent Watcher at the entrance to the Moon Cave. A figure seated on a sacred stool, it is motionless, and behind it with hands placed upon its shoulders stand two female figures robed in white and silver, one crowned with the crescent and the other with a silver star.

Merlin draws all his power through these two priestesses; he loses his rule and his power when he allows the silver priestess to usurp his divine authority, and thus Merlin fell. If we go back into Egyptian mythology we find the same warning in the tale of Isis and Ra. For the silver-footed Isis, by her craft, obtained the secret name of the great sun-god, and by so doing became possessed of his power and so his master. Beware the mastery of the silver priestess; rule *your own* subconscious mind.

Just myth and legend you may say, and with truth. But the myths and legends of this world are the earthly shadow of a happening in the shining land of the gods in the uppermost West. Listen to the song of the fairy maid who sang to Connla:

It will guard thee gentle Connla of the flowing golden hair.
It will guard thee from the druids, from the demons of the air.
My crystal boat will guard thee till we reach the western shore,
Where thou and I in love and joy shall live for ever more.

(Joyce, *Old Celtic Romances.)*

Connla forsook all to follow the fairy maiden, springing into the boat in which she stood. The King and his people watched as their prince sailed away over the bright sea to the Lands of the West. Some day this same call may well come to you, and then it is all or nothing. Death, damnation, hell and purgatory mean little to the one who can sit in that Moon Cave whither his fairy Shakti has brought him.

You are not meant to understand these pictures. If you do understand them, then the writer has failed in his purpose. They are meant to be incubated in the depths of your subconscious mind. Some day, perhaps under the stress of great love, hate or adoration, the inner fountains of your subliminal life will open up. The images that you have worked with for so long will spring into life full blown, for better or worse in your conscious life. Will you, as the lord of the Moon Wisdom, as the initiated Tehuti, use them, or will they use *you*? Knowledge is a two-edged sword.

Part 4

In the last section reference was made to a certain Kha-Em-Uas, whose statue was until recently in the Southern Egyptian Gallery of the British Museum. The name is sometimes spelt as Khamuas or Kha-m-uas. He is also called Setne or Sethon, a corruption of Sem, a sacerdotal title.

He was the son of Rameses II and his Queen Isis-Nefert, and was born about 1300 BC and died in 1246 BC some ten years before his father. He was a man of great learning. In his youth he was a soldier, later he became a priest, and then a High Priest of Ptah, and finally the head of the whole Egyptian hierarchy of his time. He was the most notable of the progeny of Rameses II.

His name has the meaning of 'Manifestation in Thebes' indicating that he was born in the southern capital, but he lived most of his life in Memphis and died there, being buried near the Great Pyramid. Had he outlived his father it is probable that he would have become Pharoah. In the Egyptian legends he played a part similar to that which Merlin played in later centuries in the medieval tales of the Round Table. There is a strange likeness in the characters of these two men.

In order to visualize the image of this great initiate more clearly, the reader is advised to buy the two photos of his statue published by the British Museum. If he can persuade the authorities who have hidden this statue in some inaccessible cellar to let him see it, so much the better, for the best contact is a personal one. There is great magnetic power in this statue.

For those not likely to see it, here is a description taken from the British Museum Guide of 1909, page 170.

> Flint agglomerate statue of Kha-em-Uaset ... The deceased wears a heavy short wig and a tunic, and holds to his sides with his arms two standards. That on the right was surmounted by a mummied form and a figure of the prince, that on the left by an object which appears to represent the box which held the head of Osiris at Abydos. In front of this object are two Uraei ... the height of the statue including the base is 4 feet 8 inches ...*

The following may also prove helpful to the building of your visualization. On page 69 of the 1930 General Guide to the Egyptian Collection in the museum we find the following:

> Another is the extraordinarily eerie tale (of a much later date) preserved in a demotic papyrus, of the magician Setme Khamuas (historically a son of Rameses II) who went down into a tomb to obtain a book of magic reported to be in it. Khamuas plays draughts with the ghosts, the stake being the precious book.

* This statue is still on display, though now in the North Gallery, the number 947 still applies and the photos are still available.

The life story of this Magus is well told by Griffith, in his now rare book *Stories of the High Priests of Memphis*, and he gives this tale in full in Chapter 11 under the heading of 'The Tale of Khamuas and Ne-Nefer-Ka-Ptah'.

As the object of these articles is to give the reader who is prepared to spend the time and trouble the chance of experiencing the ancient Mystery teaching by experimenting for himself, a few notes on the ways of thought habitual to the initiates of that time will first be given. They will be followed by a short account of the tale, which the reader should carefully visualize.

We know from historical research that the Egyptian Mysteries were divided into two grades. In the first grade were the feminine Mysteries such as those of Isis, Hathor, Mut and Sekmet. These particular cults dealt mainly with the developing of mediums and mediumship, especially in the young girls, who as the virgins of the Temple were used for psychic work, and who later became the priestly seeresses. These latter were often married into the priesthood, or if they had little ability, married to laymen selected by the Temple Authorities. A study of the funeral texts in the British Museum makes this theory almost conclusive.

In these Lesser Mysteries the phenomena, both mental and physical, were much the same as those now found in the Spiritualist Society, which seek to awaken religion through the emotions. These Mysteries were not confined to women, but they offered a quick and easy development of the subconscious through the emotions, and for this reason attracted women with their finer sensibilities rather than men.

In addition in the outer forms of the Lesser Mysteries there were beautiful rituals that were combined with song, music and dance. Here every effort was made to stir up the emotional nature and the subconscious minds of the laity in order to produce a stirring religious atmosphere.

These festivals were usually held with reference to the moon periods. The symbolism was that of the moon, water and the form-giving, negative side of nature. Though the mother principle of the macrocosm was the object of this type of worship, those who worked these Lesser Mystery cults were the more highly trained priests and priestesses of the Greater Mysteries. The hierophants who ruled had to be members of that Order which had its colleges at 'The House of Net' whose Lord was Thoth, whose main Temple was in Hermopolis, the Greek name for the ancient city of Unnu. Thoth is the 'pacifier' of the gods, that is the ruler over the chiefs of all the Mystery schools, and the arbitrator in their disputes.

The Greater Mysteries were (in Egypt but not in Greece) masculine in their nature and the gods were male, and usually considered to be the Lords of Life or Judges in the world to come. Gods such as Osiris, Anubis, Imhotep, Khnosu, Tehuti and Thoth were human rulers or divine/human saviours. They also seemed to be names for an office that was held by many hierophants ruling over a cult that may have lasted for centuries. They were the earthly representatives of the Lords of the Fields of Aalu, the Egyptian Summerland. Like the box of Thoth in the Sea of Coptos, the Summerland was surrounded by a wall of iron, broken by several doors. Here, iron stands for the boundary of the material world, the limit of the sphere of sensation in man. These gods were represented in terms of the Qabalah, the microcosmic aspect of the Greater Mysteries; that is, they dealt with the salvation of mankind in a purely religious sense.

In addition the Greater Mysteries also had their macrocosmic aspect. Here the chief gods were Amen, the Hidden One, with a subsidiary form of Min, Ra, Ptah and Khnemu as Cosmic Creators. These gods had each of them a consort of Shakti. Amen had Mut, Ra had Rat, Ptah had Sekmet. It should be noted that the feminine consorts were often the destructive aspect of the male god. In India this same idea appears as the relationship between Shiva and Kali-Durga. Most of these gods are personifications of various elemental powers, and often the benevolent Mothers of the Lesser Mysteries become the terrible destroying Mothers of the Greater Mysteries.

Controlling all Mysteries, Gods, saviours, rulers and hierophants was the Lord of Khemmennu. He ruled over the colleges in which were trained the selected initiates from the Lesser and Greater Mysteries of all Egypt. His was the earthly Order that is behind all earthly Orders. Here were trained the hierophants skilled in magic, the Kheri Heb, or priest-magicians. This was indeed the 'House of the Net', and it is still behind each and every contacted Order that comes to birth on this plane. A hierophant had to pass through the 'Net', and take the higher grades out of the body before becoming a high priest. For the highest degrees are of grace, and not by rite.

Before we try to look at the experiences of this earthly life through the eyes of the Egyptian initiates, a caution must be given. No priest, no anthropologist will allow for one moment that most of the views which I am about to put before you are anything but fancy. I can offer no proof in their support. But if you will use them as working hypotheses, you will get results that will tend to show you that they are, in the main, very sound ideas. Keep an open mind and see for yourself.

The ancient initiates being both clairvoyant and clairaudient, when fully trained, were able to function almost at will in states of consciousness other than that of the purely material. For them the seen had become a much greater reflection of the unseen. They had sought for and found the world of causes that lies behind the world of effects. They knew the lore contained in the books of The Double House of Life, and had developed objective clairvoyance and subjective awareness. In the quiet of the great temples they sought to train even further, in order to develop highly sensitive nervous, vital, emotional and mental mechanisms. They were equally careful to develop a physical body capable of withstanding the extra strain that such psychic work involves.*

For the initiate of the ancient world the inner levels were fully objective on their own plane of consciousness. He knew from experience that within those levels definite forces functioned, and wove forms that could be seen. He raised himself to the required level by using the cult symbols with which he had been conditioned, yet he never forgot that the Kingdoms of the Heavens were within himself.

After this brief, and very inadequate, explanation of the ancient initiate's viewpoint we must return to the story of Khamuas, which we shall tell in such a manner that the reader may use it for his visualization.

The first half of the narrative has perished, but it has been conjectured by Griffith to be as follows:

Setne Khamuas, the son of Pharoah Usermara, being a diligent seeker after ancient and divine writings, was informed of the existence of a book which Thoth, the god of Letters, Science and Magic had written with his own hand. He learned that this book was to be found in the cemetery of Memphis, in the tomb of Ne-Nefer-

---

* Contrary to the usual ideas, psychics are rarely 'tall, thin, pale and with the look of a starving poet'! To withstand the immense pressure of their work they need strong, sturdy bodies capable of heavy physical exertion. This applies in particular to the higher degrees.

Ka-Ptah, the son of a Pharoah named Mer-Neb-Ptah. Having succeeded in identifying and entering the tomb accompanied by his brother Anherru, he finds there the ghosts of the owner, his wife [Ahure] and child, and lying by them the coveted book. But they refuse to give it up to him. Theirs it was, for they had paid for it with their earthly lives, and its magic power availed them in good stead even within the tomb. To dissuade Setne from taking the book Ahure tells him their sad story.

Here it is necessary to give an exact definition of what the word *magic* means when used by initiates, and the meaning given to it in these articles. It has been defined thus: 'Magic is the art of causing changes to take place in accordance with the will.' Using this conception of magic it becomes evident that Khamuas and Anherru visited that tomb by means of the magical process called, or rather miscalled today, astral projection. That is why they met the ghosts on a footing of equality and were refused possession of the book. Anyone with the necessary training can do the same kind of thing today, if they will but remember that initiation is an experience that takes place *not in time or space*, and if they realize the full implication of the definition of magic just given.

Ahure tells Khamuas and Anherru that her husband, the heir apparent Ne-Nefer-Ka-Ptah, was a man of great learning who, hearing about the Book of Thoth from an elderly priest, determined to get possession of it, having learned that it was hidden in the 'Sea of Coptos'.

Note carefully the following quotation:

And the priest said unto Ne-Nefer-Ka-Ptah, 'The book named is in the middle of the Sea of Coptos in a box of iron, this same being in a box of bronze, in a box of Kete-wood, this box of Kete-wood is in a box of ivory and ebony, in a box of silver in a box of gold, wherein is the Book; there being a schoenus of every kind of serpent, scorpion, and reptile round the box wherein is the Book.

Here Griffith points out that: 'in the description of the nesting of the boxes, it is evident that the scribe has reversed the order of things' (see Part Three of this article). But *has* the scribe been careless and made a mistake? Iron for the Egyptian as well as the Celtic initiate was a symbol for the material universe, and the human sphere of sensation. They, and we, know the physical body is within the etheric, and the etheric within the astral, the astral is within the mental and the mental within the spiritual, matter being the most condensed. This is a reversal of the way the ordinary man thinks about his so-called 'inner man'. So has the scribe indeed reversed the order of things? Build the Tree of Life in your aura, and see where the golden box of Tipareth comes. The Book of Thoth is in Daath, and Daath is the Revealer of the Secrets of the Universe. A tree mirrored in water is upside down; so too is the astral when reflected in matter. Here is the key to this story and indeed to the occult. That which is miscalled the inner is outside the outer!

The subtle is more extensive than the less subtle and it is less contracted. If you do not believe this and fail to see the implications of this apparent reversal of the normal way of thinking, then look carefully at the diagrams given in Dr Kilner's book *The Human Aura*.

You may ask what is the use of visualizing this story, and trying to unravel its subtleties, what will you, in the twentieth century get out of these ancient tales of Khamuas? The answer is simple: direct contact with the minds of the greatest magicians of ancient Egypt, Ka-Em-Uas, and Ne-Nefer-Ka-Ptah.

Part 5

In the previous chapter the first part of the encounter between the two magicians was begun, and the story of the finding of the Book of Thoth was briefly summarized. The first part of the story dealing with the finding of the book and the deaths of the magician's wife and child, and his own subsequent suicide by jumping into the Nile is of no great importance to the elementary student. But it contains much that is important to the advanced student for it hints at dangers of which they should become aware when travelling these ancient by-ways. Such an awareness is often brought about by unpleasant experiences in the twilight realms of Anubis, realms that have already been described in these articles in terms of ancient symbolism that gives right of way through them, and, more importantly, the right of return.

Some students think they can neglect the technique of the return journey, but for such the price is paid in growing ill health both psychic and physical. Let us return to the story.

Ahure the wife begs Khamuas to leave the book in the tomb, saying: 'Thou hast no lot in it, whereas our term of life on earth was taken for it.' Khamuas, however, threatens to take it by force, and the story goes on ...

Ne-Nefer-Ka-Ptah raised himself on the funeral couch and said, 'Art thou Stone to whom this woman has spoken these vain words, and thou hast not harkened to her? The book named, wilt thou be able to take it by power of a good magician or by prevailing over me in a game of draughts? Let us play for it ...'

And Setne said, 'I am ready.'

They set before them the game-board with its pieces, they played at the game of fifty-two and Ne-Nefer-Ka-Ptah won one game from Setne Khamuas. He pronounced a spell upon him, causing him to sink into the floor to his feet. He did the like by the second game, and caused him to sink into the floor as far as his middle. He did the like by the third game and caused him to sink up to his ears ...

Then Setne Khamuas feeling that he was beaten sent his brother Anherru to bring from the upper world his Amulets of Ptah. As soon as these Amulets were placed upon his body he was free, and he hastened to the upper world, taking with him the Book of Thoth.

However, he did not keep the book for long; the vengeance of the dead pursued him and he soon returned humbly to their tomb to replace the book where it belonged. (Griffith, *Stories of the High Priests of Memphis*, Chapter 2.)

Now conduct your own experiment with this inner working. Picture the Book of Thoth as a roll enveloped in its own bright aura of soft moonlight. Then day by day build and rebuild this story using the visualizing properties of the human mind. Look at pictures of Egyptian tombs in order to get the image right. Try to sense the emotions of the characters concerned, try to feel the thick heavy darkness of the tomb, hidden deep in the desert sand on the western bank of the Nile. Feel the velvet blackness of the realms of the Lord of the West, Anubis.

Use composition of place as taught by Ignatius Loyola. Build each scene as if you were preparing to set it out on a stage, picture where each character will be placed. Imagine the couch on which the mummy of Ne-Nefer-Ka-Ptah is laid. Watch the mummy with its still living counterpart playing draughts with Khamuas and his brother Anherru. See the ghosts of Ahure and her child Merab, without their mummies, feel their anxiety and their fear and their joy as the game goes in their favour. Experience fear as Khamuas must have felt it. Hear Ahure weeping for the lost book and hear her despairing cry as the two brothers escape with it: 'Hail King Darkness, Farewell King Light, Every power has gone that was in the tomb.'

Sense the power and the certainty that fills the great magician as he comforts his family in the astral blackness that falls on them when the light shed by the Book of Thoth is gone. Hear his words: 'Be not grieved, I will cause him to bring the book hither once more.'

Later picture the chastized Khamuas returning humbly and saluting a much greater magician than himself. Bringing the book back causes the light of the sun to illumine the tomb once more, for where the Book of Thoth is, there also is light. As an act of repentance Khamuas brings the long-dead bodies of Ahure and Merab to join their husband and father in the tomb of Ne-Nefer-Ka-Ptah.

Once more you may ask why you should take all this trouble. Be assured this type of work is for the very few. It will go a long way towards training you to change planes of consciousness at will. By such matters you will be judged as a competent magician.

The actual forms of the gods are creations of the created, and one of the most important forms is that of Thoth. The Wise Ibis is a common symbol for the Logos and as such Thoth is Lord of Magic; that is why you have been given these pictures in such detail. If you can gain the ear of Thoth, you can work magic, i.e. you can touch the World Mind of the Great Mother whose children include man and gods alike.

In magic you must work for your play and play for your work. This is the law of alternating rhythm. For your work build upon the magical Egyptian myths; for your play build upon the Celtic myths. They too are magical, but in another way. Get in touch with nature if you want to know the gods, call on them by the names that come most easily to you. Your mind will give them form, the Great Mother will ensoul them. The following working is one that will magically enhance your 'play'.

The Gates of Horn and Ivory

It is the first week of June and spring has suddenly become summer. On the sunlit edge of a beechwood, bright with the colouring of new leaves, seated in the grass of a golden and green meadow sit two worshippers of the Great Mother. They sit in meditation seeking full communion with Her Children. Magically they are at play.

The invocations have been made, the god desired has been called upon by the wordless adoration that follows the vibration of the sacred name. He has given proof that he has heard; his presence is felt.

The sun has put off his cloak of midday brilliance and completed his journey through the eighth house of Death, now he has become the Setting Sun and sinks through the scarlet and gold cusp of the eighth and ninth houses of Heaven. The silver-grey half-moon is now with him in the house of Unmanifested Life. Between these two Great Ones is the planet Venus. She is the ruler of the star Sothis, Queen of the thirty-six constellations that formed the astronomical tables of ancient Egypt. The Isis of Netzach concealing her powers behind a veil of emerald green. She is and is not the Silver Isis of the Moon. As the Sun-God departs, the Green Isis merges into the Silver-Grey Goddess of the Evening when the Children of the Great Mother return to their play.

Now the Lord of Tipareth gives way to the Lady of Yesod, and as the summer's day merges into the silver twilight the Children of Isis wake from their day-long sleep and come peeping through the purple and green shadows that creep across the meadow.

'I am the Setting Sun,' chants the neophyte as he prepares to enter the realm of the Great Mother that is next to his own plane of existence. 'I am the Silver Isis, the dark-veiled ruler of Night,' answers his guide as she closes his eyes in the temple sleep* so that he may see with the inner eyes the Children of the Goddess who wait to see him pass between the Pillars of the East and West.

Without speaking the silent pair watch the violet shadows play across the darkening land. As each patch of light is swallowed up something seems to stir into waking life. Bright eyes look out from every bush and tree, half-seen forms flit through the undergrowth. The birds sing their sunset song until the topmost leaves are dark with shadows. Then something happens to the trees. They have become alert; the wood is alive. All the Children of the Great Mother are now awake.

In meditation, through tightly closed eyes bright forms can be seen that step out of the shadows of the wood. High above is a great swirling form of green and silver. It is the deva that rules this wooded valley, the cosmic mind that gives life and keeps order, a formless force that man personifies because he cannot do otherwise.

---

* The Temple Sleep is an ancient and important ritual still in use today.

Deeper and deeper the two watchers sink into meditation; their aims and methods are one, they have merged their consciousness into a single sphere of sensation.* Their bodies are propped against a tree, their bodily senses are slowly being put out of action for a while.

Dusk comes, and the conscious sleep grows deeper, a feeling of panic comes, a welcome sign, for this feeling of fear means that power is condensing upon their sphere of sensation. The Great Gates of Horn and Ivory loom up before the inner eyes, then swing back on soundless hinges, the Great God comes. We pass into His garden and the gates close behind us. We have invoked and He has come, the First-Born of the Great Mother, the Master, the shepherd of all Her children, except modern man. Name the God if you can, worship Him if you dare, invoke Him if you are able.

The consciousness of the pair now 'awake in sleep' is in Tir-nan-oge or Fairyland. Anyone can enter if they but take the time and trouble to prepare themselves and their minds to know and accept other spheres of existence. You will know when you have won the Key to the Gates of Horn and Ivory. You will receive there the blessing of the Great God who is the first-born love of the Great Mother. As a man thinks, so he is.

Tir-nan-oge is the Celtic fairyland, the Land of Promise, the home of the Tuatha de Danaan, who are the Children of the Goddess Danu, another name for the Great Mother. They wandered the earth and finally came to Ireland where they fought and defeated the Firbolgs, taking over the land. Later they were defeated in their turn and disappeared into the Hollow Hills of Fairyland. Today they are called the Sidhe (Shee), or the Fairy Host.

Mannanan Mac Lyr was one of their great chiefs, and Aengus Oge was their great magician, being to them what Thoth was to the Egyptians. Remember these Names of Power and brood over them. They can become a Key to the Gates. But do not try to rationalize these ideas or explain the names of power; they are seed thoughts to be buried deep in the subconscious mind. Act as if they were potent. Remember, in magic, you are what you think you are, you are where you think you are.

All one has to do to open the Gates of Horn and Ivory is, with

---

* There is a method for the merging of consciousness of two initiates on the inner levels, but *only* on the inner levels.

emotion and intention, call upon the children of the Great Mother every day. Picture Her woods, Her mountains, Her rivers and Her shores, and you will be answered if you persevere.

The Gates may remain closed at first, and you must be content to peer through them, but with work they will swing open: 'Labor Omnia Vincit.' Then you are free to roam where you will in Her lands and become aware of an ever-opening series of worlds within worlds. You can thus become unshackled from the herd law through your own efforts.

The Celtic spirit of Freedom is now permeating through the life, religion, philosophy and customs of Britain and Brittany. Much of England is as Celtic as Wales, Ireland and Scotland. Your subconscious mind, with its link with the British racial subconscious mind, is the source of your personal power. It is the driving force of the group soul of the peoples of this island. And if the following poem lifts your soul then let your Anglo-Saxon Christian conscience beware, for the Celt in you is awakening.

The Hosting of the Sidhe

The Host is riding from Knocknarea
And over the grave of Clooth-na-Bare;
Caoilte* tossing his burning hair
And Niamh† calling, Away, come away.
Empty your heart of its mortal dream.
The winds awaken, the leaves whirl round,
Our cheeks are pale, our hair is unbound,
Our breasts are heaving, our eyes are agleam,
Our arms are waving, our lips are apart.
And if any gaze on our rushing band,
We come between him and the deed of his hand,
We come between him and the hope of his heart.
The Host is rushing twixt night and day,
And where is there hope or deed as fair?
Caoilte tossing his burning hair,
And Niamh calling, Away, come away

(W. B. Yeats, *The Celtic Twilight.)*

May to September 1938

---

* Caoilte is pronounced Kilte.
† Niamh is pronounced Nia.

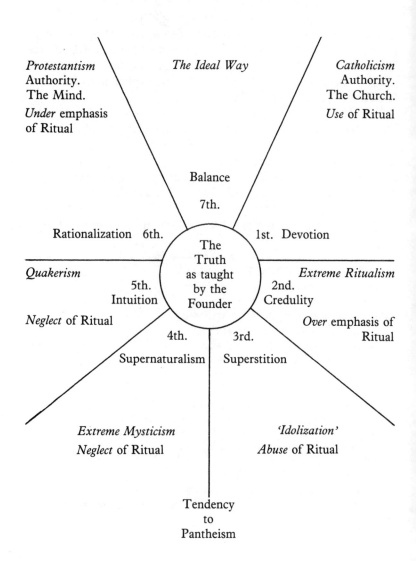

Protestantism
Authority.
The Mind.
Under emphasis
of Ritual

The Ideal Way

Catholicism
Authority.
The Church.
Use of Ritual

Balance

7th.

Rationalization   6th.

1st.   Devotion

The
Truth
as taught
by the
Founder

Quakerism

5th.
Intuition

Extreme Ritualism

2nd.
Credulity

Neglect of Ritual

Over emphasis of
Ritual

4th.

3rd.

Supernaturalism

Superstition

Extreme Mysticism
Neglect of Ritual

'Idolization'
Abuse of Ritual

Tendency
to
Pantheism

The Seven Ways of Development

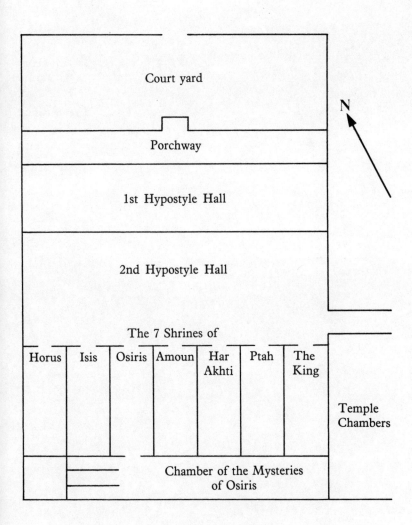

Temple of Sethy I at Abydos.
Built circa 1365 BC
(Not drawn to scale)

Index

DANCERS TO THE GODS

To Dion Fortune "mankind was . . . drawn by music to the edge of the floor . . . too self-conscious to join in yet yearning for the partner, the motion and the magic that he felt was out there . . . All he needed was the courage to forget himself and surrender to the rhythm." The ecstasy of Dion Fortune's own dance is vividly captured by **Alan Richardson** who offers a superb assessment and analysis of her work. He then considers Charles Seymour and Christine Hartley — two high grade occultists and priest and priestess within her Society of the Inner Light. The final section is a fascinating magical record of the ancient gods and discarnate entities invoked and meditated, including a naked girl's 'Willing Sacrifice' at Avebury and overwhelming bursts of power from Pan and in the Isis Rite. *Illustrated.*